Using Paired Text to Meet the Common Core

Effective Teaching across the K–8 Curriculum

William Bintz

Series Editors' Note
by Diane Lapp and Douglas Fisher

THE GUILFORD PRESS
New York   London

© 2015 The Guilford Press
A Division of Guilford Publications, Inc.
72 Spring Street, New York, NY 10012
www.guilford.com

Printed in the United States of America

This book is printed on acid-free paper.

Last digit is print number: 9   8   7   6   5   4   3   2   1

Library of Congress Cataloging-in-Publication Data is available from the publisher.

ISBN 978-1-4625-1898-2

Using Paired Text
to Meet the Common Core

Teaching Practices That Work

Diane Lapp and Douglas Fisher, Series Editors
www.guilford.com/TPTW

Designed specifically for busy teachers who value evidence-based instructional practices, books in this series offer ready-to-implement strategies and tools to promote student engagement, improve teaching and learning across the curriculum, and support the academic growth of all students in our increasingly diverse schools. Written by expert authors with extensive experience in "real-time" classrooms, each concise and accessible volume provides useful explanations and examples to guide instruction, as well as step-by-step methods and reproducible materials, all in a convenient large-size format for ease of photocopying. Recent titles have Web pages where purchasers can download and print the reproducible materials.

To Ferris and Madrean,
my heroes—

Thank you

About the Author

William Bintz, PhD, is Professor in the Department of Teaching, Learning, and Curriculum Studies at Kent State University. He has extensive classroom teaching experience, including teaching high school English in Chicago, Illinois, and San Juan, Puerto Rico; middle school language arts in Dhahran, Saudi Arabia; and grades 4–6 at an Alternative School in Bloomington, Indiana. Dr. Bintz has also been Visiting Lecturer in Language Education at the Armidale College of Advanced Education in Armidale, Australia, as well as Assistant Professor at Western Kentucky University, James Madison University, and the University of Kentucky. His professional interests include using award-winning literature to teach across the curriculum in K–12, collaborative teacher research, and reading comprehension assessment. Dr. Bintz has published numerous articles and book chapters in leading literacy journals such as *The Reading Teacher, Language Arts, Journal of Adolescent and Adult Literacy*, and *Middle School Journal*. In addition, he has presented at many international, national, and state conferences and conducted professional development workshops throughout the United States.

Series Editors' Note

As our schools continue to grow in linguistic, cultural, and socioeconomic diversity, educators are committed to implementing instruction that supports individual and collective growth within their classrooms. In tandem with teacher commitment, schools recognize the need to support teacher collaboration on issues related to implementing, evaluating, and expanding instruction to ensure that all students will graduate from high school with the skills needed to succeed in the workforce. Through our work with teachers across the country, we've become aware of the need for books that can be used to support professional collaboration by grade level and subject area. With these teachers' questions in mind, we decided that a series of books was needed that modeled "real-time" teaching and learning within classroom instruction. Thus the series Teaching Practices That Work was born.

Books in this series are distinguished by offering instructional examples that have been studied and refined within authentic classroom settings. Each book is written by one or more educators who are well connected to everyday classroom instruction. Because the series editors are themselves classroom teachers as well as professors, each instructional suggestion has been closely scrutinized for its validity.

In this book, William Bintz illustrates how to ensure that all students develop the skills needed to achieve Reading Anchor Standard 10 of the Common Core State Standards (CCSS), which calls for reading increasingly complex texts. While the "how to" of addressing this standard has perplexed teachers who realize that their students have a range of reading proficiencies, Bintz shares a viable instructional plan to make this a reality for every student. To begin with, as described in CCSS Reading Anchor Standards 7–9 (National Governors Association Center for Best Practices & Council of Chief State School Officers, 2010, p. 10), proficiency in reading involves being able to integrate, analyze, and evaluate information by making connections within and across texts:

Integration of Knowledge and Ideas

7. Integrate and evaluate content presented in diverse media and formats, including visually and quantitatively, as well as in words.
8. Delineate and evaluate the argument and specific claims in a text, including the validity of the reasoning as well as the relevance and sufficiency of the evidence.
9. Analyze how two or more texts address similar themes or topics in order to build knowledge or to compare the approaches the authors take.

Developing these proficiencies with students involves teaching them to select and consider multiple sources when reading or writing, and then how to connect these sources to scaffold the information being learned. The "how to" of this connected teaching and learning process is described in *Using Paired Text to Meet the Common Core*.

Bintz makes it very clear that the goal is to not leave some of the class behind with an easy-to-read version of a topically related text. Instead, he illustrates how scaffolded instruction can support all students in building the language and knowledge needed to read complex texts. He demonstrates how to accomplish this by initially assessing a reader's content and literacy skills, and then using his or her skills as the base for continued learning. Involved in this process is paired text that allows connected learning growth to occur. After reading this book, you will have a well-conceived plan for supporting all of your students in developing the language and content they need to read increasingly complex texts.

We invite you into the "real-time" teaching offered in this book and hope you'll find this series useful as you validate and expand your teaching repertoire.

DIANE LAPP
DOUGLAS FISHER

Acknowledgments

Mina Shaughnessy (1977), an early pioneer of writing research, once stated that "writing is something writers are always learning to do" (p. 276). Writing this book has been another opportunity for me to keep learning how to write. Fortunately, I have had much help. Over the years I have benefited greatly by collaborating with mathematicians, historians, artists, musicians, scientists, and literati of all sorts. All of these collaborators have taught me important information about their respective disciplines. They have been, and continue to be, some of my best friends and most certainly some of my best teachers. Several deserve particular acknowledgment.

I wish to acknowledge Sara D. Moore, one of my most respected and valued collaborators. Sara is a brilliant mathematician and an even more accomplished teacher and teacher educator. She taught me, with great patience, to better understand and appreciate the elegance and beauty of mathematics as a field of study, and also how to think, read, and write like a mathematician. Her voice quietly but powerfully reverberates throughout this book, especially in Part Six.

I wish to acknowledge Jill Dillard and Pam Wright for friendship and willingness to graciously share their books and their thinking about books with me.

Finally, I wish to acknowledge several of my doctoral students at Kent State University, all of whom have pushed my thinking on reading, picture books, and paired text. I want to acknowledge James Nageldinger for helping me understand the triadic relationship between oral reading fluency, award-winning literature, and content-area instruction; Lisa Ciecierski for sharing her knowledge about intertextuality and using paired text in middle grades social studies classrooms; Kathy Batchelor for sharing her thinking on writing instruction, particularly revision, and on using postmodern picture books to teach reading; and Peter Yao for making his enthusiasm for picture books contagious. I sincerely thank you all.

Contents

Purchasers can download and print copies of the materials
in the appendices from *www.guilford.com/bintz-forms*.

Introduction

Making mental connections is our most crucial learning tool, the essence of human intelligence: to forge links; to go beyond the given; to see patterns, relationship, context.
—MARILYN FERGUSON (in Maggio, 1997, p. 108)

Our fundamental task as human beings is to seek out connections. . . .
—KATHERINE PATERSON (in Maggio, 1997, p. 150)

This book is about making connections, and it has a long history. I did not know it at the time, but this book started around 30 years ago. Today, it represents my best thinking about how readers make connections across texts and how teachers can use paired text and instructional strategies to help students make connections across the curriculum efficiently and effectively. This introduction describes how this book developed over time. Specifically, it recognizes important experiences and individuals that have influenced the development of this book, identifies its aims and audience, and explains how the parts are organized.

Becoming a Father

Approximately 30 years ago I became a father for the first time, of a little girl named Ferris. I was ecstatic. I looked forward to watching Ferris take her first steps, say her first words, draw her first pictures, go to school, ride a bike, learn to swim, and roller skate. I was most excited to start reading to Ferris and eventually for her to start reading to me.

Reading Literature

Ferris had a small library of literature in her bedroom and before bedtime brought stacks of books for me to read to her. Typically, we sat side by side on a cushy couch, holding the book together. Some nights Ferris asked me to read while she turned the pages. Other nights she laid her head on my shoulder and asked me to read and also turn the pages. Still other nights she wanted to read and also turn the pages. I never knew what to expect, but we certainly enjoyed the variety.

We also enjoyed the literature that she selected from her library. She liked fairy-tales, lullabies, bedtime stories, adventure stories (*Drac and the Gremlin* [Baillie, 1989] sparked her imagination), scary stories (*Hist!* [Dennis, 1991] and *What's That Noise?* [Roennfeldt, 1987] kept her spellbound), poetry (Shel Silverstein's poems were favorites), animal books (*My Cat Maisie* [Allen, 1990] and *Scallywag* [Rowe, 1990] made her giggle), grandma and grandpa stories (*The Long Red Scarf* [Hilton, 1987] reminded her of her grandfather and *My Grandma Lived in Gooligulch* [Base, 1990] her grandmother), dragon stories (*One Dragon's Dream* [Pavey, 2009] fascinated her), nature stories (*The Wild* [Graham, 1987] sparked her interest in nature study), wordless picture books, and stories about little girls who like to play dress-up (e.g., *A Proper Little Lady* [Hilton, 1990]).

When Ferris was 5 years old, we moved to Australia for a year. During this time, our reading continued. We read stories about unfamiliar animals like *The Great Tasmanian Tiger Hunt* (Salmon, 1986) and *Kangaroo Court* (O'Toole, 1987), Australian Aboriginal legends like *The Giant Devil-Dingo* (Roughsey, 1973) and *Pigs and Honey* (Adams, 1990), Australian folktales like *Andy's Gone with Cattle* (Lawson, 1984), and lyrical poems from the famous Australian bush poet Banjo Paterson, most notably *Waltzing Matilda* (Paterson, 1998), *The Man from Snowy River* (Paterson, 2014), *The Man from Ironbark* (Paterson, 1981), *Mulga Bill's Bicycle* (Paterson, 1993), and *A Bush Christening* (Paterson, 1991).

Watching Reading Behaviors

After moving back to the United States, I continued to read to Ferris, now 6, and she continued to read with and to me. Sometimes she sat quietly listening to me reading a story and announcing at the end something like, "Daddy, that's one of my favorite stories," or "Daddy, I don't like that story." Other times, she was more active and animated during the reading. She made predictions, laughed at characters, commented on illustrations, emphasized funny words and lines, noted unfamiliar words, flipped pages back and forth, and asked endless questions. What really caught my attention, though, was that Ferris always made connections to other texts we had read.

Over time, I noticed that Ferris made both personal and textual connections across texts. For example, she stated that Maisie and Scallywag were just like our cat, Misu. They all liked to scratch things, chase mice, drink milk, eat, and sleep.

She also made textual connections, often starting with the phrase, "Daddy, this story is just like. . . ." After reading *Roxaboxen* (Cooney, 1992), Ferris noted it was like *Drac and the Gremlin* (Baillie, 1989) because both stories involved children dressing up in costumes and playing together in the backyard. Similarly, after reading *Hist!* (Dennis, 1991), she said the story was like *What's That Noise?* (Roennfeldt, 1992) because both happened late at night and were really scary and spooky. These were not isolated instances. Ferris regularly made connections across texts. I came to expect it. And yet, I asked myself: How did she learn to do this? How did she learn to do it so easily, almost effortlessly? I didn't know, but suspected it was a good thing.

Teaching Middle and High School

While learning how to parent, I was also learning how to teach English language arts (ELA) to middle and high school students. My experiences with teaching were invaluable, but challenging. The challenge was twofold: one, I taught middle and high school students who disliked, even hated, reading; and two, when they did read, they read fluently and sometimes with impressive prosody, but comprehended very little from the text. I was frustrated and perplexed. How can middle or high school students not be able to comprehend? How am I supposed to help them? After all, I am an ELA teacher, not a reading teacher. Unlike many of my students, I loved to read classical and contemporary literature and discuss my understanding of these works with others. Every day, however, I taught students who passively resisted, actively subverted, and at times even dismissed, my efforts to help them become better readers.

Asking More Questions

Around this same time I became a father for the second time, of a little girl named Madrean. I was overjoyed. I already had learned so much from Ferris about the pure enjoyment of reading to a child and looked forward to learning even more about reading from Madrean. My increasing knowledge about reading, however, was based on my own children. As a parent and a teacher, I wanted to know more about reading theory and reading instruction. How do children learn to read? How do teachers teach children to read? What materials do teachers use to teach reading? Why do some children learn to read early and easily while others struggle? Perhaps more importantly, how do children learn to comprehend? How do teachers teach comprehension? What does comprehension look like? Sound like? Why do many students, like my middle and high school students, learn to read but not learn to comprehend? I wrestled with these and other questions about reading. Finally, I stopped teaching middle and high school ELA and enrolled in a doctoral program in reading education. I entered the program with these questions and expected to leave with answers. I didn't realize that years later I would leave with more questions!

Professional Reading

In the doctoral program I read professional literature on learning theory, curriculum theory, reader response theory, language and language development, and reading theory. Again, I did not know it at the time, but these readings have influenced the writing of this book. For instance, I am influenced by the work of Lev Vygotsky (1978), specifically the notion that meaningful learning moves from the social to the personal, that is, from social engagements to individual development. I am influenced by the work of John Dewey (1963), who highlighted the importance of experience and its relationship to learning, education, and society, and the work of Douglas Barnes (1976), who stressed the importance of talk and conversation in learning. I remain inspired by the work of Jerome Harste, Virginia Woodward, and Carolyn Burke (1984), especially their seminal research on how language learners strategically develop and meaningfully use language; Frank Smith (1998) for his psycholinguistic view of reading; and Brian Cambourne (2001–2002, 2002) for identifying and promoting essential conditions for learning.

With curriculum theory, I am influenced by the work of Herbert Kliebard (1992), who outlined the history of curriculum thought and practice in the United States; Elliot Eisner (1982) for his visionary view of the arts as basic to curriculum and curriculum development; Paulo Freire (2000) for showing that literacy and curriculum are tools that can both empower and disempower learners; Michael Apple (1990) and Henry Giroux (1983) for introducing me to a critical theoretical view of curriculum; and Kathy Short and Carolyn Burke (1991) for articulating the important distinction between curriculum frameworks and curriculum documents.

With reader response theory, I am influenced by the work of Louise Rosenblatt (1994), who helped me understand the nature of text and the transactional relationships among reading, text, and reader response. Her work helped me see reading as an active, meaning-making process and how comprehension is influenced by a reader's stance, whether that stance is aesthetic (interpretive) or efferent (informational), both, or somewhere in between.

Finally, in language and language development, I am influenced by the work of M. A. K. Halliday (1975, 1978). His work helped me understand language as a social semiotic, a symbol system that allows language users to create and represent meaning. I am influenced by Don Holdaway (1979) for his work on shared book experience as a foundation of literacy; Ken Goodman (1996) for his work in whole language and miscue analysis; Constance Weaver (1994) for helping me understand that definitions of reading really matter and introducing me to different theoretical models of reading; and Frank Smith (2004, 2005) for his advocacy of using authentic literature to teach reading. Perhaps most important, I am forever inspired by the work of Jerome Harste, Kathy Short, and Carolyn Burke (Harste & Short, with

Burke, 1988; Short, Harste, & Burke, 1995) for helping me understand a socio-psycholinguistic view of reading, literature as a tool for learning, paired text as a curricular resource, and inquiry as a messy business.

Putting Names to Reading Processes and Behaviors

To be sure, reading professional literature helped me gain new knowledge. It also allowed me, for the first time, to put names to my children's reading processes and behaviors. For example, Ferris and Madrean loved to listen to me read stories to them. I learned from Jim Trelease (1990), and later from Mem Fox (2008), that *read-alouds* are important for learning to read because listening comprehension precedes print comprehension. They also loved reading to me and reading to each other, while I listened and observed. I learned from Yetta Goodman (1978) that listening to and observing children is "kid watching" and an important way to understand readers and the reading process. I did not know that I had actually been kid watching all this time. I watched and listened as Ferris and Madrean read, often mispronouncing words, ignoring words, and sometimes reading words that were not even in the story. Ken Goodman (1967) and Sandra Wilde (2000) helped me understand that these reading behaviors were not reading mistakes, but reading miscues, and offered me a new window to better understand how children develop as strategic readers. Both children also preferred to read specific kinds of books. Some favorites included *It Didn't Frighten Me* (Goss & Harste, 1993); *No Baths for Tabitha* (Thomas & Siegal, 1982); *Dog In, Cat Out* (Rubinstein, 1991); *Hattie and the Fox* (Fox, 1986); *The Spider in the Shower* (Mahy, 1988); and *The Runaway Bunny* (Brown, 2006). I learned from Lynn Rhodes (1981) that these are patterned and predictable books and are powerful tools to help children develop language, fluency, and comprehension.

Interestingly enough, I also learned much about reading and the teaching of reading from trade books. *When Will I Read?* (Cohen, 1977) introduced me to the importance of environmental print and pretend reading, as well as the language experience approach to teaching reading. *The Old Woman Who Loved to Read* (Winch, 1996) taught me that readers make the best reading teachers. *A Story for Bear* (Haseley, 2002); *Santa's Book of Names* (McPhail, 1993); *Thank You, Mr. Falker* (Polacco, 1998); *Can You Do This, Old Badger?* (Bunting, 1999); and *Once Upon a Time* (Daly, 2003) showed me that learning to read is a social engagement and always involves trusted mentors. *The Conversation Club* (Stanley, 1983) taught me the value of talk; *Least of All* (Purdy, 1993) the value of relevant reading materials; and *If I'd Known Then What I Know Now* (Lindbergh, 1994) the value of reflection. *First Grade Takes a Test* (Cohen, 1980); *Murphy, Molly, Max and Me* (Cullum, 1976); and *The Geranium on the Windowsill Just Died, but Teacher You Went Right On* (Cullum, 1971) helped me see the critical difference, and often imbalance, between teaching reading and testing it. *A Nice Walk in the Jungle* (Bodsworth, 1991) taught me to always base reading on personal interest and social inquiry.

The World That Loved Books (Parlato, 2008) showed me that, just as "we become like the company we keep" (Smith, 1998, p. 9), readers become like the literature they read. And, the evocative poem "Knowledge" (Greenfield, 1988) taught me that knowing about reading and knowing how to teach reading is a lifelong pursuit.

Finally, over the years I have remained genuinely curious about the process of making connections across texts. I learned from Julia Kristeva (1980) that this process is often referred to as intertextuality. Later, I learned from Stephanie Harvey and Anne Goudvis (2000, 2007) that making connections has another name: making text-to-text connections.

About This Book: Aim, Audience, and Organization

Collectively, these personal and professional experiences represent both the background and inspiration for this book. The aim is to provide K–8 teachers (1) a professional resource of paired text, mini-lessons, and instructional strategies that address the Common Core State Standards (CCSS) and help students make connections across texts in ELA, social studies, mathematics, and science; and (2) a set of theoretical models that teachers across the curriculum can use to develop paired text and instructional strategies to address CCSS and specific content-area standards.

Part One introduces the concept of intertextuality and describes how children, authors, picture books, and colleagues have helped me understand this important concept. It also describes the relationship between intertextuality and the Common Core State Standards for English Language Arts and Literacy in History/Social Studies, Science, and Technical Subjects (CCSS-ELA) and explains why and how picture books can support intertextuality across the curriculum with both young and older readers.

Part Two introduces the concept of paired text. It shares a mini-lesson to demonstrate the purpose of paired text and its relationship to intertextuality. It also describes the benefits of paired text, explains a rationale for using picture books as paired text across the curriculum, and identifies a number of professional resources to find high-quality and award-winning picture books that can be used to develop paired text.

Part Three focuses on using paired text to address the CCSS-ELA. It shares a mini-lesson that uses a paired text with an instructional strategy to address the Standards and a theoretical model that teachers can use to plan other lessons with paired text. It also provides additional paired text, organized by College and Career Readiness Anchor Standards for Reading (by grade levels and grade bands), and additional strategies to use with paired text in ELA.

Part Four focuses on paired text in history/social studies. It describes a mini-lesson that uses a paired text with an instructional strategy to address the CCSS for Literacy in History/Social Studies. It also shares additional paired text, organized by the CCSS Anchor Standards for Reading and the National Council of Social Studies thematic strands, and recommended grade levels and grade bands. It also identifies each text in terms of whether it represents reading literature (RL), reading informational (RI) text, or both (RL/RI). It ends with additional instructional strategies that can be used with other paired text in history/social studies.

Part Five focuses on paired text in science. It shares a mini-lesson that uses a paired text with an instructional strategy to address the CCSS for Literacy in Science and a theoretical model that teachers can use to develop other lessons with paired text in science. It also shares additional paired text, organized by the CCSS Anchor Standards for Reading and the Next Generation Science Standards, includes recommended grade levels and grade bands for each paired text, and identifies each paired text in terms of whether it represents RL, RI, or both. It ends with additional instructional strategies that can be used with other paired text in science.

Part Six focuses on using paired text in mathematics. It shares a mini-lesson that uses a paired text with an instructional strategy to address the CCSS in Mathematics. It provides a variety of paired text that is organized by mathematical content across 10 domains. It also identifies paired text in terms of whether each text represents RL, RI, or both, and ends with additional instructional strategies that can be used with other paired text in mathematics.

Intertextuality

All texts are tinted with echoes and reverberations
of other texts.
—MIKHAIL BAKHTIN (1986, p. 91)

Mikhail Bakhtin was a 20th-century Russian literary theorist and philosopher of language. His notion that all texts contain echoes and reverberations of other texts is a useful image to introduce the concept of intertextuality. I begin by describing how children, authors, picture books, and colleagues have helped me understand intertextuality. Next, I explain why and how picture books are good resources to support intertextuality across the curriculum for both young and older readers. I end by providing examples of the relationship between intertextuality and the Common Core State Standards (CCSS) for English language arts (ELA) and College and Career Readiness Standards for Reading.

What Is Intertextuality?

The concept of intertextuality is the theoretical foundation of this book. In general, the term is based on the notion that no text ever stands alone. Stated differently, "No literary text is written in a vacuum" (Orr, 1986, p. 814) and every text is the intertext of another text (Barthes, 1975, 1979). Intertextuality refers to the process of making connections with texts. It derives from the Latin word *text*, which means woven, suggesting that one text can be interwoven with other texts (King-Shaver, 2005). Practically speaking, readers make connections with past readings, prior ideas, and previous literary experiences, all of which can contribute to making sense of the current text (Chi, 2012).

Intertextuality is not a new concept. Over the years it has been defined in many formal and informal ways. Formally, Kristeva (1980), building on the work of Saussure (2012) and Bakhtin (1986), suggests that every text is the "absorption and transformation of another text" (p. 146). Allen (2000) proposes that intertextuality means that "every text has its meaning . . . in relation to other texts" (p. 6). Porter (1986; see also Hartman, 1995) posits that "texts refer to other texts and in fact rely on them for their meaning. All texts are interdependent: we understand a text only insofar as we understand its precursors" (p. 34). In essence, all written texts, and for that matter all speech, "are inherently intertextual, constituted by elements of other texts" (Fairclough, 1992, p. 170; see also Bloome & Egan-Robertson, 1993).

Informally, intertextuality is defined as "the process of interpreting one text by means of a previously composed text" (Cairney, 1990, 1992; Sipe, 2000). It is based on the notion that "past texts will be helpful in understanding current texts and making sense of current texts in light of past texts constitutes comprehension" (Harste, Woodward, & Burke, 1984, p. 170). Here, intertexuality is defined as the process of readers making connections with literary and informational texts.

Understanding Intertextuality

There are many ways to understand intertextuality. One way is to read professional literature; another is through personal experience. I have used both resources. In addition to professional literature, I have learned about intertextuality from young children, favorite authors, picture books, and content-area colleagues. I begin with a story about Kassie.

Kassie's Story

Kassie is 7 years old. Her mother, a friend of mine, recently shared this vignette with me.

> Before leaving to head to a morning meeting, I wake my 7-year-old daughter, Kassie, to say good-bye. She follows me into my office, located next to her bedroom, still half-asleep. Leaning against the door frame, watching me collect my computer and papers, she notices a picture book I just purchased, *Lily Takes a Walk* by Satoshi Kitamura, and picks it up.
>
> "Do you like this book?" I ask her. She nods, squeezing it against her chest, giving it a hug. "What do you like about it?" I ask.
>
> Kassie flips through the pages, stopping at a double-page spread where the little girl, Lily, takes her dog for a walk around her neighborhood. In the background stands a tree lurking, grinning through carefully placed leaves, bending ominously toward them with its boughs extended. Only the dog and the reader are privy to these threatening figures on each page. Kassie points at this tree, stating, "I like how there's something to notice on each page. This book reminds me of *Rosie's Walk*."
>
> "How so?" I ask.

"Well, both of the girls are being followed by something on their walk and they don't know," she states.

"What happens in *Rosie's Walk*? I'm not familiar with that story," I inquire.

"Rosie is being followed by a fox and here Lily doesn't see the things in each picture that I get to see . . . and the dog. The dog sees everything, which is probably why he gets so freaked out at the end, huh?" she laughs.

I agree. "Kassie, you are an excellent reader. Do you know why?"

She shakes her head sheepishly.

"Good readers make connections between books, and that's exactly what you did here. You found a connection between two entirely different books that you've read, and you noticed what they have in common. You stated both girls go on walks and both are unaware of the figures around them. I'm proud of you for making these connections."

She ran downstairs, book in hand, to show my husband. She said, "Dada, are you familiar with this book and *Rosie's Walk*? Well, I'll tell you what they have in common."

Kassie, like my own children and countless other children, has taught me how readers, young and old, experienced and inexperienced, make personal connections across texts so naturally, easily, almost effortlessly. She shows us how making connections is just a natural process of language learning, reading, and learning itself.

Favorite Authors

Like many readers, I have favorite authors. They include Gary Crew for his realistic fiction; Paul Jennings and Lane Smith for their humorous stories; Shaun Tan, Roberto Innocenti, and Peter Sis for their imaginative storytelling; Jeanne Baker, Anthony Browne, and Suzy Lee for their innovative illustrations; John Marsden and Eve Bunting for their commitment to important social issues; Steve Jenkins and John Locker for using art to teach science; and Cindy Neuschwander and David Schwartz for using narrative to teach mathematics.

I also have favorite poets, like J. Patrick Lewis. In *Please Bury Me in the Library* (Lewis, 2005) he includes a poem at the end of the book that acknowledges all the authors whose work he connects with and is inspired by. The last line in the acknowledgments poem caught my eye. It states:

Whose book is this? The bottom line . . .
It's partly theirs. It's partly mine.

Lewis doesn't use the term *intertextuality*. However, the entire poem is a wonderful tribute to just that. He acknowledges that his book of poems belongs as much to other authors whose books he has read, as it belongs to himself. In many ways his book of poems, like the picture books of my favorite authors, is intertextual; it contains "echoes and reverberations" (Bakhtin, 1986) of other books.

Intertextuality and Picture Books for Young Children

In addition to children and favorite authors, I have learned much about intertextuality through picture books. Many high-quality picture books have been written in such a way that they specifically invite readers to make connections to other texts. Some exemplars include *A Book* (Gerstein, 2009); *Charlie Cook's Favorite Book* (Donaldson, 2006); *Into the Forest* (Browne, 2004); *A Bear-y Tale* (Browne, 2013); *Glass Slipper, Gold Sandal: A Worldwide Cinderella* (Fleischman, 2007); *Goldie Locks Has Chicken Pox* (Dealey, 2002); *How Many, How Many, How Many* (Walton, 1993); *Naming Liberty* (Yolen, 2008); *The Flower Man* (Ludy, 2005); and *Grumbles from the Forest: Fairy-Tale Voices with a Twist* (Yolen & Dotlich, 2013). One of my favorites, however, is *A Bear-y Tale* by the award-winning author and illustrator Anthony Browne. This delightful picture book tells the tale of a little white bear and his magic pencil. While walking through a dark forest, the little bear encounters some unexpected characters: a hungry wolf, a large giant, a wicked witch, and a family of three bears. Each character, of course, is a reference to other popular stories and fairytales. With each encounter the bear cleverly and successfully draws himself out of potential danger with his magic pencil, in much the same way as the little boy does in *Harold and the Purple Crayon* (Johnson, 2005).

These picture books are entertaining and informative and also can be used to introduce intertextuality to students. However, *Where's Mum?* (Gleeson & Smith, 1992), an award-winning book recognized by the Children's Book Council of Australia as a finalist for Book of the Year in 1992, is special. Here's a summary:

> *Where's Mum?* is a delightful story about a family with a stay-at-home dad, a working mum, and three young children. One day, dad picks the children up from kindergarten. On the way home they predict Mum will arrive there first. She didn't. They wondered why. Did mum see Humpty Dumpty have a great fall? Helped Jack and Jill fetch a pail of water? Met a big bad wolf who wanted to gobble her up? Climbed a beanstalk to get the hen that lays the golden eggs? Went home with three bears to eat a bowl of porridge? Mum finally arrives home accompanied by interesting guests. Dad serves everyone tea.

This book creatively and skillfully invites readers to make intertextual connections with both language and illustrations. Throughout, the language and illustrations make references to other texts, mostly fairlytales. Mum is late because she was on a bridge and met a troll who would not let her cross is, of course, a reference to the famous Norwegian folktale *The Three Billy Goats Gruff* (Asbjornsen & Moe, 1957). Or, she is late because she needed to tell the king that the sky is falling is a reference to the story *Henny Penny* (Galdone, 1984). References to other stories are beautifully interwoven throughout the book. Children who already have knowledge of these fairytales, folktales, and nursery rhymes will make connections to them. For other children, this book can be a wonderful introduction to traditional literature.

Intertextuality and Picture Books for Older Children

Picture books are not just for young children. Oliver Jeffers, a popular and prolific author of outstanding picture books states:

> Since I began making picture books I have come to realise over time that I call them just that. Picture books. Not children's books. The reason for this is twofold: firstly, I don't believe they are just for children. I have met countless adults that collect picture books for themselves, and they are growing in confidence about openly admitting this in a book-signing queue. It's not for my daughter, or a friend's nephew. It's for me. Often these individuals are teachers, librarians, publishing employees, art college students—aspiring picture-book makers themselves. But increasingly, they are doctors, civil servants, bus drivers . . . just people who have discovered the joy of a story unfolding visually over a few dozen pages.
>
> I refrain from calling them children's books because that implies I write them specifically for children. I don't. I write them for myself. And for everyone. (2013)

Likewise, J. Patrick Lewis (2005), in his poem "A Classic," humorously states that a picture book is a classic when a child, age 6, excitedly reads it to another child, age 66. Similarly, C. S. Lewis (in Winters & Schmidt, 2001), author of the *Narnia Chronicles*, stated that "I am almost inclined to set it up as a canon that a children's story which is enjoyed only by children is a bad children's story. The good ones last. A waltz which you can like only when you are waltzing is a bad waltz" (p. 4).

The message is clear. Picture books are for all readers, young, old, and everywhere in between. Therefore, they can be used to introduce intertextuality to both younger and older readers. A series of picture books about Henry David Thoreau by D. B. Johnson is a wonderful example of using picture books to introduce intertextuality to both younger and older readers.

This series focuses on a bear named Henry, not surprisingly for Henry David Thoreau, and includes *Henry Works* (Johnson, 2004), *Henry Builds a Cabin* (Johnson, 2002), *Henry Hikes to Fitchburg* (Johnson, 2000), *Henry Climbs a Mountain* (Johnson, 2003), and *Henry's Night* (Johnson, 2009). These picture books describe the life, work, and writings of Henry David Thoreau, highlighting his life in Concord, Massachusetts, his love of nature, his walks through the woods, and his writings, most notably *Walden and Other Writings* (Thoreau, 2009). Each story highlights a different and unique aspect of Thoreau's life.

For example, *Henry Builds a Cabin* (Johnson, 2002) tells the story of how Thoreau uses only a borrowed ax and other practical, but primitive tools, to design and build his own three-room cabin. Friends worry about his excessive frugality and advise him to build a larger cabin. Thoreau believes frugality is a virtue and knows in the end his cabin will be large enough for his needs. *Henry Climbs a Mountain* (Johnson, 2003) describes the time Thoreau was stopped by a tax collector who informed him he had not yet paid his taxes. If Thoreau did not pay the taxes, the collector would take him to jail. Thoreau responded by saying that he refuses to pay taxes to a government that still believed in slavery and therefore he decides to go to jail. Thoreau spent only one night in jail because someone had paid the taxes for him. He later used the experience as the basis for his famous speech and essay entitled "Civil Disobedience."

In addition to the historical and biographical information, this series of picture books invites older readers to make intertextual connections between Thoreau and other characters. For example, in *Henry Builds a Cabin* (Johnson, 2002), Henry's friends include Emerson, Lydia, and Alcott. In reality these characters are references to the connections Thoreau had with Ralph Waldo Emerson, Lydia Emerson, Amos Bronson Alcott, and his daughter Louisa May Alcott. In actual fact, Ralph Waldo Emerson and Henry David Thoreau were somewhat "kindred spirits" (Schachner, 1998). Both enjoyed long walks and Thoreau even lived with the Emerson family for a time in exchange for room and board. Lydia was the wife of Ralph Waldo Emerson and a friend to Henry David Thoreau. Amos Bronson Alcott was a man who established an experimental school at the time and also was the father of Louisa May Alcott, the famous author of the novel *Little Women* and, not coincidentally, a student of Henry David Thoreau (Dunlap & Lorbiecki, 2002).

Similarly, in *Henry Works* (Johnson, 2004), Henry, on one of his nature walks, meets his friend Channing by a pond, Old Flint on the bank of the pond, Hawthorne by his house, and Mr. and Mrs. Hosmer at their cottage. In reality Channing is a reference to William Ellery Channing, a transcendentalist poet, friend, and frequent walking partner with Henry David Thoreau (Delbanco, 1981). Old Flint is a reference to Warren Flint, a man who allegedly would not let Thoreau use the banks of his pond as a place to write and reflect on his frequent walks, causing Thoreau to use Walden Pond instead. Interestingly enough, Walden Pond and much of the surrounding woods were owned by Thoreau's friend, Ralph Waldo Emerson (O'Neal & Westengard, 2005). Hawthorne is a reference to Nathaniel Hawthorne, a famous 19th-century American novelist and short-story writer. Like Emerson, Hawthorne was a friend and neighbor of Henry David Thoreau. Mr. and Mrs. Hosmer is a reference to Hosmer Cottage, the name of the home where the family of Amos Bronson Alcott actually lived.

Finally, in *Henry Climbs a Mountain* (Johnson, 2003), Henry, while out climbing a mountain one afternoon, meets Sam, the tax collector, who puts Henry in jail for not paying taxes. In reality Sam is a reference to Sam Staples, a constable, tax collector, and jailer in Concord, Massachusetts, who legally (illegally to Thoreau) put Thoreau in jail (Meltzer, 2006). Interestingly enough, the irony that the man who insisted that Thoreau pay his taxes or face jail time was named Sam, as in Uncle Sam, is certainly not lost in this story. *Henry David's House* (Schnur, 2002) is yet another wonderful addition to this series of interconnected picture books on Henry David Thoreau. Individually and collectively this series will engage younger and older readers, and all those in between.

Intertextuality and Picture Books for Adolescent Readers

Picture books can be used to introduce intertextuality with older readers. By older readers, I mean middle school and even high school students. For example, *The Wonders of Donal O'Donnell* (Schmidt, 2002) is a challenging story because it interweaves four traditional Irish tales. *How the Fisherman Tricked the Genie* (Sunami, 2002) is a tale within a tale within a tale. Three separate, but interwoven, tales challenge readers to make connections between each tale. *Nutcracker* (Hoffman, 1996) is another outstanding picture book in this story within a story genre. *Shortcut* (Macaulay, 1995) consists of a series of brief, interrelated, stories filled with interesting and whimsical characters. Each story includes illustrations that contain visual clues to the mysterious connections among all the stories. *Bull Run* (Fleischman, 1993) is a wonderful example of informative historical fiction. It is a fictional narrative about Bull Run, the first great battle of the Civil War. This narrative is told through the voices of 16 characters from different walks of life. Some are supportive or sympathetic to the Union Army and others to the Confederate Army. These voices invite readers to see connections among characters, perspectives, and the actual battle, as well as learn about the history of the Civil War. *Dateline: Troy* (Fleischman, 1996) provides an intertextual twist to a classic story in Greek mythology. At one level it is a retelling of the Trojan War. What makes this text so innovative is that the illustrations (collages of newspaper clippings) connect major characters and events in the Trojan War to wars in the 20th century. *Black and White* (Macaulay, 1990), like *Shortcut*, consists of brief stories that invite readers to make connections across episodes. Once connected, the episodes may tell one story or represent four parts of one story. Interweaving these episodes is challenging but enjoyable.

Voices in the Park (Browne, 1998) is a brilliantly crafted story that uses four different voices to describe a single event. The event is simple: two children, one boy and one girl, each accompanied by a parent, unexpectedly meet at a park. Each character interprets the meeting differently, and yet, all of the voices are intricately intertwined. Finally, *The Last Resort* (Innocenti & Lewis, 2002) is a mysterious story that involves an artist who has lost his imagination and seeks to find it again at a seaside hotel. There, he meets a variety of guests who, like him, are seeking something that has gone missing in their lives. The story ingeniously invites readers not only to make connections between the main character and the other guests, but also between the guests and famous literary characters like Huckleberry Finn, Long John Silver, Don Quixote, the writings of Hans Christian Anderson and Zane Grey, and the poetry of Emily Dickinson. These picture books are excellent resources to introduce and extend intertextuality to older readers. All are engaging, informative, and challenging.

Intertextuality and Picture Books across the Curriculum

Picture books are not just for young children and not just for ELA. They are for all readers and for all content areas. They use rich language, beautiful illustrations, and innovative design to tell fascinating stories and convey interesting information. They also can support intertextuality across the curriculum. I have learned this firsthand.

Over the years I have collaborated with many colleagues and teachers at different grade levels and across different content areas. These collaborations used picture books to support intertextuality and content-area material across the curriculum. For example, in mathematics, picture books were used to help students make connections among factorials, combinations, and permutations (Bintz & Moore, 2003); standard and nonstandard measurement (Bintz & Moore, 2011/2012); numbers, counting, and binary (Moore & Bintz, 2000); geometry and measurement (Moore & Bintz, 2002b); art and mathematics (Bintz & Moore, 2007); and even phonemic awareness and mathematics instruction (Bintz & Wright, 2008). In science, picture books were used to help students make intertextual connections among scientific and observational inquiry (Bintz & Moore, 2005b; Moore & Bintz, 2002a), experimental design (Bintz & Moore, 2004; Bintz, Moore, Singleton, Tuttle, & Jones, 2006), forces and motions (Moore & Bintz, 2002c), sinking and nonsinking (Bintz & Moore, 2005a), earth movement, and earth science (Bintz, Wright, & Sheffer, 2010). And, in social studies, picture books were used to explore interdisciplinary connections among longitude, latitude, and time (Bintz & Moore, 2006), as well as a framework to investigate the relationships among history, exploration, and colonialism (Bintz et al., 2008).

Intertextuality and the CCSS

Although the term is not explicitly stated, intertextuality is woven throughout the CCSS. A number of standards explicitly refer to students making connections between texts. In the next section I give an overview of the CCSS and describe the relationship between the College and Career Readiness Anchor Standards for Reading and intertextuality.

The CCSS

First and foremost, the CCSS-ELA are not a prescription but a "vision" (Valencia & Wixson, 2013, p. 182). This vision is expressed as a set of rigorous, research-based, and internationally benchmarked standards designed to "help ensure that all students are college and career ready in literacy" (National Governors Association Center for Best Practices and Council of Chief State School Officers, 2010, p. 1). The goal of these standards, or expectations, is for students to "develop the skills in reading, writing, speaking, and listening that are the foundation for any creative and purposeful expression in language" (2010, p. 1). These standards are based on an earlier attempt in 2009 to develop College and Career Readiness (CCR) standards in reading, writing, speaking, listening, and language.

CCR standards are based on a fundamental principle, namely, that literacy is a shared responsibility. Helping students to meet important reading standards (Key Ideas and Details, Craft and Structure, Integration of Knowledge and Ideas, Range of Reading and Level of Text Complexity), writing standards (Text Types and Purposes, Production and Distribution of Writing, Research to Build and Present Knowledge, Range of Writing), speaking and listening standards (Comprehension and Collaboration, Presentation of Knowledge and Ideas), and language standards (Conventions of Standard English; Knowledge of Language, Vocabulary Acquisition, and Use) is the responsibility of all teachers, not just reading teachers or ELA teachers. Moreover, CCR standards apply to reading literary and informational texts, including texts in ELA, science, history/social studies, and technical subjects.

Anchor Standards for Reading

CCR standards are also known as Anchor Standards for Reading. The 10 Anchor Standards, 9 of which focus on comprehension and 1 on text complexity, are organized around the four major categories shown in Figure 1.1.

The CCSS also include grade-specific standards for reading, writing, speaking, listening, and language. The purpose of grade-specific standards is to provide greater specificity to the CCSS Anchor Standards for Reading. In grades K–5 the standards (Reading Literature and Informational Text) are organized by single grade levels (K, 1, 2, 3, 4, 5); in grades 6–12 the standards (Reading Literature and Informational Text) are organized by 3- and 2-year grade bands (6–8, 9–10, and 11–12) to provide middle grades and high school teachers with more flexibility to use disciplinary-based literacy practices to teach ELA, history/social studies, science, and career and technical education.

Last, the CCSS refer to literature texts and range of literary text, stories, dramas, and poetry. Here, informational text is defined as "text written with the primary purpose of conveying information about the natural and social world (typically from someone presumed to be more knowledgeable on the subject to someone presumed to be less so) and having particular text features to accomplish this purpose" (Duke, 2000, p. 205).

Intertextuality and Anchor Standards for Reading

As noted earlier, this book is based on the concept of intertextuality, the process of reading and making connections across texts. The intent is not to address all Anchor Standards for Reading. Rather, it is to address those Anchor Standards for Reading (grade level and grade band) that are directly related to intertextuality. CCR Anchor Standard 9 does just that:

◆ Analyze how two or more texts address similar themes or topics in order to build knowledge or to compare the approaches the authors take.

Key Ideas and Details

1. Read closely to determine what the text says explicitly and to make logical inferences from it; cite specific textual evidence when writing or speaking to support conclusions drawn from the text.
2. Determine central ideas or themes of a text and analyze their development; summarize the key supporting details and ideas.
3. Analyze how and why individuals, events, or ideas develop and interact over the course of a text.

Craft and Structure

4. Interpret words and phrases as they are used in a text, including determining technical, connotative, and figurative meanings, and analyze how specific word choices shape meaning or tone.
5. Analyze the structure of texts, including how specific sentences, paragraphs, and larger portions of the text (e.g., a section, chapter, scene, or stanza) relate to one another and the whole.
6. Assess how point of view or purpose shapes the content and style of a text.

Integration of Knowledge and Ideas

7. Integrate and evaluate content presented in diverse formats and media, including visually and quantitatively, as well as in words.
8. Delineate and evaluate the argument and specific claims in a text, including the validity of the reasoning as well as the relevance and sufficiency of the evidence.
9. Analyze how two or more texts address similar themes or topics in order to build knowledge or to compare the approaches the authors take.

Range of Reading and Level of Text Complexity

10. Read and comprehend complex literary and informational texts independently and proficiently.

FIGURE 1.1. College and Career Readiness Anchor Standards for Reading. Copyright 2010 by the National Governors Association Center for Best Practices and the Council of Chief State School Officers. All rights reserved.

This standard expects students to be able to analyze two or more texts for various purposes, including building background knowledge, examining similarities and differences in the approaches authors take, and making connections among themes, topics, events, and characters of texts.

In many ways Anchor Standard 9 focuses on the purposes for making connections across texts. Other Anchor Standards also relate to intertextuality and focus on what is involved in making connections across texts. These include:

• *Anchor Standard 1*: making connections between two or more texts involves both literal (what the text says explicitly) and inferential (what the text says implicitly) thinking.
• *Anchor Standard 2*: making connections involves focusing on central ideas and supporting details.

◆ *Anchor Standard 5*: making connections involves understanding of texts and how portions of text relate to each other.

◆ *Anchor Standard 6*: making connections involves recognizing different points of view and purpose and how they shape content and style of text.

◆ *Anchor Standard 7*: making connections involves integrating and evaluating content.

Intertextuality and Integration of Knowledge and Ideas

CCR Anchor Standards for Reading are organized around four major categories: Key Ideas and Details, Craft and Structure, Integration of Knowledge and Ideas, and Range of Reading and Level of Text Complexity. The category Integration of Knowledge and Ideas relates directly to intertextuality since integration is an important component of making connections across texts. Like the other three, this category is present at the individual grade levels (K–5) and the 3-year grade band (6–8) and includes both literary and informational text. The following are specific standards for Integration of Knowledge and Ideas that are related to intertextuality. I list these standards by grade level and grade band and include whether the standard involves reading literature (RL) or reading informational text (RI):

Grade Levels (K–5)

Kindergarten

(RL) With prompting and support, compare and contrast the adventures and experiences of characters in familiar stories.

(RI) With prompting and support, identify basic similarities in and differences between two texts on the same topic (e.g., in illustrations, descriptions, or procedures).

Grade 1

(RL) Compare and contrast the adventures and experiences of characters in stories.

(RI) Identify basic similarities in and differences between two texts on the same topic (e.g., in illustrations, descriptions, or procedures).

Grade 2

(RL) Compare and contrast two or more versions of the same story (e.g., Cinderella stories) by different authors or from different cultures.

(RI) Compare and contrast the most important points presented by two texts on the same topic.

Grade 3

(RL) Compare and contrast the themes, settings, and plots of stories written by the same author about the same or similar characters (e.g., in books from a series).

(RI) Compare and contrast the most important points and key details presented in two texts on the same topic.

Grade 4

(RL) Compare and contrast the treatment of similar themes and topics (e.g., opposition of good and evil) and patterns of events (e.g., the quest) in stories, myths, and traditional literature from different cultures.

(RI) Integrate information from two texts on the same topic in order to write or speak about the subject knowledgeably.

Grade 5

(RL) Analyze how visual and multimedia elements contribute to the meaning, tone, or beauty of a text (e.g., graphic novel, multimedia presentation of fiction, folktale, myth, poem). Compare and contrast stories in the same genre (e.g., mysteries and adventure stories) on their approaches to similar themes and topics.

(RI) Integrate information from several texts on the same topic in order to write or speak about the subject knowledgeably.

Grade Band 6–8

Grade 6

(RL) Compare and contrast texts in different forms or genres (e.g., stories and poems, historical novels and fantasy stories) in terms of their approaches to similar themes and topics.

(RI) Compare and contrast one author's presentation of events with that of another (e.g., a memoir written by and a biography on the same person).

Grade 7

(RL) Compare and contrast a fictional portrayal of a time, place, or character and a historical account of the same period as a means of understanding how authors of fiction use or alter history.

(RI) Analyze how two or more authors writing about the same topic shape their presentations of key information by emphasizing different evidence or advancing different interpretation of facts.

Grade 8

(RL) Analyze how a modern work of fiction draws on themes, patterns of events, or character types from myths, traditional stories, or religious works such as the Bible, including describing how the material is rendered new.

(RI) Analyze a case in which two or more texts provide conflicting information on the same topic and identify where the texts disagree on matters of fact or interpretation.

Intertextuality, the Common Core, and Paired Text

In Part One, I introduced the concept of intertextuality, identified sources to better understand this concept, and described picture books as excellent resources to introduce and extend student understanding of intertextuality. I also provided an overview of the CCSS-ELA and the CCR Standards for Reading and described connections between these standards and intertextuality. In Part Two, I turn to paired text and describe how paired text is a way to support intertextuality and address the CCSS.

Paired Text

> Learning is seeing patterns that connect.
> —GREGORY BATESON (1979, p. 11)

In Part Two I introduce the notion of paired text through a variety of questions. These questions include:

- What is a paired text?
- What is the purpose of paired text?
- How can paired text address the CCSS?
- Why are types of paired text?
- Why use picture books as paired text?
- Why use picture books as paired text across the curriculum?
- How do I find high-quality picture books across the curriculum?
- How do I create paired text?
- How do I use paired text?

What Is Paired Text?

A paired text is two texts that are conceptually related in some way, for example, topic, theme, or genre (Harste & Short, with Burke, 1988). Paired text is based on the beliefs that reading is about making connections (Cross, 1999) and "readers make personal connections between the books they are currently reading and their past experiences" (Harste & Short, with Burke, 1988, p. 358).

Demonstration is an excellent way to introduce a concept (Smith, 1981; see also DeStefano, 1981). Here, I introduce the concept of paired text through a descriptive demonstration of a mini-lesson that uses a paired text with instructional strategies in ELA. The topic of the lesson is "Seeing and Thinking Differently," and it is appropriate for students across grades 3–8 depending on student background knowledge and experience with the topic, inferential thinking, and making connections across texts.

Mini-Lesson: Seeing and Thinking Differently

Materials

- Copy of paired text: *Once Upon an Ordinary School Day* (McNaughton, 2004) (RL) and *Luke's Way of Looking* (Wheatley, 2001) (RL).
- Venn Diagram (see Appendix A at the end of this book).

Procedure

- The teacher displays paired text and a large Venn diagram to the whole class.
- The teacher invites students to spend a few minutes with a partner and infer how these two books are similar and how they are different, and records student responses on the Venn diagram.
- The teacher distributes a Venn diagram to each student.
- The teacher reads aloud *Once Upon an Ordinary School Day*, stopping at strategic places (e.g., episodic changes) and inviting students to "turn and talk" about what the story means to them. After reading, students share with the class what the story means to them.
- The teacher reads aloud *Luke's Way of Looking*, following the same procedure. After reading, students work with a partner and record on the Venn diagram how these books are similar and how they are different, and later share Venn diagrams with the whole class.
- As a culminating experience, the teacher invites students to use a Problems and Pleasures sheet (see Appendix B at the end of this book) to reflect, record, and share problems and pleasures about making connections among texts.
- Note: *Just Behave, Pablo Picasso* (Winter, 2012) is an outstanding picture book that can be paired with *Once Upon an Ordinary School Day* and *Luke's Way of Looking*. This book is a short and inspirational biography of Pablo Picasso who always painted what he saw, not what others wanted him to see.

Background for the Mini-Lesson

Once Upon an Ordinary School Day (McNaughton, 2004) is a delightful story of an ordinary boy who lives an ordinary life. Every day he awakes from his ordinary dreams, gets out of his ordinary bed, eats his ordinary breakfast, and walks to his ordinary school. One day, however, his ordinary classroom became quite extraordinary. Unknown to him, his new teacher, Mr. Gee, prepared an extraordinary writing lesson. The lesson gradually transformed the ordinary students into extraordinary learners and writers. After school, the boy told Mr. Gee it was a wonderful lesson, almost magical. At home that night the ordinary boy put on his ordinary pajamas, brushed his ordinary teeth, and slept in his ordinary bed. This time, however, he had extraordinary dreams.

Luke's Way of Looking (Wheatley, 2001) is a provocative story about a boy named Luke who is frustrated with the way his rigid and overbearing art teacher, Mr. Barraclough, reacts to his artwork. Luke sees the world very differently than his classmates and Mr. Barraclough. When told to paint an apple, all of the students correctly used red or green, but Luke imaginatively chose blue. Mr. Barraclough always reacts harshly. He screams at Luke and destroys his paintings and brushes. Luke says nothing. One day, instead of going to school, Luke goes to a museum. There, Luke saw artwork created by artists who saw the world like Luke does. Later, back at school, Mr. Barraclough told the class to paint the watermelon sitting on his desk. Mr. Barraclough watched as Luke painted what he saw. This time, however, Mr. Barraclough said nothing.

Purpose of Paired Text

One purpose for paired text is to put intertextuality into action. Paired text is a curricular resource to help readers make connections across texts. By using paired text, readers "develop both an expectation for connections and strategies and for making the search for connections more productive and wide ranging" (Short & Harste, with Burke, 1996, p. 537).

Once Upon an Ordinary School Day (McNaughton, 2004) and *Luke's Way of Looking* (Wheatley, 2001) is an example of a paired text. How are these texts connected? Figure 2.1 is a Venn diagram illustrating some intertextual connections (similarities and differences) between these texts.

As for similarities, both texts are narratives with young boys as main characters. Both boys successfully overcome pervasive problems at school. One young boy (unnamed) overcomes typical boredom and monotony at school through the help of a new teacher who engages students in an exhilarating, creative writing lesson. The other boy (Luke) overcomes harsh criticism and frustration from a rigid art teacher through an inspiring visit to a public museum. Both texts involve male teachers, although one is a new teacher and the other is highly experienced, and both planned lessons for their students. Both texts have similar plots and strong story structures. The primary setting for both narratives involves a city (not the same city), a school, and a classroom. Each focuses on problem resolution and involves a circular story structure in which the story ends at the same place it begins, only this time with a new beginning (i.e., the young boy is now going to sleep to have extraordinary, not ordinary, dreams; Luke is now painting artwork that leaves Mr. Barraclough saying nothing but thinking differently). Lastly, both texts masterfully and progressively use color and image to help readers create meaning from and with the text. In fact,

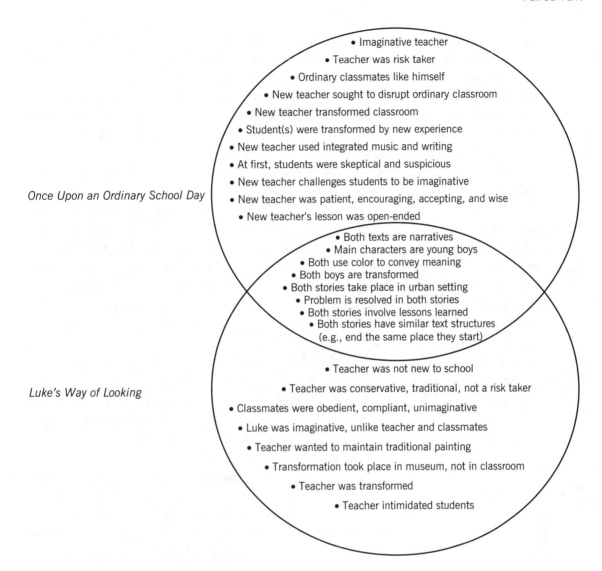

Once Upon an Ordinary School Day

- Imaginative teacher
- Teacher was risk taker
- Ordinary classmates like himself
- New teacher sought to disrupt ordinary classroom
- New teacher transformed classroom
- Student(s) were transformed by new experience
- New teacher used integrated music and writing
- At first, students were skeptical and suspicious
- New teacher challenges students to be imaginative
- New teacher was patient, encouraging, accepting, and wise
- New teacher's lesson was open-ended

- Both texts are narratives
- Main characters are young boys
- Both use color to convey meaning
- Both boys are transformed
- Both stories take place in urban setting
- Problem is resolved in both stories
- Both stories involve lessons learned
- Both stories have similar text structures (e.g., end the same place they start)

Luke's Way of Looking

- Teacher was not new to school
- Teacher was conservative, traditional, not a risk taker
- Classmates were obedient, compliant, unimaginative
- Luke was imaginative, unlike teacher and classmates
- Teacher wanted to maintain traditional painting
- Transformation took place in museum, not in classroom
- Teacher was transformed
- Teacher intimidated students

FIGURE 2.1. Venn diagram from *Once Upon an Ordinary School Day* and *Luke's Way of Looking.*

the use of color and image in both texts is one of the most important and intriguing connections between these two texts.

For example, *Once Upon an Ordinary School Day* begins with light and dark gray illustrations. These drab colors are used to convey the ordinary world of the young boy at home as he prepares to go to school, in the schoolyard before school begins, and in the classroom before students meet the new teacher, Mr. Gee. The young boy's world is a drab, black-and-white world, and devoid of any color, just ordinary. However, colors start to change with the appearance of Mr. Gee. The changes in color, from drab to bright, suggest that the young boy's ordinary world is about to change. This is beautifully conveyed as Mr. Gee enters the classroom dressed in a bright yellow suit and blue tie. As the lesson starts, the gray clothes of the boy start to slowly change. He now wears a bright blue jacket and red tie, and this is just the beginning. At this point the story starts to change dramatically. Single-page, drab illustrations become double-page and colorful. Now, other students are wearing bright clothes and writing imaginative and exciting stories. At the end of the day, the young boy returns home to a colorful, not drab, bedroom where that night he dreams extraordinary dreams. This masterful use of color, specifically the gradual change from drab to colorful colors, beautifully conveys how Mr. Gee positively changed students, especially the young boy.

Similarly, *Luke's Way of Looking* is set at school and also begins with drab, unimaginative colors, specifically light and dark brown illustrations. The art teacher, Mr. Barraclough, is dressed in a drab, dark brown suit. All of the students, including Luke, are dressed in drab, light brown uniforms with dark brown ties. Luke is an artist. His paintings, however, are colorful and imaginative, not drab. The use of color in the illustrations starts to dramatically change when Luke visits a local museum. There, yellow light flows out from the front doors and down the museum's steps, inviting Luke to enter. Inside, he sees colorful artwork everywhere, on the walls, hanging from the ceiling, and in the cafeteria. He feels welcomed there, but needs to return to school. Back at school, Luke and other students are now dressed in bright blue, not light brown, uniforms. As instructed, Luke paints a picture of a watermelon. This time, Mr. Barraclough watches Luke and ponders his painting. This time, Mr. Barraclough says nothing. Like *Once Upon an Ordinary School Day*, the use of color, specifically the gradual change from drab to colorful colors, beautifully conveys change and transformation, only in this story it conveys how Luke positively changed Mr. Barraclough.

As for differences, Mr. Gee and Mr. Barraclough are radically different. Mr. Gee is imaginative, supportive, and a risk taker. He invited and encouraged students to be imaginative. On the other hand, Mr. Barraclough is traditional, rigid, and conventional. He dominated and intimidated students, and even punished them for using imagination. Mr. Gee wanted students to think and write imaginatively. He wanted to disrupt and change the ordinary world of students. Mr. Barraclough wanted students to be conventional, compliant, and obedient. He insisted on privileging and maintaining his way of looking at the world. In addition, the young boys are also different. The unnamed, young boy was transformed at school by an inspiring teacher who used music to teach creative writing, and in the end developed a sense of voice and identity. Luke did not experience transformation, but rather confirmation in the museum, and in the end changed Mr. Barraclough rather than the other way around.

Paired Text and the CCSS

Once Upon an Ordinary School Day (McNaughton, 2004) and *Luke's Way of Looking* (Wheatley, 2001) is a paired text that helps students understand the importance of seeing and thinking differently. Along with the Venn diagram, it addresses several CCR Anchor Standards and grade-level standards for RL text.

In the CCSS-ELA category of Key Ideas and Details, making connections, like the ones described above, requires students to read closely to determine what the text says explicitly and to make logical inferences from it; determine central ideas or themes of a text and analyze their development; and analyze how and why individuals, events, or ideas develop and interact over the course of a text. In the category of Integration of Knowledge and Ideas, students are expected to integrate and evaluate content presented in diverse formats and media, including visually and quantitatively, as well as in words; and analyze how two or more texts address similar themes or topics in order to build knowledge or to compare the approaches the authors take.

With respect to grade-level standards, this paired text helps students in grade 4 (RL) compare and contrast the treatment of similar themes and topics (e.g., opposition of good and evil) and patterns of events (e.g., the quest) in stories, myths, and traditional literature from different cultures. In grade 5 (RL) students analyze how visual and multimedia elements contribute to the meaning, tone, or beauty of a text (e.g., graphic novel, multimedia presentation of fiction, folktale, myth, poem) and compare and contrast stories in the same genre (e.g., mysteries and adventure stories) on their approaches to similar themes and topics.

Types of Paired Text

Once Upon an Ordinary School Day (McNaughton, 2004) and *Luke's Way of Looking* (Wheatley, 2001) is a paired text consisting of two different narratives written by two different authors. However, there are many different types of paired text. For example, a paired text can include two books by the same author or illustrator; two books on the same story, one is a traditional version and one is a variant; two books with similar story structures or text types; two books with similar topics or themes; two books with similar content areas; and two books from the same genre (Crafton, 1991).

Paired text is also referred to as twin texts. These are two books, one fiction (literary) and one nonfiction (informational), that deal with the same or related topic (Camp, 2000, p. 400). Another type is combined-text picture books. These are books that integrate multiple genres of expository and narrative writing (Dean & Grierson, 2005, p. 456). Still another type is narrative–expository books. These are single books that present information about a specific topic using narrative as the primary means of expression (e.g., using story to teach scientific information; Ebbers, 2002, p. 46). These single books are also referred to as hybrid texts. These texts essentially have a "dual purpose" (Donovan & Smokin, 2001). They tell a story and present information at the same time (Maloch & Bomer, 2013, p. 443). *The Bumblebee Queen* (Sayre, 2005), *Big Blue Whale* (Davies, 1997), *If the Earth . . . Were a Few Feet in Diameter* (Miller, 1998), and *Energy Island* (Drummond, 2011), all in science; *One Riddle, One Answer* (Thompson, 2001) in math; and *A Wreath for Emmett Till* (Nelson, 2005) in Language arts and social studies are wonderful examples of hybrid texts.

Benefits of Paired Text

In terms of benefits of paired text, I have found it helpful to remember the words of Plotinus (*The Enneads*) who stated, "it is a wise man who can learn about one thing from another." In this instance the "things" are picture books. That said, paired texts have several benefits. They help students learn about one book from the other. They also help students learn content-area material. In fact, according to Neufeld (2005), "reading and sharing understandings of paired text contributes to learning across all subjects" (p. 302). Specifically, paired text (1) enables students to "share and extend understandings of each text differently than if only one text had been read and discussed" (Short & Harste, with Burke, 1996, p. 537); (2) enables students to "read one text and in the process build background knowledge for reading a second, related text" (Soalt, 2005, p. 680); (3) provides experiences with multiple genres and content areas; (4) demonstrates how "different genres provide students with different lenses for interpreting text" (Murray, 1968, p. 122) and therefore different ways of knowing about texts (Paretti, 1999); (5) highlights different text structures, specialized academic vocabulary, captions, diagrams, subheadings, maps, and so on; (6) increases vocabulary by seeing the same words in different contexts; and (7) increases motivation to "explore topics students are not initially interested in" (Soalt, 2005, p. 681).

Paired Text and Picture Books

According to Harvey and Goudvis (2000), "when students have practiced comprehension strategies in short text of varying genres, they are far better prepared to construct meaning from longer chapter books later" (p. 42). In other words, short text is an excellent tool to teach reading comprehension at all grade levels. Short text can include poetry, letters, newspapers, graphs, editorials, magazine articles, short stories, excerpts from chapter books, summaries of reports, and picture books. Picture books are examples of short text and excellent resources for paired text.

Simply put, a picture book is "a book in which the illustrations are as important as the text, both contributing to the telling of the story" (Harris & Hodges, 1995, p. 188). Here, picture book is defined as "a work in which the illustrations and the written text combine to form a single work of art" (Winters & Schmidt, 2001, p. 22). This definition highlights an important characteristic of picture books, namely, the integration, not the separation, of language and illustration. In a picture book language and illustration have an integrated, or symbiotic, relationship; one complements and extends the other. That is, language enriches illustrations and illustrations extend the text. Cech (1983–1984) suggests that language and illustrations conduct a "duet" in a picture book (p. 118). Metaphorically, they "dance" together (Sipe, 2011, p. 238).

In addition to integration of language and illustrations, picture books have many important and interesting physical features. For instance, a picture book is literally a short text. Typically, it consists of approximately 32 pages. They are typically small and do not weigh a great deal, unlike, for example, large, thick, and heavy anthologies and textbooks. They are comfortable to read; employ horizontal and vertical-shaped illustrations; often use the cover page to hint at mood; include front and back covers; sometimes have a dust jacket; incorporate front and back endpapers; sometimes include frames and borders on each page; use different kinds of paper (e.g., glossy, stock, matte); and employ a variety of design elements with color, line, shape, texture, and style (Sipe, 2001).

Picture books have many benefits for children, adolescents, and adults. They help teachers provide short, but powerful, demonstrations of what good readers do when they read. They also help students of all ages to read widely, deeply, and critically. For example, picture books can be used to demonstrate:

- What good reading *looks like* and *sounds like*.

- How readers strategically use comprehension strategies.

- How readers use fix-up strategies when comprehension breaks down.

- How readers distinguish between *what's interesting* (what is nice to know) versus *what's important* to know.

- How readers learn academic vocabulary (e.g., word text-based predictions in ELA, data-based hypotheses in science, and evidence-based conjectures in mathematics).

- How readers integrate text and illustrations to create meaning.

- How readers shift perspectives to create new or different understandings of the same text.

Picture books can be used to help students read widely:

- They are short and teachers can use them for read-alouds and interactive read-alouds as a regular part of classroom life.

- There are many types of picture books (e.g., narrative, informational, poetry, wordless, flip and pop-up).

- They can draw student attention to different story structures and patterns (e.g., repetitive pattern—*Fortunately* [Charlip, 1993], cumulative pattern—*The House That Jack Built* [Mayo, 2006], familiar problem—*The Three Little Pigs* [Marshall, 2000], chronological sequence—*The Grouchy Ladybug* [Carle, 1996], and rhyme and rhythm—*The Real Mother Goose* [Wright, 1994]).

- They can be used as "way-in" (Keene & Zimmerman, 1997) texts (e.g., texts that encourage student exploration of topics for which little or no interest currently exists).

- They can build background knowledge.

Picture books can help students read deeply:

♦ As part of text sets, to deepen student understanding of a particular topic, theme, genre, and so on.

♦ To make text-to-self, text-to-text, and text-to-world connections (Harvey & Goudvis, 2007).

♦ To highlight the notion of text potential, that is, any text has a variety of potential meanings.

♦ To introduce complex ideas and challenging texts (Gallagher, 2004).

♦ To promote reflection by inviting students to pause, consider, and reconsider current understandings (Opitz & Rasinski, 2008).

♦ To help students persevere and think their way through complex text.

Picture books can help students read critically:

♦ To help students understand close reading.

♦ To help students understand stance and how a reader's stance influences comprehension.

♦ To help students ask critical questions before, during, and after reading.

♦ To help students be reflexive (e.g., "actively seek alternative explanations or opposing viewpoints"; Lewison, Leland, & Harste, 2008, p. 19).

♦ To help students recognize inconsistencies and pursue anomalies.

♦ To help students challenge text propositions and author assertions.

♦ To help students question why some information was included and other information was excluded in a text.

♦ To help students understand that comprehension is based on perspective and multiple perspectives enable rich, multiple meanings.

♦ To help students expect difference and look for "surprises" (Lewison et al., 2008, p. 17).

Picture Books and Paired Text across the Curriculum

Clearly, picture books have many benefits. Two of the most important are variability and flexibility. Paired text can be two literary texts, two informational texts, or two texts—one literary and one informational, one with text and one wordless, and so forth. Another benefit is potential for interdisciplinary teaching and learning. Typically, picture books, text sets, and paired text have been used primarily for reading and writing instruction, as well as for literature discussion. To a lesser degree, they have been used for content-area instruction. This is not surprising given the fact that traditionally mathematics education has been driven more by word problems, hands-on manipulatives, and evidence-based inquiry projects rather than picture books; science education has been driven more by hands-on experiments using scientific method and observational inquiry rather than picture books; and social studies education has been driven by reading primary and secondary documents rather than picture books. This trend, however, is changing.

For some time now, there has been a proliferation of professional literature that provides excellent resources for using picture books across the curriculum. In mathematics Burns and Sheffield (2004a, 2004b) provide an extensive number of classroom-based lessons for using a variety of picture books to teach mathematical concepts across grades K–1 and 2–3. Similarly, Bresser (2004) offers picture books to teach math in grades 4–6 and Bay-Williams and Martinie (2004) for grades 6–8, as does Sheffield and Gallagher (2004) who offer lessons for math and nonfiction picture books. Whitin and Whitin (2004) and Whitin and Wilde (1992, 1995) provide excellent ideas for integrating literacy and math, K–6, as does Whitin, Mills, and O'Keefe (1991), and Mills, O'Keefe, and Whitin (1996). Pappas (1993, 1997a, 1997b, 2004) also shares short tales and simple stories designed to ignite student interest in a wide variety of mathematical topics, K–8.

In science, the use of picture books to integrate reading and science is also very popular (Baker & Saul, 1994). Royce, Morgan, and Ansberry (2012) and Morgan and Ansberry (2010, 2013) offer teachers lessons for using picture books to teach scientific inquiry, K–6. Similarly, Konieck-Moran (2013a, 2013b) presents short mystery stories for teachers to provide inquiry-based instruction in life and physical science. In social studies, Libresco, Balantic, and Kipling (2011) provide an impressive list of picture books to integrate language arts and social studies instruction. Last, an increasing amount of professional literature is available on ways to use picture books across multiple content areas. Columba, Kim, and Moe (2009) provide lessons for using picture books to teach math, science, and social studies.

To be sure, this proliferation of professional literature is a rich resource for teachers. Much of this literature focuses primarily on using single picture books, one at a time, to teach content-area material. Few resources currently exist that show how paired text can be used not only to teach content-area material but to also address the CCSS. Some research has been conducted with paired text in mathematics. For example, Whitin and Whitin (2005) used a paired text of picture books to help students make connections between mathematics and the real world; see mathematical concepts from different perspectives; and develop abilities to compare and contrast, predict, design, analyze, and evaluate. More research and professional resources are needed that focus on multiple texts, like paired text, to help students make connections across texts and learn content-area material across the curriculum at the same time.

Finding Picture Books for Paired Text across the Curriculum

To be sure, there is no single resource for finding high-quality and award-winning picture books to develop paired text. Fortunately, a number of resources already exist. One of the most accessible is the websites and journals of national professional organizations. For example, each year the National Science Teachers Association (NSTA), in cooperation with the Children's Book Council (CBC), publishes a list of Outstanding Science Trade Books, K–12. This list is organized around four Next Generation Science Standards (NGSS): earth and space science, life science, physical science, and science as inquiry (see *www.nextgenscience.org*). Each book on the list is recognized as an outstanding trade book on which to build student literacy skills and learn science content at the same time (see *www.nsta.org/publications.ostb*). In addition, two NSTA journals, *Science and Children* for primary and elementary teachers, and *Science Scope* for middle-level teachers, regularly publish articles describing how teachers use picture books to teach science. *Science and Children*, in particular, regularly includes a column in each issue entitled "Teaching Through Trade Books." Although it does not use the term *paired text*, contributors to this column identify two related trade books and describe how these books can be used with classroom activities to teach science content and address NGSS science standards.

Each year since 1972, the National Council of Social Studies (NCSS), in cooperation with the CBC, provides annotated book lists of Notable Social Studies Trade Books for Young People, K–8 (see *www.socialstudies.org/notable*). What makes these lists particularly helpful for social studies teachers is that annotators indicate how each trade book relates to one or more thematic strands in the National Curriculum Standards for Social Studies. Similarly, *Teaching Children Mathematics* and *Mathematics Teaching in the Middle School*, two journals published by the National Council of Teachers of Mathematics (NCTM), regularly include excellent articles by math teachers and researchers that describe how to use picture books to teach a variety of math concepts.

Likewise, the International Reading Association (IRA) sponsors the IRA Children's and Young Adult Book Awards and the Teachers' Choices Award (*www.reading.org*). The National Council of Teachers of English (NCTE) sponsors Notable Children's Books in the English Language Arts, and the Orbis Pictus Nonfiction Award (*www.ncte.org*).

In addition to national professional educational organizations like these, there are a number of other organizations that honor books. The American Library Association (ALA) sponsors the Robert F. Sibert Informational Book Medal, the Laura Ingalls Wilder Medal, the Schneider Family Book Award, the Pura Belpré Medal, the John Newbery Medal, the Caldecott Medal, and the Coretta Scott King Book Award (*www.ala.org*). Moreover, the Jane Addams Children's Book Award is sponsored by the Women's International League for Peace and Freedom (WILPF) and the Jane Addams Peace Association. The purpose of this award is to honor books "that effectively promote the cause of peace, social justice, world community, and the equality of the sexes and all races as well as meeting conventional standards of excellence" (*www.janeaddamspeace.org/jacba*).

Using Paired Text

In Part Two, I have provided a descriptive demonstration to introduce the concept of paired text. I have also shared definitions, purposes, and types of paired text, described a rationale for using paired text, and explained ways to find picture books to use as paired text across the curriculum. In Part Three through Part Six, I focus on using paired text across the curriculum. Specifically, I share paired text and instructional strategies that address the CCSS in ELA, social studies, science, and mathematics.

Paired Text
in English Language Arts

Intertextual study provides an interaction between text and reader
different than that provided by traditional literary study. It challenges
the reader to read responsibly, to search out and make connections,
to engage in critical thinking, and to form relationships.
—AMY BRIGHT (2011, p. 45)

In Part Three, I introduce a paired text for ELA that focuses on perspective and
point of view. I describe a mini-lesson to introduce this paired text, provide background information for the mini-lesson, use a Spokewheel as an instructional strategy to illustrate intertextual connections between these texts, and discuss how this
paired text and strategy address the CCSS for ELA. I also share additional paired
text, organized by the CCSS Anchor Standards for Reading, and include recommended grade levels and grade bands for each paired text, as well as identify each
text in terms of whether it represents reading literature (RL), reading informational
text (RI), or both (RL/RI). I end by sharing additional instructional strategies that
can be used with other paired text in ELA, as well as other content areas.

Mini-Lesson: Perspective and Point of View

Materials

- Copy of paired text: *Duck! Rabbit!* (Rosenthal & Lichtenheld, 2009) (RL) and
  Daft Bat (Willis & Ross, 2008) (RL).
- Spokewheel (see Appendix C at the end of this book).

Procedure

- ◆ The teacher displays the paired text and a large Spokewheel to the whole class.

- ◆ The teacher invites students to infer how these two books are similar and how they are different, and records similarities in the interior sections of the Spokewheel and differences in the outer sections.

- ◆ The teacher provides each student with a copy of the Spokewheel.

- ◆ The teacher reads aloud *Duck! Rabbit!* stopping at strategic places (e.g., illustrations where the creature is viewed as both a duck and rabbit depending on the reader's point of view) and inviting students to "chitchat" about their interpretations of whether it is a duck or a rabbit.

- ◆ The teacher invites students to share their interpretations and how they are related to perspective and point of view.

- ◆ The teacher reads aloud *Daft Bat*, following the same procedure. After reading, students work in pairs and use a Spokewheel to record similarities and differences between these texts and then share them with the whole class.

- ◆ The teacher uses *Once Upon a Time, the End (asleep in 60 seconds*; Kloske, 2005) to invite students to write a retelling of each story. This delightful book tells the story of an exhausted father who, instead of reading several classic fairytales to his little girl at bedtime, shortens each to a few sentences to get her to finally fall asleep. These shortened versions of fairytales are entertaining just by themselves, but can be used as humorous examples of how to write very short retellings of stories, like *Duck! Rabbit!* and *Daft Bat*, that can be read in 60 seconds or less.

- ◆ As a culminating event, the teacher invites students to use New Insights and New Questions (see Appendix D at the end of this book) to reflect, record, and share new insights (lightning bolts) and new questions (question marks) about the process of making connections between texts.

Background for the Mini-Lesson

Duck! Rabbit! (Rosenthal & Lichtenheld, 2009) is a clever and thoroughly entertaining narrative because it involves optical illusion. On each full-page spread, text and illustrations work together to describe two unseen and unidentified narrators arguing over a simple question: Is the creature a duck or a rabbit? One narrator sees a duck, the other sees a rabbit. In the end both narrators learn that the creature can be both. It all depends on perspective and point of view.

Daft Bat (Willis & Ross, 2008) is a delightful and humorous book about a group of wild animals that meet a young bat. Owl asks the animals to get Bat a welcome gift. The animals inquire what Bat would like as a gift. Her answers are odd and so are her explanations. Bat says an umbrella is a nice gift because it will keep her feet dry and protect her from rain clouds in the sky below. A rain hat would be nice, but it would fall off into the grass above. The animals are confused. Clouds are not below and grass is not above. The animals tell Owl that Bat is daft because she gets everything turned upside down. Owl asks the animals to see things from Bat's perspective. They do and end up seeing her in a very different way. The story ends with an upside-down illustration of Bat to remind readers of this important lesson about perspective.

Intertextual Connections

Figure 3.1 is a Spokewheel that illustrates some similarities and differences between these two texts. A Spokewheel is an organizational device to record connections between two texts. The sections inside the circle identify similarities and sections on the outside identify differences.

In terms of similarities, both texts involve animal characters and illustrations are whimsical, almost cartoon-like. Both include unidentified narrators, although *Duck! Rabbit!* (Rosenthal & Lichtenheld, 2009) includes two narrators and *Daft Bat* (Willis & Ross, 2008) only one. Both depict animals in natural habitats doing the kinds of things these animals do (e.g., Bat hangs upside down from a tree limb). Both texts focus on the topic of perspective and point of view. Last, both end with narrators and characters learning a lifelong lesson: It is important to see things from different perspectives.

In terms of differences, *Duck! Rabbit!* is essentially an argument between two unidentified narrators. They argue over dueling perceptions: Is it a duck? Is it a rabbit? It has a cyclical story structure, that is, the ending starts a new beginning. There is no plot and no specific time sequence that provides a clear beginning, middle, and end. The setting is a residential neighborhood near a swamp, a pond, and grassy fields. The illustrations are full page with light blue and white colors throughout. In the end both narrators see the creature differently because they shift perspective. The duck might actually be a rabbit and the rabbit might actually be a duck. This new perspective is temporary, however, lasting only until both see another curious creature. One argues it is an anteater, and the other a brachiosaurus. And the argument continues.

Unlike *Duck! Rabbit!*, *Daft Bat* is a narrative with a clear plot, time sequence, and explicit problem–solution story structure. The problem is not dueling perceptions, but a single misperception, namely, all the animals think Bat is looney. The setting is an expansive, open plain with large trees, rivers, grasslands, and high mountains. The illustrations are single page and multicolored. One unidentified narrator introduces the story, but then turns narration over to the animals. The ending shows the animals transformed. Instead of seeing Bat as looney, the animals see Bat as perfectly normal.

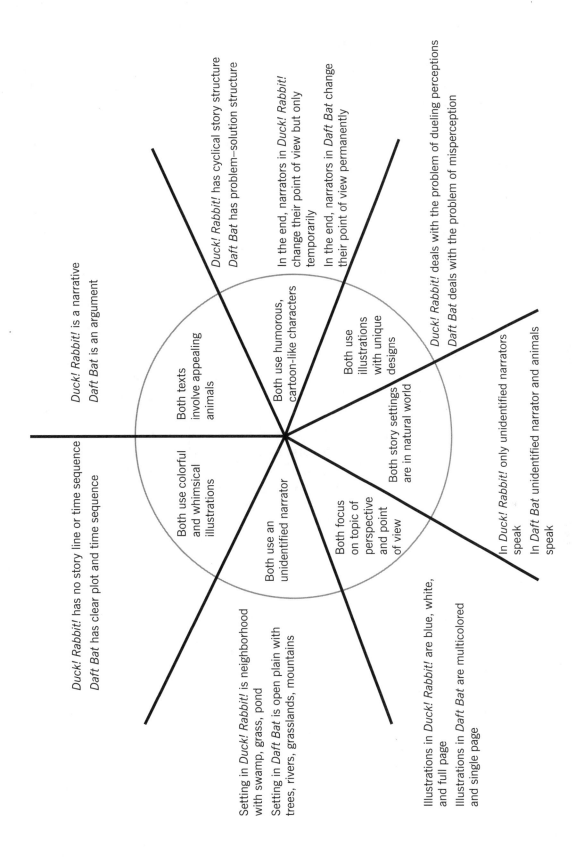

FIGURE 3.1. Spokewheel for *Duck! Rabbit!* and *Daft Bat.*

Paired Text, Intertextual Connections, and the CCR Anchor Standards

Duck! Rabbit! (Rosenthal & Lichtenheld, 2009) and *Daft Bat* (Willis & Ross, 2008) is a paired text that addresses several CCR Anchor Standards for Reading in the categories of Key Ideas and Details, Craft and Structure, and Integration of Knowledge and Ideas. These standards include:

Key Ideas and Details

1 Read closely to determine what the text says explicitly and to make logical inferences from it; cite specific textual evidence when writing or speaking to support conclusions drawn from the text.

2 Determine central ideas or themes of a text and analyze their development; summarize the key supporting details and ideas.

Both texts invite readers to create explicit and implicit understandings. In *Duck! Rabbit!* it is explicitly stated that images on each page are viewed as a duck or a rabbit. Both animals have identical heads and ears. One sniffs, eats a carrot, hides in the grass, and flies in the air, thus, it is a rabbit; one quacks, wades through a swamp, and eats a piece of bread, thus, it is a duck. And, in *Daft Bat* it is explicitly stated that young Bat hangs upside down naturally. That is why she needs an umbrella to protect her feet from getting wet when it rains, why her ears will get wet when it rains because the river will rise, and why a rain hat will only fall into the grass above. At the same time, both books invite implicit understanding and inferential thinking. They imply the major idea or lesson learned, namely, it is important to see things from different perspectives.

Craft and Structure

3 Assess how point of view or purpose shapes the content and style of a text.

Both texts are connected by point of view. In *Duck! Rabbit!* this connection is represented primarily through illustrations. The same creature is depicted but two narrators make two different interpretations. Is one interpretation right and the other wrong? Maybe both are right. It all depends on point of view. In *Daft Bat* this same connection is communicated through text and illustrations. Owl taught the animals to look from Bat's point of view. Then, they would understand that Bat is not as looney as everybody first thought.

Integration of Knowledge and Ideas

4 Analyze how two or more texts address similar themes or topics in order to build knowledge or to compare the approaches the authors take.

Both texts, albeit in different and unique ways, are based on the theme of understanding perspective and point of view.

Additional Paired Text on Perspective and Point of View

In addition to *Duck! Rabbit!* (Rosenthal & Lichtenheld, 2009) and *Daft Bat* (Willis & Ross, 2008), other paired texts focus on perspective and point of view. Here are a few:

Grades K–3

- *A Box Story* by Kenneth Kit Lamug (RL)
- *Not a Box* by Antoinette Portis (RL)

Texts take readers on a visual, imaginary journey in which a simple box is anything but simple in the hands and minds of creative thinkers.

- *Dear Mr. Blueberry* by Simon James (RL)
- *Not a Stick* by Antoinette Portis (RL)

Texts pay tribute to the power of perspective and creative thinkers who prefer imagination over fact.

- *Hansel and Gretel* by Paul Zelinsky (RL)
- *Into the Forest* by Anthony Browne (RL)

Texts provide two different perspectives on a popular fairytale: one traditional and one with an intriguing, updated twist.

- *Pablo the Artist* by Satorshi Kitamura (RL)
- *The Art Lesson* by Tomie dePaolo (RL)

Texts highlight two perspectives on what it means to be an artist. One stresses the value of unconventionality and imagination, and the other highlights the need to see multiple perspectives.

Grades 4–5

- *Seven Blind Mice* by Ed Young (RL)
- *All I See* by Cynthia Rylant (RL)

Texts highlight the lure of seeing differently and the power of seeing the world in unique ways.

- *Knots on a Counting Rope* by Bill Martin, Jr. (RL)
- *The Seeing Stick* by Jane Yolen (RL)

Texts promote the idea that seeing, really seeing, does not just occur with the eyes.

- *Two Bad Ants* by Chris Van Allsburg (RL)
- *The Other Side* by Jacqueline Woodson (RL)

Texts show the value of seeing familiar things and familiar problems in unfamiliar ways.

- *Goldilocks and the Three Bears* by James Marshall (RL)
- *Me and You* by Anthony Browne (RL)

Texts provide two different versions of a popular fairytale: one traditional and entertaining, and the other unconventional and thought provoking.

Grades 6–8

- *Voices in the Park* by Anthony Browne (RL)
- *A Walk in the Park* by Anthony Browne (RL)

Texts use elaborate illustrations to show innovative ways to see single events from multiple perspectives.

- *Black and White* by David Macauley (RL)
- *Shortcut* by David Macauley (RL)

Texts with humorous and colorful illustrations integrate seemingly isolated events into multiple stories from different perspectives.

- *The Viewer* by Gary Crew (RL)
- *The Watertower* by Gary Crew (RL)

Texts include rich, multilayered stories told with haunting illustrations and innovative book design.

- *The Girl in Red* by Roberto Innocenti (RL)
- *Honestly, Red Riding Hood Was Rotten: The Story of Little Red Riding Hood as Told by the Wolf* by Trisha Speed Shaskan (RL)

Texts provide two different versions of the famous fairytale: one a humorous version, and the other a contemporary and provocative version unlike any other.

- *Mirror* by Jeanne Baker (RL)

I add this single book for several reasons. It is a beautiful book, informative, artful, and thoroughly unique in design. It presents two interrelated stories in one book. At one level, both stories describe two boys and their families during a typical day of shopping. In one story, the setting is Sydney, Australia, and the other is Morocco. Each is told as a wordless story. However, the genius of this book is in the design. Unlike traditional picture books, these two wordless stories are designed to be read in a unique way. One is read from left to right, and the other from right to left. In essence, the book opens up in the middle and the reader turns two pages simultaneously, one to the left, and the other to the right. On the left is the wordless story in Australia and on the right is the wordless story in Morocco. Both stories describe a series of similar shopping events. However, each is told from a different cultural perspective and invites readers to make intertextual connections. The stories mirror each other, thus, the title.

Theoretical Model

A theoretical model is one way to visually represent a complex concept and process. In this instance the concept is paired text and the process is using them to develop and implement standards-based instruction. Figure 3.2 is a theoretical model that illustrates the relationships among the CCR Anchor Standards for Reading, K–12; the CCSS-ELA standards for grade levels (K–5) and grade bands (6–8); and paired text. It is inspired by and adapted from a whole-language model of reading (Goodman, 2006). This model uses three concentric circles to illustrate three cueing systems of language: graphophonemics, syntax, and semantics. The center circle is semantic,; the next circle is syntax, and the outer circle is graphophonemics. A wedge cuts across all three circles to represent how any instance of reading can integrate all three cueing systems.

In the model presented here the outside circle identifies major categories of the CCR Reading Anchor Standards: Craft and Structure, Key Ideas and Details, Integration of Knowledge and Ideas, and Range of Reading and Level of Text Complexity. The inner circle identifies major categories of the CCSS-ELA standards across grade levels (K–5) and grade bands (6–8), including reading (RL/RI), writing, speaking and listening, and language. The wedge extending across both circles illustrates how paired text can be used as a curricular resource to integrate selected CCR Anchor Standards and selected CCSS-ELA grade-level and grade-band standards.

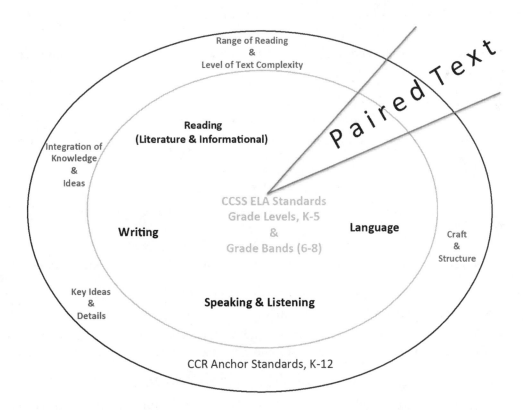

FIGURE 3.2. Theoretical model for ELA paired text.

Teachers can use this model to develop and use paired text for standards-based instruction.

Paired Text for ELA Standards by Grade Levels and Grade Bands

Duck! Rabbit! (Rosenthal & Lichtenheld, 2009) and *Daft Bat* (Willis & Ross, 2008) is a literary paired text that involves reading literature. The CCSS also focus on RI. Therefore, what follows is an extensive list of recommended paired text presented in two sections. Section One identifies paired text and CCSS-ELA standards with RL in grade levels K–5 and in grade bands 6–8. Section Two identifies paired text and CCSS-ELA standards with RI in K–5 and 6–8. Both sections address standards related to the CCSS category Integration of Knowledge and Ideas.

Section One: Paired Text for Reading Literature

Reading Literature K–5

Kindergarten

With prompting and support, compare and contrast the adventures and experiences of characters in familiar stories (CCSS.ELA-Literacy.RL.K.9).

▪ *Knuffle Bunny: A Cautionary Tale* (RL) and *Knuffle Bunny Too: A Case of Mistaken Identity* (RL) by Mo Willems

Texts describe the endearing relationship between children and their favorite stuffed pet animal.

▪ *Peter's Chair* by Ezra Jack Keats (RL)
▪ *Knuffle Bunny: A Cautionary Tale* by Mo Willems (RL)

Texts describe a chair and a bunny, each a beloved friend to two different children.

▪ *My Crayons Talk* by Patricia Hubbard (RL)
▪ *The Day the Crayons Quit* by Drew Daywalt (RL)

Texts include colors that come alive, some with pride and some with protest.

▪ *I Want My Hat Back* (RL) and *This Is Not My Hat* (RL) by Jon Klassen

Texts use visual humor and simple stories to invite readers in on an entertaining joke.

▪ *New Shoes for Silvia* by Johanna Hurwitz (RL)
▪ *Grandpa's Slippers* by Joy Watson (RL)

Texts provide lessons in imagination and courage: one with a little girl and her new red shoes, and the other with a grandpa and his old gray slippers.

▪ *I Went Walking* (RL) and *Let's Go Visiting* (RL) by Sue Williams

Texts, one original and the other a companion, are adventure stories that include counting, guessing, colorful animals, and a wild-haired boy.

■ *Oops! A Preston Pig Story* (RL) and *Suddenly! A Preston Pig Story* (RL) by Colin McNaughton

Texts present not-so-mysterious characters from popular fairytales, all of whom get outsmarted and the good guy wins in the end.

Grade 1

Compare and contrast the adventures and experiences of characters in stories (CCSS.ELA-Literacy.RL.1.9).

■ *Deep in the Forest* by Brinton Turkle (RL)
■ *Believe Me, Goldilocks Rocks!: The Story of the Three Bears as Told by Baby Bear* by Nancy Loewen (RL)

Texts present two variations of the favorite fairytale: one wordless, and the other told from the perspective of a familiar, but unlikely, character.

■ *Dreadful David* by Sally Farrell Odgers and Craig Smith (RL)
■ *No David!* by David Shannon (RL)

Texts describe the hilarious antics of two lively, endearing little boys as they test the patience of a mother and grandmother who love them.

■ *Geraldine's Blanket* by Holly Keller (RL)
■ *Owen* by Kevin Henkes (RL)

Texts show that old blankets really never get too old for their owners no matter how old their owners get.

■ *The Little Black Truck* by Libba Moore Gray (RL)
■ *The Rusty, Trusty Tractor* by Joy Cowley (RL)

Texts teach that even old broken-down trucks and rusty tractors can be renewed.

■ *Mary Marony and the Snake* by Suzy Kline (RL)
■ *Hooway for Wodney Wat* by Helen Lester (RL)

Texts treat young children's challenges with pronunciation and stuttering in a humorous and respectful way.

■ *The Recess Queen* by Alexis O'Neill (RL)
■ *Mean Soup* by Betsy Everitt (RL)

Texts teach that being mean and bullying people isn't always necessary or effective

■ *Where's Stripey?* by Wendy Binks (RL)
■ *Edwina the Emu* by Sheena Knowles (RL)

Texts present humorous stories of loving parents who learn important lessons about parenting from their emu children.

■ *Edward the Emu* (RL) and *Edwina the Emu* (RL) by Sheena Knowles

Texts combine the original and the sequel about two emu parents who learn important lessons about what it means to be yourself.

■ *I Ain't Gonna Paint No More!* by Karen Beaumont (RL)
■ *Don't Say That Word* by Alan Katz (RL)

Texts show how one active boy keeps painting and keeps saying words he should not say, despite being told to stop.

■ *Tough Boris* by Mem Fox (RL)
■ *Pirates Don't Change Diapers* by Melinda Long (RL)

Texts show a very different side of pirates. Pirates cry? Pirates change diapers? Who is left digging for treasure?

■ *On the First Day of Grade School* by Emily Brenner (RL)
■ *The Night before First Grade* by Natasha Wing (RL)

Texts present a classic song and a classic tale to help a teacher and a child get ready for first grade.

■ *Ping* by Marjorie Flack (RL)
■ *The Runaway Bunny* by Margaret Wise Brown (RL)

Texts describe two young animals that seek adventure only to return to the comforts of home and the ones that love them.

■ *I Feel a Foot* by Maranke Rinck (RL)
■ *Seven Blind Mice* by Ed Young (RL)

Texts tell stories of animals trying to identify an unknown creature and ultimately realize they need to look not just at the parts but at the whole.

■ *It Happens to Everyone* by Bernice Myers (RL)
■ *First Day Jitters* by Julie Danneberg (RL)

Texts show nervousness about starting school, for children and teachers.

■ *A Proper Little Lady* by Nette Hilton (RL)
■ *Dreadful David* by Sally Farrell Odgers and Craig Smith (RL)

Texts describe the contrast between a little girl, all prim and proper, and a little boy, all busy and boisterous.

■ *Grandmother* by Jeanne Baker (RL)
■ *Our Granny* by Margaret Wild (RL)

Texts provide different but endearing images of one of the most influential persons in a child's life.

■ *A Place for Grace* by Jean Davies Okimoto (RL)
■ *Officer Buckle and Gloria* by Peggy Rathmann (RL)

Texts show the tender relationship between dogs and their owners, especially one owner with physical challenges.

■ *What's That Noise?* by Mary Roennfeldt (RL)
■ *Hist!* by C. J. Dennis (RL)

Texts use rich, figurative language to create a night mystery involving eerie noises.

- *Sophie* by Mem Fox (RL)
- *The Two of Them* by Aliki (RL)

Texts tell tender stories of the relationship between granddaughter and grandfather and their challenges as they both grow older.

- *Friends* by Eric Carle (RL)
- *My Friends* by Taro Gomi (RL)

Texts portray the beauty of true friendship.

- *Sebastian Lives in a Hat* by Thelma Catterwell (RL)
- *Diary of a Wombat* by Jackie French (RL)

Texts describe the life of a wombat in different forms and from different perspectives.

Grade 2

Compare and contrast two or more versions of the same story (e.g., Cinderella stories) by different authors or from different cultures (CCSS.ELA-Literacy.RL.2.9).

- *Goldilocks and the Three Bears* by James Marshall (RL)
- *Goldie Locks Has Chicken Pox* by Erin Dealey (RL)

Texts show two variations of the traditional fairytale: both are humorous and one is hilarious.

- *The Three Billygoats Gruff and Mean Calypso Joe* by Cathrene Valente Youngquist (RL)
- *The Three Billy Goats Gruff* by Paul Galdone (RL)

Texts show two variations of the traditional tale: one involves the meanest troll on an island.

- *Goldilocks and the Three Bears* by James Marshall (RL)
- *Somebody and the Three Blairs* by Marilyn Tolhurst (RL)

Texts share different perspectives on the story of Goldilocks: one from the bears' perspective, and the other from the Blairs' perspective.

- *Little Red Snapperhood* by Neal Gibertson (RL)
- *Little Red Riding Hood: A Newfangled Prairie Tale* by Lisa Campbell Ernst (RL)

Texts provide two variations of the traditional tale: one from deep in the sea, and the other from out on the prairie.

- *The Ugly Duckling* by Hans Christian Andersen (RL)
- *The Sissy Duckling* by Harvey Feinstein (RL)

Texts present two versions of the popular tale. One is traditional, and the other shows a softer side of an endearing duckling.

- *Old MacDonald Had a Farm* by Jane Cabrera (RL)
- *Old MacDonald Had a Workshop* by Lisa Shulman (RL)

Texts show a humorous and informative alternative to the traditional song.

- *Adelita* by Tomie dePaola (RL)
- *Princess Furball* by Charlotte Huck (RL)

Texts present two different versions of *Cinderella*: one from Mexico, and the other from the land of kings, queens, princesses, and an ogre.

- *Cinder Edna* by Ellen Jackson (RL)
- *Prince Cinders* by Babette Cole (RL)

Texts present two different versions of *Cinderella* using wordplay to describe the main characters.

- *Little Red Writing* by Joan Holub (RL)
- *Carmine: A Little More Red* by Melissa Sweet (RL)

Texts show clever variations of *Little Red Riding Hood*. One is a fractured tale of a red pencil in search of a good story, and the other is about a young painter riding a bike to her grandmother's house.

- *The Rough-Face Girl* by Refe Martin (RL)
- *Dinorella: A Prehistoric Fairy Tale* by Pamela Duncan Edwards (RL)

Texts present different versions of *Cinderella* in both time and topic. One is an Algonian Indian version, and the other takes place in prehistoric time.

- *The Three Little Javelinas* by Susan Lowell (RL)
- *The Three Little Wolves and the Big Bad Pig* by Eugene Trivizas (RL)

Texts illustrate two intriguing versions of the traditional tale: one in the American southwest, and the other a reversal—there is a big bad pig!

- *The Three Pigs* by David Weisner (RL)
- *The Three Horrid Little Pigs* by Liz Pichon (RL)

Texts show different sides to characters in *The Three Little Pigs*. One side shows clever and hardworking pigs, and the other has pigs so horrid their own mother sends them away.

Grade 3

Compare and contrast the themes, settings, and plots of stories written by the same author about the same or similar characters (e.g., in books from a series; CCSS. ELA-Literacy.RL.3.9).

- *Don't Let the Pigeon Drive the Bus!* (RL) and *Don't Let the Pigeon Stay Up Late!* (RL) by Mo Willems

Texts hilariously describe how the untypical behavior of a pigeon remarkably resembles the typical behavior of young children.

- *Brown Bear, Brown Bear: What Do You See?* (RL) and *Polar Bear, Polar Bear: What Do You Hear?* (RL) by Bill Martin, Jr.

Texts are patterned books focusing on senses, colors, and animals.

- *First Day Jitters* (RL) and *First Day Letters* (RL) by Julie Danneburg

  Texts, one original and the other a sequel, describe the angst of the first day of school for both teacher and students.

- *Saving Sweetness* (RL) and *Raising Sweetness* (RL) by Diane Stanley

  Texts, one original and the other a sequel, tell the adventures of a heroine named Sweetness, a lovable, kindhearted, and rambunctious orphan who likes to save the day.

- *David Gets in Trouble!* (RL) and *No David!* (RL) by David Shannon

  Texts describe the behavior of an active, but endearing little boy who enjoys mischief and mayhem.

- *Diary of a Worm* (RL) and *Diary of a Worm: Teacher's Pet* (RL) by Doreen Cronin

  Texts use the format of a diary to share individual stories of worms in two different situations.

- *Click, Clack, Moo: Cows That Type* (RL) and *Giggle, Giggle, Quack* (RL) by Doreen Cronin

  Texts tell the story of Duck and his animal friends that know what they want and how to get it, be it through collective bargaining or downright subterfuge.

- *Home* (RL) and *Window* (RL) by Jeanne Baker

  Texts, both wordless, show change over time with artful, three-dimensional collage illustrations.

- *Hidden Forest* (RL) and *Where the Forest Meets the Sea* (RL) by Jeanne Baker

  Texts include three-dimensional collage illustrations to highlight important environmental issues on the land and under the sea.

- *Night in the Country* (RL) and *When I Was Young in the Mountains* (RL) by Cynthia Rylant

  Texts describe in rich, evocative language the sights, sounds, and beauty of country living.

- *Dear Mr. Blueberry* (RL) and *Dear Greenpeace* (RL) by Simon James

  Texts tell the story of little Emily who writes letters back and forth to her teacher when she discovers a whale in her backyard, but when that doesn't help her cause, she decides to write letters to Greenpeace for advice on how to protect the whale.

- *Zen Ties* (RL) and *Zen Shorts* (RL) by John Muth

  Texts include beautiful watercolor illustrations to introduce Zen Buddism.

- *The Three Questions* (RL) and *Stone Soup* (RL) by John Muth

  Texts include beautiful watercolor illustrations to introduce Zen Buddism.

- *Mama, Do You Love Me?* (RL) and *Papa, Do You Love Me?* (RL) by Barbara M. Joosse

  Texts highlight the theme of parents' unconditional love for their children: one the love of an Eskimo mother, and the other the love of an African father.

- *Yo! Yes?* (RL) and *Ring! Yo?* (RL) by Chris Raschka

   Texts are unconventional but conventional in theme: Both describe how two young boys become acquainted and eventually friends.

- *Miss Malarkey Won't Be in Today* (RL) and *Miss Malarkey Doesn't Live in Room 10* (RL) by Judy Finchler

   Texts follow the day-to-day activities of a fictional teacher and provide insights into the real lives of teachers.

- *Ish* (RL) and *The Dot* (RL) by Peter Reynolds

   Texts describe gentle stories of characters building confidence enough to take risks.

Grade 4

Compare and contrast the treatment of similar themes and topics (e.g., opposition of good and evil) and patterns of events (e.g., the quest) in stories and myths, and traditional literature from different cultures (CCSS.ELA-Literacy.RL.4.9).

PATTERNS OF EVENTS—MYTHS

- *The Gods and Goddesses of Olympus* by Aliki (RI)
- *Mount Olympus Basketball* by Kevin O'Malley (RL)

   Texts with colorful, cartoon-like illustrations introduce the troubles between gods and mortals. One is an informational text, and the other describes a lively basketball game between determined competitors.

- *Hercules* by Robert Burleigh (RL)
- *Hercules: The Man, the Myth, the Hero* by Kathryn Lasky (RL)

   Texts show different versions of the biography of the famous hero.

- *King Midas: A Golden Tale* by John Warren Stewig (RL)
- *King Midas: The Golden Touch* by Demi (RL)

   Texts show different versions of the king who could turn things to gold with a single touch.

- *Storm Boy* (RL) and *Frog Girl* (RL) by Paul Owen Lewis

   Texts use northwest Native American motifs to describe visits to a mysterious, supernatural world.

- *The Giant Devil-Dingo* (RL) and *The Rainbow Serpent* (RL) by Dick Roughsey

   Texts are dreamtime stories based on Australian Aboriginal traditions.

- *Greek Myths* by Marcia Williams (RL)
- *Wings* by Jane Yolen (RL)

   Texts are retellings of famous myths in comic book format and highlight one myth in narrative form.

- *Theseus and the Minotaur* by Leonard Everett Fisher (RL)
- *Theseus and the Minotaur* by Warwick Hutton (RL)

Texts show richness of this myth from two different perspectives.

- *Cyclops* by Leonard Everett Fisher (RL)
- *Odysseus and the Cyclops* by Warwick Hutton (RL)

Texts use different types of illustrations to tell the story of a man-eating monster.

- *Persephone* retold by Warwick Hutton (RL)
- *Persephone and the Pomegranate* by Kris Waldherr (RL)

Texts tell the same myth, a trip to the underworld, in various ways with different types of illustrations. One shows a dream-like world, and the other uses beautiful watercolors.

- *The Way of the Stars: Greek Legends of the Constellations* (RL) and *The Shining Stars: Greek Legends of the Zodiac* (RL) by Ghislaine Vautier

Texts connect traditional Greek legends to constellations of stars in the sky.

PATTERNS OF EVENTS—QUESTS

- *Don Quixote and the Windmills* by Eric A. Kimmel (RL)
- *Miguel de Cervantes' Don Quixote* retold by Marcia Williams (RL)

Texts tell an old story from different perspectives and with new pictorial formats.

TRADITIONAL LITERATURE FROM DIFFERENT CULTURES

- *Kamishibai Man* by Allen Say (RL)
- *The Storytellers* by Ted Lewin (RL)

Texts describe the history of storytelling through the words of two storytellers: one from Japan, and the other from Morocco.

- *Lon Po Po: A Red Riding Hood Story from China* by Ed Young (RL)
- *The Orphan: A Cinderella Story from Greece* by Anthony Manna (RL)

Texts show different versions of the famous fairytale: one from China, and the other from Greece.

- *Domitila: A Cinderella Story from the Mexican Tradition* by Jewell Reinhart Coburn (RL)
- *Adelaida: A Cuban Cinderella* by Ana Monnar (RL)

Texts show different versions of the famous fairytale: one from Mexico, including proverbs in the margins, and the other from Cuba with an unexpected twist.

- *The Egyptian Cinderella* (RL) and *The Korean Cinderella* (RL) by Shirley Climo

Texts show different versions of the famous fairytale: one from Egypt, and the other from Korea.

- *The Golden Sandal: A Middle Eastern Cinderella* by Rebecca Hickox (RL)
- *The Persian Cinderella* by Shirley Climo (RL)

Texts show different versions of the famous fairytale from the Middle East: one exquisitely illustrated from Iraq, and the other from ancient Persia, now Iran.

- *Yeh-Shen: A Cinderella Story from China* by Ai-Ling Louie (RL)
- *Moss Gown* by William Hooks (RL)

Texts with beautiful, even haunting illustrations, of *Cinderella*: one from China, and the other from the American southern tradition.

TALES

- *The Pot That Juan Built* by Nancy Andrews-Coebel (RL)
- *Dave the Potter: Artist, Poet, Slave* by Laban Carrick Hill (RL)

Texts depict the artistry and significance of making pots by artists who live in different times and from different cultures.

- *The Girl Who Loved Wild Horses* (RL) and *Death of the Iron Horse* (RL) by Paul Goble

Texts depict tales of the life, times, and traditions of Native American Indians.

FOLKTALES

- *Goha the Wise Fool* by Denys Johnson-Davies (RL)
- *A Donkey Reads* by Muriel Mandell (RL)

Texts describes important and different historical figures from the Middle East.

FAIRYTALES

- *Grumbles Forest: Fairy-Tale Voices with a Twist* by Jane Yolen and Rebecca Kai Dotlich (RL)
- *The Stinky Cheese Man and Other Fairly Stupid Tales* by John Scieszka (RL)

Texts provide a very different twist on very old fairytales.

- *The Emperor's New Clothes* by Hans Christian Andersen (RL)
- *The Principal's New Clothes* by Stephanie Calmenson (RL)

Texts show two different versions of the popular fairytale: one traditional, and one contemporary.

- *The Very Smart Pea and the Princess-to-Be* by Mini Grey (RL)
- *The Pea and the Princess* by Lauren Child (RL)

Texts reveal different perspectives on this traditional fairytale: one from the princess, and one from the pea.

- *The Three Billy Goats Gruff* by Carol Ottolenghi (RL)
- *Three Cool Kids* by Rebecca Emberley (RL)

Texts show different perspectives on a popular fairytale: one with goats and a troll in the country, and the other in the city.

- *James Marshall's Cinderella* retold by Barbara Karlin (RL)
- *The Turkey Girl: A Zuni Cinderella Story* by Penny Pollock (RL)

Texts show different versions of the fairytale: one traditional, and one from the Native American tradition.

- *Jack and the Beanstalk* retold by Steven Kellogg (RL)
- *Jack and the Wonder Beans* by James Still (RL)

  Texts show different versions of the fairytale: one traditional (more or less), and one from Appalachia.

TRICKSTER TALES

- *Iktomi and the Berries* (RL) and *Iktomi and the Boulder* (RL) by Paul Goble

  Texts show the attempts of the famous mischief maker in the Native American tradition.

BALLADS

- *The Drover's Dream* illustrated by Deborah Niland and written by A. B. Paterson (RL)
- *Andy's Gone with Cattle* by Henry Lawson (RL)

  Texts tell different traditional ballads from the Australian outback.

- *Mulga Bill's Bicycle* (RL) and *Waltzing Matilda* (RL) by A. B. Paterson

  Texts tell different traditional ballads from the Australian outback.

- *The Man From Snowy River* (RL) and *The Man from Ironbark* (RL) by A. B. Paterson

  Texts tell different traditional ballads from the Australian outback.

FABLES

- *Fables* by Arnold Lobel (RL)
- *Squids Will Be Squids* by Jon Scieszka (RL)

  Texts combine entertaining traditional and nontraditional fables.

- *Fables* by Arnold Lobel (RL)
- *Fables Aesop Never Wrote* by Robert Kraus (RL)

  Texts combine traditional Aesop fables with fables Aesop never actually wrote.

- *Buddha Stories* (RL) and *Demi's Reflective Fables* (RL) by Demi

  Texts combine thoughtful and reflective tales and fables from ancient China.

- *The Lion and the Mouse* (RL) and *The Tortoise and the Hare* (RL) by Jerry Pinkney

  Texts, one wordless, provide beautifully illustrated adapted versions of famous fables.

- *The Crow and the Pitcher* by Aesop (RL)
- *The Crow and the Pitcher* retold and illustrated by Stephanie Gwyn Brown (RL/RI)

  Texts show different versions of a famous fable: one traditional, and the other integrating literacy and science.

- *William Tell* by Leonard Everett Fisher (RL)
- *William Tell* by Margaret Early (RL)

  Texts describe different versions of the famous Swiss folk hero, both beautifully illustrated.

TALL TALES

- *The Bunyans* by Audrey Wood (RL)
- *Paul Bunyan* retold and illustrated by Steven Kellogg (RL)

Texts describe the rollicking ride of a famous tall-tale hero who created many natural wonders across America. Or did he?

- *Pecos Bill* (RL) and *Mike Fink* (RL) retold and illustrated by Steven Kellogg

Texts depict a rowdy cowboy and a Mississippi riverman through large, colorful illustrations showing characters as larger-than-life figures.

- *The Legend of the Indian Paintbrush* (RL) and *The Legend of the Bluebonnet* (RL) by Tomie dePaola

Texts describe different but related tall tales. One is about a unique plant and how it got its name, and the other describes a unique flower and how it found a home as the Texas state flower.

- *Johnny Appleseed* (RL) and *Sally Ann Thunder Ann Whirlwind Crockett* (RL) retold and illustrated by Steven Kellogg

Texts present two characters. One is a brave, daring, and accomplished heroine, and the other is an appealing and traveling hero.

Grade 5

Analyze how visual and multimedia elements contribute to the meaning, tone, or beauty of a text (e.g., graphic novel, multimedia presentation of fiction, folktale, myth, poem) (CCSS.ELA-Literacy.RL.5.7).

- *The Little Red Fish* by Taeeun Yoo (RL)
- *Red Flower Goes West* by Ann Turner (RL)

Texts use the color red with two different objects (fish and geranium) and in two different times and settings to highlight the power of imagination.

- *A Sweet Smell of Roses* by Angela Johnson (RL)
- *Red Flower Goes West* by Ann Turner (RL)

Texts use the color red with two different objects (fish and roses) and in two different time and settings. One involves African American children marching during the civil rights movement, and the other describes a family migrating to the American West. Both highlight the power of imagination concerning a new future.

- *Rose Blanche* by Roberto Innocenti (RL)
- *A Sweet Smell of Roses* by Angela Johnson (RL)

Texts use the voices of children living in different times and places to describe the injustices of the Holocaust and racism.

- *Erika's Story* by Ruth Vander Zee (RL)
- *Rose Blanche* by Roberto Innocenti (RL)

Texts use color, penetrating illustrations, and provocative stories to discuss the horrors of the Holocaust.

- *Mirror* (RL) and *Shadows* (RL) by Suzy Lee

Texts use innovative design formats and shadowing techniques to highlight the importance of play, imagination, and reflection.

Compare and contrast stories in the same genre (e.g., mysteries and adventure stories) on their approaches to similar themes and topics (CCSS.ELA-Literacy.RL.5.9).

- *If Not for the Cat* by Jack Prelutsky (RL/RI)
- *Haiku Hike* written and illustrated by fourth-grade students at Massachusetts St. Mary's Catholic School (RL/RI)

Texts teach Haiku as a form of poetry.

- *Dear Mrs. LaRue: Letters from Obedience School* by Mark Teague (RL)
- *Messages in the Mailbox: How to Write a Letter* by Loreen Leedy (RI)

Texts use narrative and informational text. One tells the story of a dog that wants to leave obedience school, and the other explains how to write letters.

- *Blueberry Bear* by Rebecca Kaler (RL)
- *Little Blue and Little Yellow* by Leo Lionni (RL)

Texts beautifully use a spirit of inquiry and complementary colors to tell different stories. One is a story of friendship, and the other describes what happens when colors are mixed.

- *Wave* (RL) and *The Zoo* (RL) by Suzy Lee

Texts include innovative design formats to tell stories of innocence and wonder. One is wordless, and the other uses rich language and beautiful illustrations.

- *The House* by Roberto Innocenti and J. Patrick Lewis (RL)
- *Home* by Jeannie Baker (RL)

Texts highlight the theme of change over time by following the history of two homes: one old home in the country, and one new home in the city.

- *Home in the Sky* (RL) and *Millicent* (RL) by Jeanne Baker

Texts are gentle stories detailing two different perspectives about living in a city and the people who live there.

- *Rose Blanche* by Roberto Innocenti (RL)
- *Let the Celebrations Begin* by Margaret Wild (RL)

Texts show different perspectives about innocent people who experienced the Holocaust.

- *Troy Thompson's Excellent Poetry Book* (RL) and *Troy Thompson's Excellent Prose Folio* (RL) by Gary Crew

  Texts humorously display the writing of one middle school student who learns different ways to write poetry and prose.

- *June 29, 1999* (RL) and *Flotsam* (RL) by David Weisner

  Texts include a visual feast of beautiful, artful illustrations to stimulate imaginations, young and old.

- *The Dot* by Peter Reynolds (RL)
- *The Clever Stick* by John Lechner (RL)

  Texts include illustrations that uniquely and perfectly complement the story lessons of imagination and risk taking.

- *Bear's Magic Pencil* (RL) and *A Bear-y Tale* (RL) by Anthony Browne

  Texts include ingenious illustrations to show how a magic pencil can get a little bear out of trouble.

- *Those Bottles!* by M. L. Miller (RL)
- *The Big Orange Splot* by Daniel Pinkwater (RL)

  Texts use colorful and whimsical illustrations to highlight the value of and respect for difference.

- *The Incredible Book Eating Boy* by Oliver Jeffers (RL)
- *The World That Loved Books* by Stephen Parlato (RL)

  Texts share the love of books and how reading books can transform lives.

- *One Scary Night* by Antoine Guillope (RL)
- *Mysteries of Harris Burdick* by Chris Van Allsburg (RL)

  Texts use evocative and suspenseful illustrations to tell different, as well as similar, stories set in mysterious and scary settings.

- *The Last Resort* by Roberto Innocenti (RL)
- *The Collector of Moments* by Quint Buchholz (RL)

  Texts illuminate the wonders of imagination. One describes a search for imagination lost, and the other a discovery of imagination left behind.

- *The Mysteries of Harris Burdick* (RL) and *The Z Was Zapped* (RL) by Chris Van Allsburg

  Texts use stunning black-and-white drawings with evocative shadows to present story mysteries and mysteries of performances.

Reading Literature 6–8

Grade 6

Compare and contrast texts in different forms or genres (e.g., stories and poems, historical novels and fantasy stories) in terms of their approaches to similar themes and topics (CCSS.ELA-Literacy.RL.6.9).

- *Rosa* by Nikki Giovanni (RL/RI)
- *A Wreath for Emmett Till* by Marilyn Nelson (RL/RI)

Texts provide narrative accounts of two important historical events in the struggle for civil rights. One is in story format about Rosa Parks, and the other is in a collection of interwoven sonnets about the tragic death of Emmett Till.

- *Carl Sandburg: Adventures of a Poet* by Penelope Niven (RL)
- *Poetry for Young People: Carl Sandburg* edited by Frances Schoonmaker Bolin (RL)

Texts present the life and poetry of one of America's greatest poets from two different perspectives. One highlights Sandberg's life, and the other discusses his lyrical and thoughtful poetry.

- "How to Eat a Poem" by Eve Merriam (RL)
- *The Incredible Book Eating Boy* by Oliver Jeffers (RL)

Texts, although different (one is a poem, and the other is a narrative), use a similar metaphor about the need for readers to digest, not just read, good literature.

- *Something Permanent* by Cynthia Rylant (RI/RL)
- *Tight Times* by Barbara Shook Hazen (RL)

Texts describe difficult times for people during the Depression era through different genres. One uses black-and-white photographs and is accompanied by poetry, and the other uses black-and-white illustrations in a gentle but compelling narrative.

- *William Shakespeare and the Globe* by Aliki (RI)
- *The Boy, the Bear, the Baron, the Bard* by Gregory Rogers (RL)

Texts introduce information about the life and work of William Shakespeare. One is a colorful and engaging picture book, and the other is an imaginative, wordless picture book.

- *Diary of a Baby Wombat* (RL) and *How to Scratch a Wombat* (RL/RI) by Jackie French

Texts show two different perspectives on the wombat: one shares information, and the other is a narrative on one of Australia's most endearing animals.

- *The Wombat Who Talked to the Stars* (RL/RI) and *Koala Number One* (RL) by Jill Morris

Texts use different formats and perspectives to share important and interesting information about the lovable wombat.

■ "The Midnight Ride of Paul Revere" by Henry Wadsworth Longfellow engraved and painted by Christopher Bing (RL/RI)
■ *Paul Revere's Midnight Ride* by Stephen Krensky (RL/RI)

Texts provide fascinating information about an important historical event during the Revolutionary War period. One presents the famous poem and is accompanied by award-winning illustrations, and the other is a beautifully illustrated narrative.

■ *Uptown* by Bryan Collier (RL)
■ *Harlem* by Walter Dean Myers (RL)

Texts share unique, but different, perspectives on a historical time and important place in New York called Harlem.

■ "The Negro Speaks of Rivers" by Langston Hughes (RL)
■ *Langston's Train Ride* by Robert Burleigh (RL)

Texts present two perspectives on the life and work of Langston Hughes. One is a poem written by the poet, and the other is an insightful biography.

■ *Visiting Langston* by Willie Perdomo (RL)
■ *Coming Home from the Life of Langston Hughes* by Floyd Cooper (RL)

Texts are two biographies that depict the famous author in various ways and from different perspectives.

■ *Duke Ellington* by Andrea Davis Pinkney (RL)
■ *Ellington Was Not a Street* by Ntozake Shange (RL)

Texts are biographical narratives with beautiful and informative illustrations. One is about the life of the famous musician, and the other discusses the author's fellow artists and community.

■ *When I Heard the Learned Astronomer* and *Nothing but Miracles* by Walt Whitman (RL)
■ *Walt Whitman: Words for America* by Barbara Kerley (RL)

Texts provide a rich portrait of the life and work of Walt Whitman. One highlights two of the author's famous poems, and the other presents an extensive biographical account of the man behind the poetry.

■ *I Dream of Trains* by Angela Johnson (RL)
■ "Crossing" by Philip Booth (RL)

Texts provide insights into the majesty and lure of trains. One is told as a first-person narrative of a young boy who dreams of a special train and a historical engineer, and the other is told in a third-person poem of people who watch and count the different cars of an almost magical freight train.

■ *Train Song* by Diane Siebert (RL)
■ *Trains* by Gail Gibbons (RI)

Texts celebrate trains. One uses a song that pays aesthetic tribute to the sights and sounds of trains and the people who rode them. The other is an informational tribute to the history of trains, identifies different kinds of trains, and explains how trains run and what cars they pull.

Compare and contrast a fictional portrayal of a time, place, or character and a historical account of the same period as a means of understanding how authors of fiction use or alter history (CCSS.ELA-Literacy.RL.7.9).

Texts with marginalia and hybrid texts, while technically not paired text, are good resources to address this standard. Simply put, texts with marginalia are narratives that also include related information in margins of a text. Hybrid texts are single books that integrate literary and informational text.

MARGINALIA

■ *Magic in the Margins* by W. Nikola-Lish (RL/RI)

Text tells a story set in the Medieval Ages about the beautiful art and historical practice of marginalia.

■ *Starry Messenger* by Peter Sis (RL/RI)

Text combines a narrative about Galileo and rich information in the book's margins about the famous philosopher, scientist, and mathematician.

■ *Snowflake Bentley* by Jacqueline Briggs Martin (RL/RI)

Text combines a beautifully told narrative about the man who discovered that no two snowflakes are the same with interesting informational text in the book's margins about his life, perseverance, and amazing photographs.

■ *The Other Mozart: The Life of the Famous Chevalier de Saint-George* by Hugh Brewster (RL/RI)

Text describes a little-known but fascinating historical character study about a talented musician who was compared with Amadeus Mozart.

■ *Python* by Christopher Cheng (RL/RI)

Text uses a narrative format to follow a day in the life of a python snake in the Australian outback and includes informational text about the behaviors, habitats, and activities of pythons.

HYBRID TEXT—TIME

■ *The Cats in Krasinski Square* by Karen Hesse (RL/RI)

Text combines a beautifully told narrative describing a courageous instance of Jewish resistance during World War II in Warsaw.

■ *The Donkey of Gallipoli: A True Story of Courage in World War I* by Mark Greenwood (RL/RI)

Text combines a colorful and engaging narrative with a historical account of the battle of Gallipoli during World War I from British and Turkish perspectives, told by a special soldier and an even more special donkey.

■ *Mei Ling in China City* by Icy Smith (RL/RI)

Text combines a compelling narrative for ELA teachers about a bonding relationship between two girls, one Chinese and the other Japanese, and informational text for social studies teachers to introduce the controversial issue of Japanese American internment camps during World War II.

■ *Kamishibai Man* by Allen Say (RL/RI)

Text combines a heartwarming narrative for ELA teachers about a grandfather who was once a master picture storyteller, and provides informational text for social studies teachers to introduce paper theater, the practice of public storytelling and the role it played during World War II in Japan.

PAIRED TEXT—CHARACTER

■ *The Watcher* by Jeanette Winter (RL)
■ *Me, Jane* by Patrick McDonnell (RL)

Texts are both narratives from different narrators that describe the extraordinary, lifelong work of Jane Goodall who studied behaviors of chimpanzees.

■ *A Taste of Colored Water* by Matt Faulkner (RL/RI)
■ *Ruth and the Green Book* by Calvin Alexander Ramsey (RL/RI)

Texts poignantly describe racism and discrimination occurring in the Deep South during the 1950s and 1960s. One introduces Jim Crow laws, and the other introduces a little-known but historically significant green book.

■ *When Marian Sang* (RL/RI) and *Amelia and Eleanor Go for a Ride* (RL/RI) by Pam Muñoz Ryan

Texts introduce Marian Anderson, one of America's finest opera singers, and describe her relationship with Eleanor Roosevelt at one of the most important times in U.S. history.

Section Two: Paired Text for Reading Informational Text

This section identifies paired text that focuses on RI and addresses ELA standards for K–5 and 6–8.

Reading Informational Text K–5

Kindergarten

With prompting and support, identify basic similarities in and differences between two texts on the same topic (e.g., in illustrations, descriptions, or procedures) (CCSS. ELA-Literacy.RI.K.9).

■ *Charlie Anderson* by Barbara Abercrombie (RL/RI)
■ *Six-Dinner Sid* by Inga Moore (RL/RI)

Texts tell different stories about two cats and the secrets they share. One of the stories gently touches on the topic of two sisters living in two homes.

Grade 1

Identify basic similarities in and differences between two texts on the same topic (e.g., in illustrations, descriptions, or procedures; CCSS.ELA-Literacy.RI.1.9).

ALPHABET

- *ABC: What Do You See?* by Arlene Alda (RL/RI)
- *Alphabet City* by Stephen T. Johnson RL/RI)

Texts include unique, real-life illustrations that teach the letters of the alphabet in very innovative ways.

- *The Graphic Alphabet* by David Pelletier (RL/RI)
- *The Z Was Zapped* by Chris Van Allsburg (RL/RI)

Texts show unique and visually appealing techniques for introducing and learning the letters of the alphabet. One presents a dazzling display of alphabetic letters as they have never been seen before, and the other presents a performance never witnessed before.

- *Q Is for Duck: An Alphabet Guessing Game* by Mary Elting (RL/RI)
- *A Is for Angry: An Animal and Adjective Alphabet* by Sandra Boynton (RL/RI)

Texts use a guessing-game format to teach the letters of the alphabet while using prediction as part of the learning process.

- *Animalia* by Graeme Base (RL/RI)
- *Aster's Aardvark's Alphabet Adventure* by Steven Kellogg (RL/RI)

Texts use gorgeous illustrations to teach the letters of the alphabet in unforgettable ways.

- *Alphabeasts* by Wallace Edwards (RL/RI)
- *Animalia* by Graeme Base (RL/RI)

Texts use gorgeous illustrations to teach the letters of the alphabet in unforgettable ways.

ALPHABETIC LETTERS

- *The Vowel Family: A Tale of Lost Letters* by Sally M. Walker (RL/RI)
- *The War between the Vowels and Consonants* by Priscilla Turner (RL/RI)

Texts tell two clever and entertaining stories with vowels and consonants as the main characters to show the important differences between them.

ALLITERATION

- *Some Smug Slug* (RL/RI) and *Four Famished Foxes and Fosdyke* (RL/RI) by Pamela Duncan Edwards

Texts use narrative to teach alliteration in a fun and frolicking way.

- *Watch William Walk* by Ann Jonas (RL/RI)
- *The Worrywarts* by Pamela Duncan Edwards (RL/RI)

Texts use simple narratives to teach alliteration in a humorous way.

WORD STUDY

■ *There's an Ant behind Anthony* (RL/RI) and *There's an Ape behind the Drape* (RL/RI) by Bernard Most

Texts provide a fun and entertaining introduction to word study, particularly by seeing little words inside bigger words.

Grade 2

Compare and contrast the most important points presented by two texts on the same topic (CCSS.ELA-Literacy.RI2.9).

PARTS OF SPEECH

■ *Kites Sail High: A Book of Verbs* by Ruth Heller (RL/RI)
■ *Add It, Dip It, Fix It: A Book of Verbs* by R. M. Schneider (RL/RI)

Texts teach the same part of speech, verbs, from two different perspectives using rhyming text.

■ *Hairy, Scary, Ordinary: What Is an Adjective?* by Brian P. Cleary (RL/RI)
■ *Many Luscious Lollipops: A Book about Adjectives* by Ruth Heller (RL/RI)

Texts teach the same part of speech, adjectives, from two different perspectives using rhyming text.

■ *Dearly, Nearly, Insincerely: What Is an Adverb?* by Brian P. Cleary (RL/RI)
■ *Up, Up and Away: A Book about Adverbs* by Ruth Heller (RL/RI)

Texts teach the same part of speech, adverbs, from two different perspectives using rhyming text.

■ *A Mink, a Fink, a Skating Rink: What Is a Noun?* by Brian P. Cleary (RL/RI)
■ *Nouns and Verbs Have a Field Day* by Robin Pulver (RL/RI)

Texts teach the same part of speech, nouns and verbs: one uses rhyming text, and the other is a narrative with nouns and verbs as the main characters.

PUNCTUATION

■ *Punctuation Take a Vacation* by Robin Pulver (RL/RI)
■ *Twenty-Odd Ducks: Why Every Punctuation Mark Counts* by Lynn Truss (RL/RI)

Texts teach the value of punctuation and the different functions of punctuation marks. One is a narrative, and the other uses single illustrations with a delightful play on words.

■ *Elephants Aloft* by Kathi Appelt (RL/RI)
■ *Rosie's Walk* by Pat Hutchins (RL/RI)

Texts tell simple narratives about characters on a big adventure. One story is about being in the air, and the other takes place on land, and in the process both teach prepositional phrases.

- *Over, under and through* by Tana Hoban (RI)
- *Under, over, by the Clover* by Brian P. Cleary (RL/RI)

Texts teach prepositions in a simple, direct way.

INTERESTING INFORMATIONAL TEXTS

- *The Berry Book* by Gail Gibbons (RI)
- *Kiernan's Jam* by Nancy Delano Moore (RL/RI)

Texts combine an informational book about berries and a heartwarming narrative about a little boy and his grandparents making jam.

- *Popcorn at the Palace* by Emily Arnold McCully (RL)
- *The Popcorn Book* by Tomie dePaola (RI)

Texts combine an informational book on the history of popcorn with a delightful narrative about the history of a common crop used in uncommon ways.

Grade 3

Compare and contrast the most important points and key details presented in two texts on the same topic (CCSS.ELA-Literacy.R.3.9).

PARTS OF SPEECH

- *Pitch and Throw, Grasp and Know: What Is a Synonym?* by Brian P. Cleary (RL/RI)
- *Antonyms, Synonyms and Homonyms* by Kim Rayevsky and Robert Rayevsky (RI)

Texts teach synonyms: one uses rhyming text, and the other adds antonyms and homonyms to the mix.

- *A Cache of Jewels and Other Collective Nouns* (RL/RI) and *Merry-Go-Round: A Book about Nouns* (RL/RI) by Ruth Heller

Texts use rhyming text to teach the meaning and function of nouns.

- *A Chocolate Moose* (RL/RI) and *The King Who Rained* (RL/RI) by Fred Gwynne

Texts teach homonyms through delightful, playful, and humorous wordplay.

- *How Much Can a Bare Bear Bear? What Are Homonyms and Homophones?* by Brian B. Cleary (RL/RI)
- *Dear Deer: A Book of Homophones* by Gene Baretta (RL/RI)

Texts teach the definition and show examples of homophones: one uses rhyming text, and the other contains a unique collection of unusual homophones.

- *Mine, All Mine: A Book about Pronouns* by Ruth Heller (RL/RI)
- *I and You and Don't Forget Who: What Is a Pronoun?* by Brian P. Cleary (RL/RI)

Texts use rhyming text to teach the meaning and function of pronouns.

PUNCTUATION

- *Greedy Apostrophe: A Cautionary Tale* by Jan Carr (RL/RI)
- *The Girl's Like Spaghetti: Why You Can't Manage without Apostrophes!* by Lynne Truss (RL/RI)

Texts teach the importance of apostrophes in two different ways. One is a cautionary tale, and the other uses single illustrations with a delightful play on words.

- *Greedy Apostrophe: A Cautionary Tale* by Jan Carr (RL/RI)
- *Alfie the Apostrophe* by Moira Rose Donohue (RL/RI)

Texts show the value of apostrophes in different ways. One is a cautionary tale, and the other is a lively, dramatic narrative.

FIGURES OF SPEECH

- *My Momma Likes to Say* by Denise Brennan-Nelson (RL/RI)
- *Figures of Speech* by Mervyn Peake (RL/RI)

Texts provide interesting, informative, and popular figures of speech.

Grade 4

Integrate information from two texts on the same topic in order to write or speak about the subject knowledgeably (CCLS.ELA-Literacy.RI.4.9).

PARTS OF SPEECH

- *Thesaurus Rex* by Laya Steinberg (RL/RI)
- *Antonyms, Synonyms and Homonyms* by Kim Rayevsky and Robert Rayevsky (RI)

Texts teach synonyms. One follows a day in the life of a young dinosaur with lots of similar words to describe his activities, and the other introduces synonyms while adding antonyms and homonyms to the mix.

VOCABULARY

- *Double Trouble in Walla Walla* by Andrew Clements (RL/RI)
- *Miss Alaineus: A Vocabulary Disaster* by Debra Frasier (RL/RI)

Texts use humor and wordplay to teach vocabulary: one is a lively narrative, and the other uses the main character to provide an interesting and entertaining play on vocabulary words.

INTERESTING INFORMATIONAL TEXTS

- *Sweet Clara and the Freedom Quilt* by Deborah Hopkinson (RL/RI)
- *Follow the Drinking Gourd* by Jeannette Winter (RL/RI)

Texts include beautiful illustrations and rich text to provide two different versions on the underground railroad.

Grade 5

Integrate information from several texts on the same topic in order to write or speak about the subject knowledgeably (CCLS.ELA-Literacy.RI.5.9).

SIMILE

- *Crazy Like a Fox: A Simile Story* by Loreen Leedy (RL/RI)
- *Muddy as a Duck Puddle and Other American Similes* by Laurie Lawlor (RL/RI)

Texts introduce the concept of simile. One is a delightful story of Rufus who is not only a fox but is crazy like a fox, and the other isa collection of similes as crazy and zany as Rufus.

INTERESTING INFORMATIONAL TEXTS

- *Armadillo Trail: The Northward Journey of the Armadillo* by Stephen R. Swinburne (RL/RI)
- *The Armadillo from Amarillo* by Lynn Cherry (RL)

Texts describe the journeys and adventures of armadillos. One uses rhyming text, and the other is a narrative that follows an armadillo that faces and overcomes dangers along the way.

Reading Informational Text 6–8

Grade 6

Compare and contrast one author's presentation of events with that of another (e.g., a memoir written by and a biography on the same person; CCLS.ELA-Literacy.RI.6.9).

- *The Edmund Fitzgerald: The Song of the Bell* by Kathy-Jo Wargin (RL/RI)
- *The Gulls of the Edmund Fitzgerald* by Tres Seymour (RL/RI)

Texts share two perspectives on a famous maritime disaster. One is a narrative account that describes the travels and later sinking of a huge transport ship on Lake Superior. The other is a narrative with black-and-white and colored illustrations that focus on the gulls of Lake Superior, birds that warn of danger only if sailors take notice.

- *Abraham Lincoln* by Amy L. Cohn and Suzy Schmidt (RL/RI)
- *A. Lincoln and Me* by Louise Borden (RL/RI)

Texts insightfully portray one of America's greatest presidents. One is a biography accompanied with colorful illustrations, and the other is a contemporary narrative told by a young boy who shares similar attributes as Abraham Lincoln starting with that they were born on the same day.

- *Abe's Honest Words: The Life of Abraham Lincoln* by Doreen Rappaport (RL/RI)
- *Abraham Lincoln's Gettysburg Address* by Jack Levin and Mark Levin (RL/RI)

Texts represent a unique combination. One is a biography told in two voices (third person by the author and first person by Abraham Lincoln) and accompanied with stunning illustrations. The other is an evocative, black-and-white illustrated version of Lincoln's historic Gettysburg Address, the 10-sentence, 268-word speech that challenged a nation.

- *Young Abe Lincoln* by Cheryl Harness (RL/RI)
- *Abe Lincoln Remembers* by Ann Turner (RL/RI)

Texts share simple and interesting introductions to the fascinating life and times of Abraham Lincoln. One is told with realistic, colorful illustrations and third-person narration, and the other is told through limited text and artistic paintings from Lincoln's own point of view.

- *On a Beam of Light: A Story of Albert Einstein* by Jennifer Berne (RL/RI)
- *Odd Boy Out: Young Albert Einstein* by Don Brown (RL/RI)

Texts provide two differently illustrated biographies on one of the most famous scientists in the world. Both show the life, work, and struggles of the scientist and each highlights different scientific discoveries including theory of relativity, speed of light, and atomic energy leading to the development of the atomic bomb.

- *Galileo's Journal: 1609–1610* by Jeanne K. Pettenati (RL/RI)
- *I, Galileo* by Bonnie Christensen (RL/RI)

Texts use biographies through different formats to introduce the life and times of Galileo. One is in journal format, as Galileo might have kept, and the other is a first-person narrative in which the famous scientist speaks for himself.

- *Galileo* by Leonard Everett Fisher (RL/RI)
- *Galileo's Treasure Box* by Catherine Brighton (RL/RI)

Texts are beautifully illustrated biographies of the historical figure. One is designed in evocative black-and-white with rich information about Galileo's life and work. The other is a tapestry of rich pictures and rich text that slowly reveals through the eyes and words of his daughter the mysterious items in Galileo's famous treasure box.

- *Martin's Big Words* by Doreen Rappaport (RL/RI)
- *My Brother Martin: A Sister Remembers Growing Up with the Rev. Dr. Martin Luther King Jr.* by Christine King Farris (RL/RI)

Texts present beautiful and respectful narratives accompanied by artful and symbolic illustrations about the life and times of Martin Luther King, Jr. One combines a third-person narration about Dr. King and includes inspirational quotes from the civil rights leader. The other is a beautifully crafted narrative and reflection told by Dr. King's sister.

Grade 7

Analyze how two or more authors writing about the same topic share their presentations of key information by emphasizing different evidence or advancing different interpretations of facts (CCLS.ELA-Literacy.RI.7.9).

- *John Muir: America's Naturalist* by Thomas Locker (RL/RI)
- *Sierra* by Diane Siebert (RL/RI)

Texts share complementary perspectives dealing with the life and times of John Muir. One includes short, rich descriptions of Muir's travels in the Sierra Nevada Mountains of California, particularly Yosemite, and is accompanied with painted landscape illustrations. The other provides a lyrical description of the beautiful Sierra Nevada Mountains as told from the perspective of one of the mountains in the range.

- *Where Poppies Grow: A World War I Companion* by Linda Granfield (RL/RI)
- *In Flanders Fields* by Norman Jorgensen (RL/RI)

Texts combine to provide both a snapshot and an expansive view of soldier's life during World War I. One uses a red robin to describe a single, unexpected, life-altering experience for soldiers (and the world) on both sides of the war. The other uses a collection of photographs, paintings, postcards, and magazine advertisements to provide a sweeping history of a war that affected people from all walks of life and from many countries.

- *We're Riding on a Caravan* by Laurie Krebs (RL/RI)
- *The Silk Route: 7000 Miles of History* by John S. Major (RL/RI)

Texts describe a historically important trade route. One is a rhyming tale of a family that travels along the route and learns about different cultures along the way. The other covers the history and purpose of the Silk Route based on caravan journeys that stop in major towns and cities.

- *Sam Patch Daredevil Jumper* by Paul E. Johnson (RL/RI)
- *Queen of the Falls* by Chris Van Allsburg (RL/RI)

Texts delightfully introduce the legends of two real-life daredevils who jumped over Niagara Falls. One tells the story of a man supposedly born to jump, and the other relates the unexpected story of an elderly woman, the first person ever to go over Niagara Falls in a barrel.

- *Piggybook* by Anthony Browne (RL)
- *Pigsty* by Mark Teague (RL)

Texts are humorous accounts with colorful and whimsical illustrations describing lessons learned on manners, respect, and working together.

Grade 8

Analyze a case in which two or more texts provide conflicting information on the same topic and identify where the texts disagree on matters of fact or interpretation (CCLS.ELA-Literacy.RI.8.9).

- *Henry's Freedom Box: A True Story from the Underground Railroad* by Ellen Levine (RL/RI)
- *Freedom Song: The Story of Henry "Box" Brown* by Sally M. Walker (RL/RI)

Texts provide different descriptions on the same event, namely, a young slave boy who, out of desperation, literally mails himself to freedom.

- *Rosa* by Nikki Giovanni (RL/RI)
- *Back of the Bus* by Aaron Reynolds (RL/RI)

Texts share different versions and interpretations of one of the most important events in the civil rights movement, differing somewhat on just where Rosa Parks sat on the bus.

■ *Wangari's Trees of Peace: A True Story from Africa* by Jeanette Winter (RL/RI)
■ *Planting the Trees of Kenya: The Story of Wangari Maathai* by Claire A. Nivola (RL/RI)

Texts include similar and different information about the life of Wangari Maathai, an environmentalist, conservationist, and winner of the 2004 Nobel Peace Prize for work in her native Kenya reconnecting people's health to their environment.

■ *The Librarian of Basra* by Jeannette Winter (RL/RI)
■ *Alia's Mission: Saving the Books of Iraq* by Mark Alan Stamaty (RL/RI)

Texts describe different versions and interpretations of the heartwarming story of a courageous woman from Basra (Iraq) whose love of books overshadowed the dangers of war and her own well-being. One shares the story through limited text and colorful illustrations, and the other uses extensive text in a graphic novel format.

■ *The Tale of Pale Male: A True Story* by Jeanette Winter (RL/RI)
■ *Pale Male: Citizen Hawk of New York City* by Janet Schulman (RL/RI)

Texts include similar and different information about the true story of two red-tailed hawks that build a nest, live, and mate on a balcony of a building overlooking Central Park in New York City. One tells the story briefly with limited text and colorful, pastel illustrations, and the other uses extensive text about the two hawks and informational text about the unusual characteristics of the red-tailed hawk.

■ *Fly High!: The Story of Bessie Coleman* by Louise Borden and Mary Kay Kroeger (RL/RI)
■ *Talkin' about Bessie: The Story of Aviator Elizabeth Coleman* by Nikki Grimes (RL/RI)

Texts include similar and different information about the life of Bessie Coleman, the first African American, man or woman, to earn a pilot's license.

Additional Instructional Strategies

In addition to Spokewheel, Listening and Connecting, and Similarities and Differences are other strategies to help students make intertextual connections with paired text. Listening and Connecting (see Appendix E at the end of this book) is a strategy that introduces students to the expectation that readers make connections to text before, during, and after reading. In the left column students record words, phrases, sentences, quotes, and so forth that trigger connections from the text and in the right column describe the connections that were triggered. Similarities and Differences (see Appendix F at the end of this book) is a strategy for readers to record the similarities and differences between a paired text.

PART FOUR

Paired Text
in History/Social Studies

Readers use texts to understand other texts.
—LAWRENCE R. SIPE AND JEFFREY BAUER
(2001, p. 332)

Literature puts flesh on the bare bones of history.
—JIM TRELEASE (1990)

In Part Four, I introduce a paired text for history/social studies that focuses on drummer boys in the Civil War. I describe a mini-lesson to introduce this paired text, provide background information for the mini-lesson, use an H-Map as an instructional strategy to illustrate intertextual connections between these texts, and discuss how this paired text and strategy address the CCSS for Literacy in History/Social Studies. I also share additional paired text, organized by the CCSS Anchor Standards for Reading and the NCSS standards. I include recommended grade levels and grade bands for each paired text and identify each text in terms of whether it represents reading literature (RL), reading informational text (RI), or both (RL/RI). I end with additional instructional strategies that can be used with other paired text in history/social studies and other content areas.

Mini-Lesson: Drummer Boys in the Civil War

Materials

- ◆ Copy of paired text: *Drummer Boy: Marching to the Civil War* (Turner, 1998) (RL) and *Red Legs: A Drummer Boy of the Civil War* (Lewin, 2001) (RL).

- ◆ H-Map (see Appendix G at the end of this book).

Procedure

◆ The teacher displays the paired text and a large H-Map to the whole class.

◆ The teacher invites students to infer how these two books are similar and how they are different, and records both on the H-Map with similarities in the middle of the H-Map and differences in the left and right columns.

◆ The teacher provides each student with a copy of an H-Map.

◆ The teacher reads aloud *Drummer Boy: Marching to the Civil War*, stopping at strategic places (e.g., the boy's first encounter in battle, the boy's change of mind about Abraham Lincoln) and inviting pairs of students to Swap Hypotheses (see Appendix H at the end of this book) about what is happening in this story. After reading, the teacher invites students to share with the whole class the record of hypotheses that were swapped and whether these hypotheses were confirmed or disconfirmed.

◆ The teacher reads aloud *Red Legs: A Drummer Boy of the Civil War* following the same procedure. After reading, students work in pairs and use the H-Map to record how these texts are similar and how they are different, and share their completed H-Map with the whole class.

◆ As a culminating experience, the teacher invites students to use an Aha! Sheet (see Appendix I at the end of this book) to reflect, record, and share new "Ahas!" about the process of making connections between texts.

Background for the Mini-Lesson

Drummer Boy (Turner, 1998) is an informative and provocative story of a young boy who was inspired by Abraham Lincoln to join the Union Army and become a drummer boy, even though he was not old enough to enlist. The boy soon learns about the real meaning of war. He sees and hears soldiers marching, bullets flying, drums beating, and horses and soldiers dying in battle. Day after day, battle after battle, the boy marches on, doing his job, drumming his drum. Unlike when he first enlisted, the boy waits for the war to end so he can go home and tell Mr. Lincoln why no boy should ever see what he saw.

Red Legs (Lewin, 2001) is a story about a young boy named Stephen, a drummer boy in the Union Army. At the campsite he prepares for tomorrow's battle between the Union and Confederate armies. The next morning Stephen beats his drum, first calling the units into line and then into battle. A drummer boy in the Confederate Army is doing the same. Both drummer boys watch from afar as soldiers from both armies fall and die from rifle and cannon fire. Tragically, Stephen falls, apparently shot by a Confederate soldier. Suddenly, the shooting stops and the battle ends because something very unexpected is about to happen.

Intertextual Connections

Drummer Boy (Turner, 1998) and *Red Legs* (Lewin, 2001) is a paired text about the Civil War, particularly about the nature and purpose of drummer boys. Each is an entertaining and informative read. Together, however, they offer readers an opportunity to make important intertextual connections. One way readers can represent connections is with an H-Map (Hadaway & Young, 1994). An H-Map is a visual way to record connections (similarities and differences), identify important information, and support inferential thinking. Figure 4.1 illustrates an H-Map with several similarities and differences between *Drummer Boy* and *Red Legs*.

As for similarities, both texts include young boys as main characters. Both were drummer boys in the Union Army who wrote letters to parents about their upcoming involvement in battle. Both boys know the purpose of their jobs as drummer boys, namely, to rally soldiers and relay orders to troops from commanding officers. Both stories describe uncommon situations for many young boys. They participate in fierce and deadly battles. One boy is involved in an important scene where a mysterious helping hand is extended to a wounded, presumably dying, soldier. Finally, both stories provide an afterword containing interesting historical notes about drummer boys.

As for differences, *Drummer Boy* is told with first-person narration, occurs during the Civil War period, is told from the perspective of a drummer boy in the Union Army, takes place over an undetermined period of time, and ends with the boy dramatically changing his view of war due to his experiences as a drummer boy. *Red Legs* is told in the third person, has a more contemporary timeline, includes both Union and Confederate perspectives, takes place in a single day, and ends with the boy maintaining, not dramatically changing, his view of the war.

In many ways similarities and differences on the H-Map represent evidence of reading comprehension. This evidence can be used by students to discuss these texts in literature circles and also create written retellings. For example, teachers can invite students to use differences recorded in the left and right columns to write a retelling of each story using a prompt like:

> "Suppose our principal unexpectedly sticks his or her head into our classroom and asks, 'What are you all doing today?' And we say, 'We just read *Drummer Boy* and *Red Legs*. And he or she says, 'I don't know those books. What are they about?' What would we say? Let's tell our principal what these books are all about in writing [or sketching, etc.]."

Likewise, similarities recorded in the middle of the H-Map can be used by students to compose a piece of writing (e.g., "quick write," an extended summary) that identifies and describes intertextual connections between these texts. Students can also use art (sketch), performance art (improvise, tableaux), or technology (Power-Point presentation) to represent important intertextual connections. These exten-

Book 2: *Red Legs*

- Story takes place in today's time.
- Story includes two perspectives: the Union Army and the Confederate Army.
- Timeline for the whole story covers 1 day.
- Wrote a mental letter, not an actual one, to his mother telling her not to worry and that he would make her proud.
- Battle wasn't real—it was a reenactment.
- Soldiers, including the boy, pretended they were shot and died.
- Stephen's father participates in the battle.
- After the reenactment, Stephen and others go home happy and satisfied.
- Story describes an educational experience for Stephen.
- In the end, Stephen was a pretend hero.
- Stephen, his father, and the other characters in the story were reenactors or living historians.
- Perspective on war and life doesn't dramatically change due to the reenactment.
- Story is based on the life of a real person who served as a drummer boy in the Civil War.

- Both boys wrote letters to parents about their upcoming involvement in the war.
- Both were drummer boys in the Union Army.
- Both stories describe fierce battles.
- Both stories describe uncommon situations for many young boys.
- In both stories a helping hand was extended to a wounded soldier.
- Both boys know their job as drummer boys is to rally the soldiers and relay orders to the troops.
- Both stories include historical notes at the end.

Book 1: *Drummer Boy*

- Story takes place during the time of the actual Civil War, 1860–1864.
- Story is told from the perspective of a drummer boy in the Union Army.
- Timeline for the whole story covers several months, maybe years.
- Saw and heard Abraham Lincoln campaigning on his way to Washington.
- Inspired by Lincoln to join the Union Army and fight to against slavery.
- Wrote an actual letter to his father before he volunteered to join the army.
- Lied about his age to join the army.
- Brother left home earlier and enlisted in the Union Army.
- "Pa" didn't believe boy would be much use in the war, unlike the boy's brother, Jed.
- Battle was real.
- Experienced death of fellow soldiers.
- After the Civil War ended, boy blames Lincoln for his experiences as a drummer boy.
- Coming-of-age story.
- In the end, the boy was a real hero.
- Perspective on war and life changes dramatically over time due to the war.

FIGURE 4.1. H-Map for *Drummer Boy* and *Red Legs*.

sions can be followed with other paired text to broaden and extend student understanding about drummer boys, but also about other important information about the Civil War. Here are recommended paired text for this purpose:

- *Drummer Boy: Marching to the Civil War* by Ann Warren Turner (RL/RI)
- *The Last Brother: A Civil War Tale* by Trinka Hakes Noble (RL/RI)

Texts describe the lives of young boys as buglers and drummer boys in the Civil War. One is a narrative about a single drummer boy, and the other is also a narrative but about two brothers: a bugler and a foot soldier.

- *Diary of a Drummer Boy* by Marlene Targ Brill (RL/RI)
- *A Civil War Drummer Boy: The Diary of William Bircher, 1861–1865 (Diaries, Letters, Memoirs)* by William Bircher (RL/RI)

Texts use the genre of diary to provide interesting and informative depictions of life as a drummer boy.

- *Civil War Drummer Boy* by Verla Kay (RL/RI)
- *Lil Dan, the Drummer Boy: A Civil War Story* by Romare Bearden (RL/RI)

Texts describe the lives of young boys as drummer boys in the Civil War: both are narratives and one is accompanied by music.

Theoretical Model

Figure 4.2 is a theoretical model that illustrates the relationships among the CCR Anchor Standards in Reading, NCSS thematic strands, and paired text. Like the ELA model presented in Part Three, this was also inspired by and adapted from a whole-language model of reading (Goodman, 2006). In the model presented here, the outer circle identifies four major categories (Key Ideas and Details, Craft and Structure, Integration of Knowledge and Ideas, and Range of Reading and Level of Text Complexity) of the CCR Anchor Standards for Reading, K–12. The inner circle identifies the 10 NCSS thematic strands, and the wedge represents how paired text can be used as a curricular resource with instructional strategies to address both sets of standards.

The CCSS, the NCSS, and Paired Text

The CCSS do not specify ELA Standards in History/Social Studies in grades K–5, but they do for grades 6–8. In the following section I describe paired text in two ways: (1) I identify paired text for grades K–5 based on the NCSS thematic strands, and (2) I identify paired text for grades 6–8 that address specific ELA Standards in History/Social Studies.

FIGURE 4.2. Theoretical model for history/social studies and paired text.

Paired Text in Grades K–5 by NCSS Thematic Strands

The NCSS standards identify 10 thematic strands: Culture; Time, Continuity, and Change; People, Places, and Environments; Individual Development and Identity; Individuals, Groups, and Institutions; Power, Authority, and Governance; Production, Distribution, and Consumption; Science, Technology, and Society; Global Connections; and Civic Ideals and Practices. I identify each strand, provide a short NCSS description of each strand, and identify paired text that can be used to address each strand.

Culture

This strand states that "social studies programs should include experiences that provide for the study of culture and cultural diversity" (NCSS, p. 14). Specifically, it focuses on how human beings create, learn, share, and adapt to culture; how culture changes over time; important elements of culture; and similarities and differences among cultural groups.

Grades K–5

■ *Grandpa, Is Everything Black Bad?* by Sandy Lynne Holman (RL)
■ *We All Have a Heritage* by Sandy Lynne Holman (RL)

Texts address the recognition and value of people of every color.

■ *Masai and I* by Virginia Kroll (RL)
■ *The Hello-Goodbye Window* by Norton Juster (RL)

Texts describe living in two different cultures.

■ *The Other Side* (RL) and *Each Kindness* (RL) by Jacqueline Woodson

Texts discuss excluding others because of race or social status and opportunities missed and taken.

■ *Smoky Night* by Eve Bunting (RL)
■ *A Chair for My Mother* by Vera B. Williams (RL)

Texts describe the tragedy of a fire on a home and an apartment complex and the unexpected benefits that result. One brings a mother and father closer together, and the other brings different cultures together.

■ *Friends from the Other Side* by Gloria Anzaldua (RL)
■ *A Day's Work* by Eve Bunting (RL)

Texts describe the real-life, everyday challenges of individuals and families who cross the border from Mexico to the United States. One describes the relationship between a Mexican American girl and a Mexican boy, and the other is about the warm relationship between a Mexican American boy and his grandfather, who he tries to help find work.

■ *Django: World's Greatest Jazz Guitarist* by Bonnie Christensen (RL)
■ *Megan's Year: An Irish Traveler's Story* by Gloria Whelan (RL)

Texts describe the life and time of real-life travelers from two different cultures. One describes Irish travelers who travel in caravans around Ireland as a way of life, and the other is about a world famous jazz guitarist and member of a traveling gypsy family.

■ *First Day in Grapes* by L. King Pérez (RL)
■ *Harvesting Hope* by Kathleen Krull (RL)

Texts depict the hardships of adults and children working as migrant workers and one person who fought for their rights.

■ *Dolores Huerta: A Hero to Migrant Workers* by Sarah Warren (RL)
■ *Harvesting Hope* by Kathleen Krull (RL)

Texts provide illuminating biographies of two historical figures and champions of protecting the rights of migrant workers.

■ *Dolores Huerta: A Hero to Migrant Workers* by Sarah Warren (RL)
■ *Brave Girl: Clara and the Shirtwaist Makers' Strike of 1909* by Michelle Markel (RL)

Texts describe two little-known historical characters, both brave women, from different cultural backgrounds who led and organized workers in a strike to better working conditions. One is about workers in the grape fields, and the other is about workers in a garment factory.

- *Circle Unbroken* by Margot Theis Raven (RL)
- *A Net to Catch Time* by Sara Harrell Banks (RL)

Texts provide a wonderful introduction to the Gullah culture. One is about the history of sweetgrass baskets in the Gullah culture, and the other is a contemporary story of how one young boy learns the importance of these baskets.

- *Grandfather Counts* by Andrea Cheng (RL)
- *Two Mrs. Gibsons* by Toyomi Igus (RL)

Texts tell tender stories of young girls who grew up in biracial worlds. One is a narrative about a loving relationship between a little girl and her Chinese grandfather, and the other is a tribute to the author's Japanese mother and her African American grandmother.

- *Two Sandals, Four Feet* by Karen Lynn Williams (RL)
- *One Green Apple* by Eve Bunting (RL)

Texts are beautifully told and sensitive accounts of the power of friendship in two very different cultural settings. One is a narrative about two girls growing up in a refugee camp in Pakistan, and the other is about a girl attending a new school without knowing the language and culture of her classmates.

- *The Whispering Cloth: A Refugee's Story* by Pegi Deitz Shea (RL/RI)
- *Dia's Story Cloth: The Hmong People's Journey of Freedom* by Dia Cha (RL/RI)

Texts address the experiences of children in refugee camps. One is a narrative about a young girl in a Hmong refugee camp in Thailand, and the other is a narrative about a story cloth that chronicles the life of the Hmong people and their emigration to the United States.

- *Sami and the Time of the Troubles* by Florence Parry Heide and Judith Heide Gilliland (RL)
- *The Silence in the Mountains* by Liz Rosenberg (RL)

Texts describe the devastating effects of war on families. One narrative deals with a young boy making adjustments after his family left its war-torn country, and the other is a gorgeously illustrated narrative about a young boy trying to live safely in his war-torn country.

- *Tea with Milk* (RL) and *Grandfather's Journey* (RL) by Allen Say

Texts describe the challenges of characters living in two different cultures.

Grades 6–8

- *It Doesn't Have to Be This Way* by Luis Rodriguez (RL)
- *Your Move* by Eve Bunting (RL)

Texts describe the lure of gangs, pressures to join, and events that sway people to get in or get out. One involves gang life in a barrio, and the other takes place in a tough city neighborhood.

- *Just One Flick of a Finger* by Marybeth Lorbiecki (RL)
- *Your Move* by Eve Bunting (RL)

Texts describe the lure of gangs, pressures to join, and events that sway people to get in or get out with both narratives showing tough inner-city life.

- *Encounter* by Jane Yolen (RL)
- *Squanto's Journey* by Joseph Bruchas (RL)

Texts tell the stories of two important historical events. One is a narrative about Christopher Columbus's trip to the New World told from the Taino Indian point of view. The other is a narrative about the landing of Pilgrims and the first Thanksgiving told from the Native American Indian perspective.

- *Bright Path: Young Jim Thorpe* by Don Brown (RL)
- *Jim Thorpe's Bright Path* by Joseph Bruchac (RL)

Texts provide different, overlapping biographies of one of the most important figures in Native American history.

- *Cheyenne Again* by Eve Bunting (RL)
- *Home to Medicine Mountain* by Chiori Santiago (RL)

Texts address the topic of enthnocentrism sensitively but directly with both narratives telling stories of a dominant culture trying to strip the cultural identity of Native American individuals.

- *Amazon Boy* (RL) and *Sacred River* (RL) by Ted Lewin

Texts, beautifully told and illustrated, give a wonderful introduction to the indigenous cultures that live along two different rivers: the Amazon River in South America and the Ganges River in India.

- *The Dalai Lama* by Demi (RL)
- *Tibet: Through the Red Box* by Peter Sis (RL)

Texts provide an engaging and detailed introduction to the land, people, and culture of Tibet. One focuses on the Dalai Lama, who is the spiritual leader of the country. The other gives a description of Tibet told through the writings of the author's father who lived and traveled throughout the country.

Time, Continuity, and Change

This strand states that "social studies programs should include experiences that provide for the study of the past and its legacy" (NCSS, p. 15). It focuses on understanding the human story across time, and analyzing causes and consequences of historical events and developments.

Grades K–5

- *The Little House* by Virginia Burton (RL)
- *Window* by Jeanne Baker (RL)

Texts across two different times and settings tell the stories of one house and one window in a house. Both beautifully illustrate the theme of change over time, change that is embraced, and change that is resisted.

- *Rosa* by Nikki Giovanni (RL/RI)
- *If a Bus Could Talk: The Story of Rosa Parks* by Faith Ringgold (RL/RI)

Texts present two different versions of one of the most important historical events in American history and how this event impacted the struggle for civil rights.

- *Tight Times* by Barbara Shook Hazen (RL)
- *Gettin' through Thursday* by Melrose Cooper (RL)

Texts present compelling narratives about the challenges faced by families during the time of the Depression era in the United States and its consequences on children.

- *Angels in the Dust* by Margot Theis Raven (RL/Rl)
- *Leah's Pony* by Elizabeth Freidrich (RL/RI)

Texts discuss the difficult effects of droughts in the Oklahoma region known at the time as the Dust Bowl, its devastating effects on families and children, and the ways they coped with these developments.

- *Fly Away Home* by Eve Bunting (RL)
- *We Are All in the Dumps with Jack and Guy: Two Nursery Rhymes with Pictures* by Maurice Sendak (RL)

Texts delicately but directly address the topic of homelessness. One is a narrative describing the seemingly endless time a father and son spend living in an airport. The other two interrelated nursery rhymes are accompanied by colorful, cartoon-like illustrations about a historical time when homelessness was common.

- *Let Them Play* by Margot Theis Raven (RL/RI)
- *A Home Run for Bunny* by Richard Anderson (RL/RI)

Texts describe the challenging experiences of young players who used baseball to overcome racism.

Grades 6–8

- *The Matchbox Diaries* by Paul Fleischman (RL/RI)
- *Small Beauties* by Elvira Woodruff (RL/RI)

Texts address in similar and dissimilar ways the topic of immigration. One narrative tells the story of a little girl arriving in America from Ireland who uses a variety of small things ("beauties") to remind her of home. The other tells the story of a grandfather, an immigrant from Italy, who shares items in an old cigar box with his granddaughter as a way for them to learn about each other.

- *Wingwalker* by Rosemary Wells (RL/RI)
- *The Babe and I* by David A. Adler (RL/RI)

Texts provide different perspectives of life during the American depression in the early 1900's.

- *Anno's Medieval World* by Mitsumasa Anno (RL/RI)
- *The Middle Ages* by Giovanni Caselli (RL/RI)

Texts, both masterfully illustrated, provide interesting and informational perspectives on a major period in world history. One highlights the advancements made by people at the time, and the other discusses the effects those advancements had on the future.

- *Senefer: A Young Genius in Old Egypt* by Beatrice Lumpkin (RL/RI)
- *The History of Counting* by Denise Schmandt-Besserat (RL/RI)

Texts integrate social studies and mathematics. One is a colorfully illustrated biography of Senefer, a young boy who lived in ancient Egypt and grew up to be a famous mathematician. The other is a historical account of our system of counting as seen through different cultures around the world, highlighting how and why counting evolved over time.

People, Places, and Environments

This strand is based on the belief that "social studies programs should include experiences that provide for the study of people, places, and environments" (NCSS, p. 16). It highlights the study of people, places, and environments, and examines changes in the relationships among people, places, and environments over time.

Grades K–5

- *Mozart: Scenes from the Childhood of a Great Composer* by Catherine Brighton (RL/RI)
- *Before Mozart: The Life of the Famous Chevalier de Saint-George* by Hugh Brewster (RL/RI)

Texts provide entertaining and enlightening biographies. One is about the special world and childhood experiences of the great composer Wolfgang Amadeus Mozart, and the other is about a fascinating and amazingly talented, but little-known, violinist known as the "other Mozart."

- *Wilma Unlimited* by Kathleen Krull (RL/RI)
- *Queen of the Track: Alice Coachman, Olympic High-Jump Champion* by Heather Lang (RL/RI)

Texts describe two extraordinary women athletes. One is a narrative about Wilma Rudolph who was stricken with polio as a child, yet through courage and perseverance overcomes the affliction and becomes an Olympic track champion. The other is about Alice Coachman, a track-and-field champion and the first American woman to win an Olympic gold medal.

- *Black Is Brown Is Tan* by Arnold Adoff (RL)
- *The Hello, Goodbye Window* by Norton Juster (RL)

Texts simply and honestly address the topic of living in an interracial family.

■ *Brave Harriet* (RL/RI) and *Sky High: The True Story of Maggie Gee* (RL/RI) by Marissa Moss

Texts tell truly inspiring biographies of two daring women. One is about a female pilot who was the first to fly solo across the English Channel in the early 20th century. The other is about a Chinese American female pilot who was selected to train in the WASP program, the Women Airforce Service Pilots in World War II.

■ *Fishing Day* by Andrea Davis Pinkney (RL)
■ *Each Kindness* by Jacqueline Woodson (RL)

Texts beautifully told and illustrated present two similar yet dissimilar evocative stories. One is a narrative about two pairs of people, one pair is white, one pair is black, who spend the day fishing but not talking to one another, yet the story ends on a hopeful note. The other is a narrative about children ignoring another child because she is different from them, yet once she leaves, the children realize their missed opportunity.

■ *Right Here on This Spot* by Sharon Hart Addy (RL)
■ *We Played Marbles* by Tres Seymout (RL)

Texts take a different perspective on learning history by starting with a present location and unraveling the history of that place. There is a particular focus on a special location that was the site of major battles during the Civil War.

■ *Who Came Down That Road?* (RL) and *Dreamplace* (RL) by George Ella Lyon

Texts take a different perspective on learning history by starting with a present location and unraveling the history of that place.

■ *Major Taylor Champion Cyclist* by Lesa Cline-Ransome (RL/RI)
■ *Sixteen Years in Sixteen Seconds: The Sammy Lee Story* by Paula Yoo (RL/RI)

Texts introduce two little-known but highly accomplished athletes. One is the biography of an African American cyclist who overcame racism on his way to victory, and the other is the biography of a Korean American man who became a physician and Olympic platform diver champion.

■ *Passage to Freedom: The Sugihara Story* by Ken Mochizuki (RL/RI)
■ *Four Feet, Two Sandals* by Karen Lynn Williams and Khadra Mohammed (RL/RI)

Texts poignantly reveal the difficult life and times of individuals who have been displaced from their homelands by the tragedy of war and now live in refugee camps.

■ *Emma's Poem* by Linda Glaser (RL/RI)
■ *Coming to America* by Betsy Maestro (RL/RI)

Texts provide inspirational text, poetry, and narrative about immigration, highlighting the welcoming spirit of America and the determination of those who make the difficult trip.

■ *At Ellis Island: A History of Many Voices* by Louise Peacock (RL/RI)
■ *When Jessie Came across the Sea* by Karen Hest (RL/RI)

Texts both address the history of immigration in America. One provides an introduction to the process of immigration at Ellis Island, and the other is a portrait of one family that made it to Ellis Island by sea.

■ *A Memory Coat* by Elvira Woodruff (RL)
■ *Dreaming of America: An Ellis Island Story* by Eve Bunting and Ben Stahl (RL)

Texts provide different perspectives on immigration, highlighting the challenges of immigrating to America.

■ *Going Home* by Eve Bunting
■ *Good-Bye Havana! Hola New York!* by Edie Colon

Texts share the common theme of Home, one leaving home and the other going home.

Grades 6–8

■ *The Other Mozart: The Life of the Chevalier de Saint-George* by Hugh Brewster (RL/RI)
■ *Before There Was Mozart: The Story of Joseph Boulogne Chevalier de Saint-George* by Lesa Cline-Ransome (RL/RI)

Texts provide another combination describing the story of Joseph Boulogne, the only child of a black slave who grew into an immensely talented artist and violinist.

■ *Teammates* by Peter Golenbeck (RL/RI)
■ *Testing the Ice* by Sharon Robinson (RL/RI)

Texts tell the story of Jackie Robinson as the first African American to play in the major leagues. One is a narrative about his relationship with Pee Wee Reese, a white teammate, and the other is a loving account of Jackie Robinson's family life as told by his daughter.

■ *Molly Bannaky* by Ann McGill (RL/RI)
■ *Dear Benjamin Banneker* by Andrea Davis Pinkney (RL/RI)

Texts present interrelated stories. One is from 17th-century England about a young woman who was exiled to colonial America because she could read and later married an African slave, and the other is an insightful biography into the remarkable life of her grandson, the famous Benjamin Banneker.

■ *Ellis Island: New Hope in a New Land* by William Jay Jacobs (RL/RI)
■ *Landed* by Milly Lee (RL/RI)

Texts tells the history of two immigration entry sites. One is a narrative about well-known Ellis Island, the place where immigrants arriving on the east coast entered the United States. The other is about little-known Angel Island, the place where immigrants arriving on the west coast entered the United States.

■ *Ellis Island: New Hope in a New Land* by William Jay Jacobs (RI)
■ *The Arrival* by Shaun Tan (RL)

Texts address the topic of immigration from very different perspectives. One presents the history of Ellis Island as told from an American point of view, and the other is a wordless account of immigration told from an immigrant's perspective.

■ *Terrible Things* by Eve Bunting (RL/RI)
■ *The Little Boy Star: An Allegory of the Holocaust* by Rachel Hausfater (RL/RI)

Texts use allegory in different ways to introduce important lessons about the Holocaust.

■ *The Letter Home* by Thomas Decker (RL/RI)
■ *Where Poppies Grow: A World War 1 Companion* by Linda Granfield (RL/RI)

Texts combine a provocative narrative and inferential text. One is about a trench soldier in World War I who writes a letter to his son to comfort the boy during his absence and uses rich illustrations and inferential text to communicate information about the war. The other is a beautifully illustrated, scrapbook-style text about this tragic war.

■ *Thomas Jefferson: Life, Liberty and the Pursuit of Everything* by Maira Kalman (RL/RI)
■ *Thomas Jefferson Builds a Library* by Barb Rosenstock (RL/RI)

Texts provide complimentary and little-known information about the fascinating life of Thomas Jefferson.

Individual Development and Identity

This strand is based on the belief that "social studies programs should include experiences that provide for the study of individual development and identity" (NCSS, p. 17). It focuses on how personal identities are shaped, and the relationships among human behavior, social norms, and ethical action.

Grades K–5

■ *Each Kindness* by Jacqueline Woodson (RL)
■ *So Close* by Natalia Columbo (RL)

Texts focus on the importance of kindness, one in which kindness is extended and the other kindness is denied.

■ *The Name Jar* by Choi (RL)
■ *The Crow Boy* by Taro Yashima (RL)

Texts address the need for appreciation of individual differences. One is a narrative about a little girl from Korea who is starting school in America but nobody can pronounce her name. After considering alternative names and with the help of a friend, she decides to keep her real name. The other is a touching narrative about a Japanese boy who is an outcast at school but through perseverance, he teaches his classmates to appreciate differences in others.

■ *Max* by Rachel Isadora (RL)
■ *Baseball Ballerina* by Katherine Cristaldi (RL)

Texts share a twist: one is a delightful narrative about a boy who likes to play baseball but also takes ballet lessons, and the other is a narrative about a girl who likes ballet but also practices baseball.

■ *William's Doll* by Charlotte Zolotow (RL)
■ *Oliver Button Is a Sissy* by Tomie dePaola (RL)

Texts present beautiful and thought-provoking stories about young boys who wish for a doll despite those who don't understand why.

- *The Big Orange Splot* by Daniel Manus Pinkwater (RL)
- *Those Bottles!* by M. L. Miller (RL)

Texts use colorful, cartoon-like whimsical illustrations to address a singular theme, namely, to appreciate the differences of others.

- *Amazing Grace* by Mary Hoffman (RL)
- *Hue Boy* by Rita Phillips Mitchell (RL)

Texts present two courageous characters who overcome personal challenges with dignity and grace. One is a narrative about a young African American girl who refuses to accept that she cannot play Peter Pan in the play because she is not white. The other is about a young Caribbean boy who overcomes ridicule from his classmates about his small size.

- *Like Jake and Me* by Mavis Jukes (RL)
- *The Memory String* by Eve Bunting (RL)

Texts address the relationship between children and stepparents. One is about a stepfather and stepson who create a new relationship by focusing on similarities and differences. The other is about a young girl who uses buttons as memories of her deceased mother and as opportunities to build a meaningful relationship with her new stepmother.

- *Across the Alley* by Richard Michelson (RL)
- *The Bat Boy and His Violin* by Gavin Curtis (RL)

Texts address acceptance of individual differences. One is a narrative about two young boys who live across an alley, one African American and one Jewish, who teach each other their special talents, one baseball and the other the violin. The other is a narrative about a young boy who loves to play the violin but his father needs a bat boy; in the end, the boy accomplishes both.

- *Come See the Ocean* by Estelle Condra (RL)
- *The Hickory Chair* by Lisa Rowe Fraustino (RL)

Texts presents two endearing characters who are blind. One is about a young girl who can see more than her brothers realize. The other is about a young boy who can still see, smell, and hear his adoring grandmother.

- *My Brother Sammy* by Becky Edwards (RL)
- *What's Wrong with Timmy?* by Maria Shriver (RL)

Texts lovingly portray two young boys who both have challenges to deal with. One tells the story of an autistic boy and the brother who learns to accept him. The other is about a young girl who learns to understand and accept differences in others.

Grades 6–8

- *Brothers in Hope: The Story of the Lost Boys of the Sudan* by Mary Williams (RL/RI)
- *The Boy Who Harnessed the Wind* by William Kamkwamba and Bryan Mealer (RL/RI)

Texts address the courage and ingenuity of young boys caught in the middle of catastrophic events. One is a narrative about boys dealing with the hardships of war, and the other is a narrative about a young boy who saves his people and country from drought and starvation.

■ *Each Kindness* by Jacqueline Woodson (RL)
■ *I Never Knew Your Name* by Sherry Garland (RL)

Texts address the theme of missed opportunity with different characters and settings. One is a narrative about a young boy who does not befriend an older boy in time. The other is a narrative about young girls who do not befriend a new girl in time.

■ *Way Home* by Libby Hathorn (RL)
■ *Woolvs in the Sitee* by Margaret Wild (RL)

Texts share dark, provocative stories about young boys who are alone in the city: one boy is homeless, and the other boy has a home that he leaves not knowing what awaits him.

■ *Grandpa Green* by Lane Smith (RL)
■ *The Sunsets of Miss Oliva Wiggins* by Lester Laminack (RL)

Texts treat the topic of forgotten memories by the elderly with dignity and respect.

■ *Sachiko Means Happiness* by Kimiko Sakai (RL)
■ *Wilfred Gordon McDonald Partridge* by Mem Fox (RL)

Texts treat the topic of forgotten memories by the elderly with dignity and respect.

■ *Girl Wonder* by Deborah Hopkinson (RL)
■ *Mighty Jackie* by Marissa Moss (RL)

Texts delightfully tell the stories of two young girls who grow up to be mighty baseball pitchers and who strike out some of the greatest players of the time.

■ *Ruby's Wish* by Shirin Yim (RL)
■ *The Girl Who Loved Caterpillars* by Jean Merrill (RL)

Texts relate inspiring tales of unconventional thought. One is a narrative about a 12th-century Japanese girl who challenges conventions for girls at that time and instead insists on following her dreams. The other is a narrative about a Chinese girl who challenges expectations and conventions to attend university despite family objections.

■ *The Drover's Boy* by Ted Egan (RL)
■ *Rough, Tough, Charley* by Verla Kay (RL)

Texts, both surprising and entertaining, tell the stories of a drover and a cowboy, but with a twist. One is a narrative about a girl who is a drover in Australia, and the other is about a tough, stagecoach driver who is also a girl.

Individuals, Groups, and Institutions

This strand is based on the belief that "social studies programs should include experiences that provide for the study of individuals, groups, and institutions" (NCSS, p. 18). It focuses on formal and informal institutions (political, social, economic), and how these institutions are formed, maintained, and changed.

Grades K–5

- *Elizabeth Leads the Way* by Tanya Lee Stone (RL/RI)
- *Let Them Play* by Margot Theis Raven (RL/RI)

Texts share the theme of challenging institutions. One is a biography of Elizabeth Cady Stanton who successfully challenged institutions that prohibited women from voting. The other is a narrative about one little league baseball team that successfully challenged institutions that prohibited African American teams from competing in the national Little League World Series.

- *Players in Pigtails* by Shana Corey (RL/RI)
- *Dirt on Their Skirts: The Story of the Young Women Who Won the World Championship* by Doreen Rappaport (RL/RI)

Texts describe the stories of women baseball teams that successfully challenged the all-male institutions of baseball and ultimately started the All-American Girls Professional Baseball League.

- *The Tuskegee Airmen Story* by Lynn Holman (RL/RI)
- *Wind Flyers* by Angela Johnson (RL/RI)

Texts describe different versions of the underrecognized accomplishments of the famous Tuskegee airmen during World War II.

- *The Orphan Train* by Verla Kay (RL/RI)
- *Train to Somewhere* by Eve Bunting (RL/RI)

Texts describe from different perspectives a little-known historical event in American history. One tells the long train journey of orphans from the east hoping to be adopted by families in the midwest and west. The other tells the story of three siblings with no family left but that hopes to stay together.

- *The Bracelet* by Yoshiko Uchida (RL/RI)
- *A Place Where Sunflowers Grow* by Amy Lee-Tai (RL/RI)

Texts address the controversial topic of Japanese American internment camps during World War II. One is a beautiful account of the importance of a bracelet for one young girl to stay connected to the outside world. The other is an account of the difficulties one young girl experiences trying to be artistic while living in an internment camp.

- *They Called Her Molly Pitcher* by Anne Rockwell (RL/RI)
- *Nurse, Soldier, Spy: The Story of Sarah Edmonds, a Civil War Hero* by Marissa Moss (RL/RI)

Texts provide fascinating stories of women who exhibited great courage in the face of battle and became heroes of the Civil War.

- *They Called Her Molly Pitcher* by Anne Rockwell (RL/RI)
- *Hold the Flag High* by Catherine Clinton (RL/RI)

Texts tell inspiring stories of two little-known but courageous individuals. One is about a woman, not a soldier, who exhibited great courage in the face of battle during the Revolutionary War. The other is a striking narrative of a man, a soldier, who also exhibited great courage in the face of battle during the Civil War and went on to be the first African American to receive the Congressional Medal of Honor.

Grades 6–8

■ *Leagues Apart: The Men and Times of the Negro Baseball League* by Lawrence Ritter (RL/RI)
■ *Negro Leagues: All-Black Baseball* by Laura Driscoll (RL/RI)

Texts provide an introduction to the history of the Negro leagues: one is in the form of a narrative, and the other is a school report.

■ *Leagues Apart: The Men and Times of the Negro Baseball League* by Lawrence Ritter (RL/RI)
■ *We Are the Ship: The Story of Negro League Baseball* by Kadir Nelson (RL/RI)

Texts delve deeply into the history, players, and controversies in the Negro Baseball League.

■ *Words Set Me Free: The Story of Young Frederick Douglass* by Lesa Cline-Ransome (RL/RI)
■ *Alec's Primer* by Mildred Pitts Walter (RL/RI)

Texts use words and reading as metaphors for freedom. One is a biography that shares the words of Frederick Douglass, and the other is a narrative based on a true story of a young slave boy who learned to read and gained his freedom.

■ *Music for Alice* (RL/RI) and *Home of the Brave* (RL/RI) by Allen Say

Texts address the topic of Japanese American internment camps during World War II. One is a beautifully illustrated narrative of a Japanese woman who loved to dance, but once the war started she found herself surviving the camp rather than dancing the waltz. The other is a complex narrative with much symbolism of a man who confronts the horrors of his family's incarceration in an internment camp.

■ *The Poppy Lady: Moina Belle Michael and Her Tribute to Veterans* by Barbara Walsh (RL/RI)
■ *America's White Table* by Margot Theis Raven (RL/RI)

Texts present inspirational stories with powerful symbols. One is a narrative that uses a red poppy to honor and remember soldiers who served in World War I. The other is a narrative that uses a white table to do the same for soldiers who served in the Vietnam War.

■ *Sacagawea* by Lisa Erdrick (RL/RI)
■ *My Name Is York* by Elizabeth Van Steenwyk (RL/RI)

Texts provide in-depth views of two major historical figures in the early history of the United States. One is a beautifully illustrated biography about Sacagawea and her life on the Lewis and Clark trail. The other is a detailed biography about a slave named York and his life on the Lewis and Clark trail.

■ *Seaman's Journal: On the Trail with Lewis and Clark* by Patricia Reeder Eubank (RL/RI)
■ *How We Crossed the West: The Adventures of Lewis and Clark* by Rosalyn Schanzer (RL/RI)

Texts generate interest in the story of Lewis and Clark. Both include brightly colored illustrations with descriptive text in journal format.

- *Animals Charles Darwin Saw* by Sandra Markle (RL/RI)
- *Animals Marco Polo Saw* by Sandra Markle (RL/RI)

Texts focus on the intriguing animals that two famous historical figures saw on their adventures. One is a narrative about Charles Darwin and features the animals he saw in the Galapagos lslands that were instrumental in developing his theory of evolution, and the other is a narrative about the exotic animals Marco Polo saw on his famous journey on the silk road.

- *Animals Marco Polo Saw* by Sandra Markle (RL/RI)
- *Marco Polo* by Demi (RL/RI)

Texts present two different perspectives on Marco Polo. One is a gorgeously illustrated narrative about the life, times, and adventures of the famous explorer, and the other is a narrative with informational text specifically about the animals that lived in the 13th century.

Power, Authority, and Governance

This strand is based on the belief that "social studies programs should include experiences that provide for the study of how people create, interact with, and change the structures of power, authority, and governance" (NCSS, p. 19). It highlights civic competence, political thought, structures of power, authority, and governance, and how these structures evolve over time.

Grades K–5

- *Up the Learning Tree* by Marcia Vaughn (RL)
- *The Wednesday Surprise* by Eve Bunting (RL)

Texts share the common theme of the power of reading. One is a narrative about a young slave who befriends a teacher and learns to read while hiding in a tree outside the school. The other is a narrative about a granddaughter who teachers her grandmother how to read.

- *The Conquerors* by David McKee (RL)
- *Rebel* by Allan Baillie (RL)

Texts tell stories that read like fables about the futility of war and a call for peace. One is about a general who conquers nations one by one but in the end is conquered by them, and the other is about a general who conquers all except one very young rebel.

- *Sélavi, That Is Life: A Haitian Story of Hope* by Youme Landowne (RL)
- *Fly Away Home* by Eve Bunting (RL)

Texts share different perspectives on the topic of homelessness. One is a narrative about a poor young boy in Haiti, and the other is a narrative about a boy and his father who are homeless in an airport.

- *A Taste of Colored Water* by Matt Faulkner (RL/RI)
- *White Water* by Michael S. Bandy and Eric Stein (RL/RI)

Texts use water fountains as a central symbol to address racism and Jim Crow laws. One is a narrative that takes place in the Deep South, told from two children's point of view. The other is a narrative about a young boy who learns about discrimination on a trip to his grandma's house.

■ *These Hands* by Margaret H. Mason (RL/RI)
■ *Brick by Brick* by Charles R. Smith, Jr. (RL/RI)

Texts use hands as an important symbol to address racial discrimination in different historical settings. One is a narrative about an African American man who works at the Wonder Bread factory in the 1950s and 1960s. He is not allowed to mix the bread dough or touch the baked bread but overcomes discrimination with the help of a labor union. The other is a narrative about slaves building with their own hands a residence for the president of the new country.

■ *Ben and the Emancipation Proclamation* by Pat Sherman (RL/RI)
■ The Emancipation Proclamation by Abraham Lincoln (RI)

Texts combine literary and information to address abolishment of slavery. One is a beautiful and inspiring narrative about a young slave boy who secretly teaches himself to read and later reads the Emancipation Proclamation to other adult slaves who cannot read. The other is the text of the famous document written and read by Abraham Lincoln.

■ *Ben and the Emancipation Proclamation* by Pat Sherman (RL/RI)
■ *A Band of Angels* by Deborah Hopkinson (RL/RI)

Texts provide background for the little-known but legendary Jubilee Singers at Fisk University. One is a narrative about the life and times of Benjamin C. Holmes who as a young child taught himself how to read and later read a copy of the Emancipation Proclamation to adult slaves. The other is a narrative of the history and people, including Benjamin C. Holmes, who were the Jubliee Singers.

■ *Belle, the Last Mule at Gees Bend: A Civil Rights Story* by Calvin Alexander Ramsey and Bettye Stoud (RL/RI)
■ *The Cart that Carried Martin* by Eve Bunting (RL/RI)

Texts provide fascinating background information about the mule that pulled the famous cart at the funeral of Martin Luther King.

■ *Freedom on the Menu* by Carole Boston Weatherford (RL/RI)
■ *Grandmama's Pride* by Becky Birtha (RL/RI)

Texts describe two different instances of how African-Americans peacefully protested against discrimination.

■ *White Socks Only* by Evelyn Coleman (RL/RI)
■ *A Taste of Colored Water* by Matt Faulkner (RL/RI)

Texts introduce and illustrate the nature of Jim Crow laws in the deep South during the 1960's.

■ *White Socks Only* by Evelyn Coleman (RL/RI)
■ *White Water* by Michael S. Bandy and Eric Stein (RL/RI)

Texts illustrate how Jim Crow laws were enforced during the 1960's.

■ *Freedom Summer* by Deborah Wiles (RL/RI)
■ *The Other Side* by Jacqueline Woodson (RL/RI)

Texts provide penetrating, long-lasting lessons on how friendship can overcome discrimination.

- *The Story of Ruby Bridges* by Robert Coles (RL/RI)
- *Through My Eyes* by Ruby Bridges (RL/RI)

Texts provide different perspectives on an important historical event dealing with Civil Rights.

- *The Other Side* by Jacqueline Woodson (RL/RI)
- *Across the Alley* by Richard Michelson (RL/RI)

Texts provide different perspectives on the topic of discrimination and the role friendship plays in overcoming it.

- *Sachel Paige* by Lesa Cline-Ransome (RL/RI)
- *Coming Home* by Nanette Mellage (RL/RI)

Texts describe two popular baseball players who overcame discrimination and segregation.

Grades 6–8

- *Home and Away* by John Marsden (RL/RI)
- *Ziba Came on a Boat* by Liz Lofthouse (RL/RI)

Texts describe two different instances of parents and children having to leave their home countries due to war.

- *One Green Apple* by Eve Bunting (RL/RI)
- *Nasreen's Secret School: A True Story from Afghanistan* by Jennette Winter (RL/RI)

Texts discuss the stories of two girls going to school under difficult circumstances. One is a colorful narrative of a young girl in Afghanistan whose grandmother enrolls her in a secret school for girls, and the other is a narrative about a young Muslim girl who experiences difficulties at school because she is from a different culture and does not know the English language.

- *Freedom School, Yes!* by Amy Littlesugar (RL/RI)
- *Sister Anne's Hands* by Marybeth Lorbiecki (RL/RI)

Texts provide penetrating descriptions of the hurtfulness of discrimination across two different time periods.

- *Freedom School, Yes!* by Amy Littlesugar (RL/RI)
- *Freedom Summer* by Deborah Wiles (RL/RI)

Texts describe racial tensions around the civil rights movement of the 1960s in American history. One is a poignant narrative about a young white woman who teaches at the Freedom School as part of the Mississippi Summer Project of 1964 but is resisted by both white and black people in the segregated town. The other is a penetrating narrative about two young boys (one white and one black) who experience discrimination in the aftermath of the Civil Rights Act of 1964.

- *The Composition* by Antonio Skarmeta (RL/RI)
- *The Stamp Collector* by Jennifer Lanthier (RL/RI)

Texts address the topic of dictatorship and show the consequences of this form of government. One is a narrative about a young boy from somewhere in Latin America whose friend's father is unexpectedly arrested. His arrest is followed by a visit to the boy's school by a soldier asking children to write a composition about what their families do at night. The other is a narrative with extraordinary illustrations about two boys in China who take different paths in life but learn the same lesson about the importance of free speech.

■ *Heroes* (RL/RI) and *Baseball Saved Us* (RL/RI) by Ken Mochizuki

Texts address the issue of personal consequences of war. One is a compelling narrative about a young Japanese American boy who is regarded and treated by other boys at school like the Japanese military, an enemy, and looks to his elders to understand why. The other is a narrative about a young Japanese American boy and his family dealing with the hardships of living in an internment camp by playing baseball.

■ *Harvesting Hope* by Katherine Krull (RL/RI)
■ *Si, Se Puede! Yes, We Can!* by Diana Cohn (RL/RI)

Texts share inspiring stories of little-known historical figures instrumental in fighting for workers' rights. One is a narrative about a young Hispanic boy whose mother is a janitor and through his voice tells the story of the janitor's strike of Los Angeles in 2000, and the other is an inspiring narrative about Cesar Chavez, a champion of the rights of migrant workers.

■ *The Bracelet* by Yoshiko Uchida (RL/RI)
■ *So Far from the Sea* by Eve Bunting (RL/RI)

Texts address the topic of Japanese American internment camps during World War II. One is a narrative of a young Japanese American girl who loses a bracelet given to her by a friend as a symbol of their friendship. The other is a touching narrative about a young Japanese American girl whose family once lived in an internment camp and now visits her grandfather's grave to finally say good-bye.

■ *Nelson Mandela* by Kadir Nelson (RL/RI)
■ *Toussaint L'Ouverture: The Fight for Haiti's Freedom* by Jacob Lawrence and Walter Dean Myers (RL/RI)

Texts provide inspirational narratives about well-known and little-known national heroes who led their respective countries to freedom. One is a biography of Nelson Mandela who courageously led South Africa to freedom from apartheid, and the other is a biography of Toussaint L'Ouverture, a freed slave who determinedly led Haiti to independence from France.

■ *Duel of the Ironclads: The Monitor vs. the Virginia* (RL/RI) and *The Great Ships* (RI) by Patrick O'Brien

Texts share interesting information about some of the greatest ships in the world. One focuses on two historical ships, the *Monitor* and the *Virginia*, that fought in a great battle during the Civil War period, and the other about a variety of famous battle ships.

Production, Distribution, and Consumption

This strand is based on the belief that "social studies programs should include experiences that provide for the study of how people organize for the production, distribution, and consumption of goods and services" (NCSS, p. 20). It focuses on economics, distribution of resources, goods and services, wants versus needs, and factors of production (land, labor, capital, and entrepreneurship).

Grades K–5

PRODUCTION

- *Robert Fulton: From Submarine to Steamboat* by Steven Kroll (RL/RI)
- *Pancakes, Pancakes* by Eric Carle (RL/RI)

Texts provide different examples and explanations of what it means to actually produce something.

- *Sweet Potato Pie* by Kathleen D. Lindsey (RL/RI)
- *Tight Times* by Trina Schart Hyman (RL/RI)

Texts shares different versions of creative problem solving. One is a narrative about a family that may lose their farm due to a drought but creates a successful business despite harsh financial times. The other is about a family living in a city in the 1930s during tough financial times due to the Depression but finds unexpected ways to help one another.

- *Charlie Needs a Cloak* by Tomie dePaola (RL)
- *Basket Moon* by Barbara Cooney (RL)

Texts show the art and value of creating products out of natural resources. One narrative tells the story of a shepherd who goes through the entire process of making a new red cloak. The other narrative depicts a father who makes and sells baskets, and in the process connects his life with his son's.

- *Uncle Jed's Barbershop* by Margaree King Mitchell (RL)
- *Arthur's Pet Business* by Marc Brown (RL)

Texts discuss the process of starting a new business. One is a narrative about an African American barber in the Depression of the 1920s who saves his money over time to open his own barbershop. The other is a delightful tale of a mouse that starts a pet-sitting business not so much for profit but to prove he is responsible.

- *Amelia Works It Out* by Marissa Moss (RL/RI)
- *How the Second Grade Got $8,205.50 to Visit the Statue of Liberty* by Nathan Zimelman (RL/RI)

Texts address the topic of earning money. One narrative deals with a young girl who, despite earlier attempts, successfully learns how to make a profit, and the other deals with a class trying to earn money for a class trip and highlights the concepts of expenses and profits.

■ *Abuela's Weave* by Omar S. Castaneda (RL)
■ *Charlie Needs a Cloak* by Tomie dePaola (RL)

Texts address the topics of manufacturing and selling products. One narrative deals with a grandmother and granddaughter from Guatemala who make and sell traditional weavings, and the other tells the story of a shepherd who goes through the entire process of making a new red cloak.

■ *Boss of the Plains* by Laurie Carlson (RL/RI)
■ *Levi Strauss and Blue Jeans* by Nathan Olson (RL/RI)

Texts describe two major figures in the business world. One narrative introduces the famous John Stetson who created the Stetson hat, a tall, wide-brimmed hat perfect for cowboys in the wild, wild west. The other is about Levi Strauss who created the famous blue jeans perfectly suited for those speculators rushing to the west in search of gold.

■ *Levi Strauss and Blue Jeans* by Nathan Olson (RL/RI)
■ *Levi Strauss Gets a Bright Idea: A Fairly Fabricated Story of a Pair of Pants* by Tony Johnston (RL/RI)

Texts use different formats to introduce the creator of the now famous blue jeans. One is a biography in narrative form, and the other is a biography in a graphic novel format about the life and times of the legendary man.

DISTRIBUTION

■ *Me and You* (RL/RI) and *Voices in the Park* (RL/RI) by Anthony Browne

Texts include fascinating illustrations with limited text to address the controversial topic and tensions between the haves and have-nots in British society. Both contain implications for other societies as well.

■ *Voices in the Park* (RL/RI) and *A Walk in the Park* (RL/RI) by Anthony Browne

Texts include fascinating illustrations with limited text to address the controversial topic and tensions between the haves and have-nots in British society. Both contain implications for other societies as well.

CONSUMPTION

■ *My Piggy Bank* by Tom Lewis (RL/RI)
■ *Rock, Brock, and the Savings Shock* by Sheila Bair (RL/RI)

Texts provide different examples of the value of savings and investment. One is a narrative in which an investor chooses investment over toys, and the other is about twin boys who learn the value of savings and investment from their grandfather.

■ *The Lunch Line* by Karen Berman Nagel (RL/RI)
■ *The Big Buck Adventure* by Shelley Gill and Deborah Tobola (RL/RI)

Texts address the economic principle of opportunity costs. One narrative describes a young girl who consider costs when she has to buy her own lunch at school, and the other is about a young girl who struggles over the fact that she has many things to buy but has only one dollar.

- *Who Taught You about Money?* by Richard Harris (RL/RI)
- *Alexander, Who Used to Be Rich Last Sunday* by Judith Viorst (RL)

Texts share basic money concepts. One focuses on a young boy who experiences the consequences of ignoring some of these concepts, and the other about the wisdom of knowing about money.

- *The Boston Tea Party* by Stephen Kroll (RL/RI)
- *The Boston Coffee Party* by Doreen Rappaport (RL/RI)

Texts show how one important event in American history can be used to teach both history and economics. One is a narrative about the causes and effects of the Boston Tea Party, and the other is a narrative about the concepts of the effects of supply and demand on coffee during the Revolutionary War.

- *Sold!: A Mathematics Adventure* by Nathan Zimelman (RL/RI)
- *Auction!* by Tres Seymour (RL/RI)

Texts introduce the concept of an auction. One is a humorous narrative about two women who love auctions as much for the items as for the rivalry between them, and the other is a narrative about a boy who successfully bids on items at an auction but has second thoughts about their value.

- *Cycle of Rice, Cycle of Life: A Story of Sustainable Farming* by Jan Reynolds (RL/RI)
- *One Hen: How One Small Loan Made a Big Difference* by Katie Smith Milway (RL/RI)

Texts address the economic benefits of sustainable farming. One narrative describes a young boy in Ghana who takes a loan and strategically and wisely uses it to create a profitable farm. The other is a narrative about cultural, environmental, and economic practices of successful rice farming in Bali, Indonesia.

- *Pony Express* by Steven Kroll (RL/RI)
- *Wanted: A Few Bold Riders: The Story of the Pony Express* by Darice Bailer (RL/RI)

Texts provide an introduction to the history of the Pony Express and the historical depictions of those daring and adventurous men known as the Pony Express riders.

Grades 6–8

- *Death of the Iron Horse* by Paul Goble (RL/RI)
- *Coolies* by Yin (RL/RI)

Texts provide historical accounts of western expansion, building the transcontinental railroad, and the men, particularly the Chinese railroad workers, who built the railway line in the mid-1800s.

- *Coolies* by Yin (RL/RI)
- *Ten Mile Day: And the Building of the Continental Railroad* by Mary Ann Fraser (RL/RI)

Texts provide another perspective on western expansion and the building of the transcontinental railroad. One is the wonderful story about the completion of the railroad, and the other describes a bet waged about laying 10 miles of track in a single day.

Science, Technology, and Society

This strand is based on the belief that "social studies programs should include experiences that provide for the study of relationships among science, technology, and society" (NCSS, p. 21). It focuses on the relationship between science and technology and its influence on the nature and rate of social, cultural, and technological change.

Grades K–5

- *Those Building Men* by Angela Johnson (RL/RI)
- *Sky Boys: How They Built the Empire State Building* by Deborah Hopkinson (RL/RI)

Texts address the topic of monuments of architecture. One is a general narrative about the men who built great pieces of architecture like the Erie Canal, railroads, and skyscrapers of all sorts and designs. The other is a narrative told through the voice of a child about the men who constructed the Empire State Building in New York City in the 1930s.

- *Those Building Men* by Angela Johnson (RL/RI)
- *Pop's Bridge* by Eve Bunting (RL/RI)

Texts address the topic of monuments of architecture. One is a general narrative about the men who built great pieces of architecture like the Erie Canal, railroads, and skyscrapers of all sorts and designs. The other is a narrative about a young boy whose father is building the Golden Gate Bridge in San Francisco, California.

- *The Man Who Walked between the Towers* by Mordicai Gerstein (RL/RI)
- *Up Goes the Skyscraper!* by Gail Gibbons (RI)

Texts combine literary and information about the majesty of tall buildings. One is a narrative about a famous aerialist who walked between the World Trade towers on a high wire, and the other is an informational text that describes the process of building a skyscraper from beginning to end.

Grades 6–8

- *The Boy Who Harnessed the Wind* by William Kamkwamba and Bryan Mealer (RL/RI)
- *Energy Island: How One Community Harnessed the World and Changed Their World* by Allan Drummond (RL/RI)

Texts address the benefits of harnessing the wind. One is a narrative from Malawi about a young boy who responds to the loss of crops in his village from drought by teaching himself about windmills and how they harness the wind. The other is a narrative about a small town in Denmark that wisely and effectively harnessed the wind and became completely energy independent.

- *Close to the Wind: The Beaufort Scale* by Peter Malone (RI)
- *The Man Who Made Time Travel* by Katherine Lasky (RL/RI)

Texts combine literature and information in stories about a famous man, a famous clock, and a famous scale to help sailors successfully navigate the globe.

- *The Great Wall of China* by Leonard Everett Fisher (RL/RI)
- *Talking Walls* by Margy Burns Knight (RI)

Texts provide two perspectives on the notion of great walls of the world. One is a narrative describing the history and construction of one of the greatest walls in the world, the Great Wall of China. The other is an informational text that provides interesting information about different cultures through various walls around the world.

Global Connections

This strand is based on the belief that "social studies programs should include experiences that provide for the study of global connections and interdependence" (NCSS, p. 22). It focuses on global interdependence and its consequences at local, national, and international levels, as well as costs, benefits, and tensions involved with important global issues.

Grades K–5

- *Ghandi* by Demi (RL)
- *I Have a Dream* by Martin Luther King, Jr., and illustrated by Kadir Nelson (RL)

Texts present two world icons who fought against discrimination and for social justice. One is a beautiful biography with gorgeous illustrations of Mohandas Ghandi, an advocate of social justice through nonviolence. The other is a wonderful biography of Martin Luther King, Jr., who was dedicated to equality and social justice and was influenced by the life and teachings of Ghandi.

- *Ghandi* by Demi (RL)
- *Nelson Mandela* by Kadir Nelson (RL)

Texts address human rights and equality. One is a beautiful biography with gorgeous illustrations about Mohandas Ghandi, an advocate of social justice through nonviolence. The other is a biography with unforgettable illustrations about Nelson Mandela, a long-imprisoned political activist and patriot who dedicated his life to social justice and the elimination of apartheid in South Africa.

- *Nelson Mandela* by Kadir Nelson (RL)
- *Mandela: From the Life of the South African Statesmen* by Floyd Cooper (RL)

Texts provide two different but complementary biographies of the person who dedicated his life to the abolishment of white suppression known as apartheid and later was elected to be the president of democratic South Africa.

- *Fly Away Home* by Eve Bunting (RL)
- *The Caged Birds of Phnom Penh* by Frederick Lipp (RL)

Texts use birds as a symbol and metaphor for freedom. One is a narrative about a homeless young boy and his father who live undetected in an airport. One day the boy sees a bird fly out of the airport and hopes he and his father will do the same. The other is a narrative about a young girl in Cambodia who saves her money to free caged birds and at the same time hopes she and her family will be free one day, too.

- *Always with You* by Ruth Vander Zee (RL)
- *Journey Home* by Lawrence McKay, Jr. (RL)

Texts depict two young girls with the courage to survive the tragedy of war. One is a narrative about a young girl whose mother was killed by an explosion during the Vietnam War. She was taken by soldiers to an orphanage where, with the help of others, learned to survive. The other is a narrative about a biracial young girl born in Vietnam who travels back to her native country in search of her birth family only to learn from an old kite maker than both her birth parents were killed in an explosion during the war.

Grades 6–8

- *The Butterfly* by Patricia Polacco (RL/RI)
- *The Yellow Star: The Legend of King Christian X of Denmark* by Carmen Agra Deedy (RL/RI)

Texts address the terror and tragedy of Nazi occupation and racism in World War II. One is a narrative about a young French girl who one night meets a little "ghost," but is actually a young girl hiding from the Nazis. Over time their friendship is revealed as is the brutality and inhumanity of Nazi Germany. The other is a biography of the courageous king of Denmark who used the yellow star to fearlessly protect people from Nazi Germany.

- *Gleam and Glow* by Eve Bunting (RL/RI)
- *Petar's Song* by Pratima Mitchell (RL/RI)

Texts address the topic of forced exile. One narrative uses figurative text and evocative illustrations to describe a family forced into exile from their war-torn country only to return with renewed hope. The other is a narrative about a young boy named Petar who loves to play the violin and one day leaves his war-torn country with his family only to return to hear music again.

Civic Ideals and Practices

This strand is based on the belief that "social studies programs should include experiences that provide for the study of the ideals, principles, and practices of citizenship in a democratic republic" (NCSS, p. 23). It highlights democratic principles, freedoms, and ideals; democratic practices; and citizenship.

Grades K–5

- *Henry Climbs a Mountain* by D. B. Johnson (RL/RI)
- *Ghandi* by Leonard Everett Fisher (RL/RI)

Texts share biographies of different historical characters. One is from America (Henry David Thoreau), and the other is from India (Mohandas Ghandi); both share the same civic ideals, namely, freedom.

- *Duck for President* by Doreen Cronin (RL/RI)
- *Daffy Duck for President* by Chuck Jones (RL/RI)

Texts address the process and complexities of running for office. One is a humorous tale about a duck that runs not as the leader of farm animals but governor of a state. The other is a humorous story with cartoon-like illustrations about the nature and function of government, particularly the separation of powers.

- *Daffy Duck for President* by Chuck Jones (RL/RI)
- *We the Kids* by Alan Katz (RI)

Texts address important concepts in a democracy. One is a humorous story with cartoon-like illustrations about the nature and function of government, particularly the separation of powers. The other is a whimsical yet understandable interpretation of the Preamble to the U.S. Constitution.

- *Liberty's Voice: The Emma Lazarus Story* by Erica Silverman (RL/RI)
- *Naming Liberty* by Jane Yolen (RL/RI)

Texts share an emphasis on the concept of liberty and its most endearing symbol, the Statue of Liberty. One is a biography of the poet Emma Lazarus who authored the famous poem inviting all to America, and the other is an integrated story told by two different characters making the arduous trip to freedom.

- *Emma's Poem* by Linda Glaser (RL/RI)
- *The Story of the Statue of Liberty* by Betsy Maestro (RL/RI)

Texts provide two different but complementary perspectives on the Statue of Liberty. One is a biography of Emma Lazarus who wrote a sonnet from the voice of the statue itself, and the other is a narrative with rich information about the history of the statue.

Additional Instructional Strategies

I have shared H-Maps with students at a variety of grade levels. While many students like H-Maps, they often propose some interesting alternatives. For example, an A-Map (see Appendix J at the end of this book) invites students to record similarities between a paired text inside the letter *A* and differences outside. Similarly, a K-Map (see Appendix K at the end of this book) allows students to record differences at the top and bottom of the letter *K* and similarities in the middle. An M-Map (see Appendix L at the end of this book) invites students to record similarities at the top and outside of the letter *M* and differences inside. Finally, a Z-Map (see Appendix M at the end of this book) enables students to record differences at the top and bottom lines of the letter *Z* and similarities (e.g., how they are connected) on the connecting line.

Paired Text in Science

Putting science trade books into the hands of children is an important step in the process of supporting science learning with literacy.
—AMELIA E. EL-HINDI (2003, p. 537)

Books used in science instruction do matter. They are significant for literacy and for science.
—CHRISTINE C. PAPPAS (2006, p. 229)

In Part Five, I introduce a paired text for science based on the question "How do scientists do science?" and describe a mini-lesson to use with this paired text. I also provide background information for the mini-lesson, use a Category Chart as an instructional strategy to illustrate intertextual connections between these texts, and discuss how this paired text and strategy address the CCSS for Literacy in Science, grades 6–8. Then, I share additional paired text, organized by the CCSS Anchor Standards for Reading and the Next Generation Science Standards and include recommended grade levels and grade bands for each paired text, as well as identify each paired text in terms of whether it represents reading literature (RL), reading informational text (RI), or both (RL/RI). I end by sharing additional instructional strategies that can be used with paired text in science and other content areas.

Mini-Lesson: How Do Scientists Do Science?

Materials

- Copy of paired text: *Snowflake Bentley* (Martin, 2009) (RL/RI) and *Starry Messenger* (Sis, 2000) (RL/RI).
- Category Chart (see Appendix N at the end of this book).

Procedure

- The teacher displays the paired text and a large Category Chart to the whole class.
- The teacher invites students to think about major categories that might represent how these two books are connected and records these categories at the top of the Category Chart.
- The teacher distributes a Category Chart to each student.
- The teacher reads aloud *Starry Messenger*, stopping at strategic places (e.g., where characters, settings, and episodes change, or where illustrations and marginalia reveal significant turning points in the life and work of Galileo, and inviting students to "say something" (Short, Harste, & Burke, 1995) to a partner about how Galileo did science. After reading, students share with the whole class some of the important ways Galileo did science.
- The teacher reads aloud *Snowflake Bentley*, following the same procedure. After reading, students work in pairs and use the Category Chart to record categories that represent similar ways Galileo and Wilson Bentley both did science and share their chart with the whole class.
- The teacher invites students to briefly explain in the boxes below how each text is connected to that category.
- As a culminating strategy, the teacher invites students to use a Eureka! Sheet (see Appendix O at the end of this book) to reflect, record, and share new findings or surprises about the process of making connections between texts. Note: *Eureka* is the Greek word for "I have found it," and allegedly was the word Archimedes shouted running naked through the streets of Athens after he stepped into a bath, observed that the water rose, and discovered displacement.

Background for the Mini-Lesson

Starry Messenger (Sis, 2000) portrays the life of Galileo, famous scientist, mathematician, astronomer, philosopher, and physicist. Even as a young boy, Galileo was always curious, especially about planets and stars. Later, as a young man, Galileo built his own telescopes to observe the natural world, but especially the universe. He wrote about his observations in a book, *Starry Messenger*. The book made him famous. In fact, one of his observations made him infamous. Galileo observed that the sun, not the earth, was the center of the universe. This idea contradicted the conventional thinking at the time and the accepted teachings of the church. He was tried in the pope's court, found guilty, and condemned to spend the rest of his life locked in his house under guard. Soon after, he lost his sight and his desire to see stars in the sky. However, more than 300 years later the church pardoned Galileo, admitting that he was right. His scientific discoveries changed the way we see the universe.

Snowflake Bentley (Martin, 2009) is a fascinating story about the life of Wilson Bentley, a farmer scientist who photographed snowflakes in order to study their interesting and unique formations. Growing up in rural Vermont, Bentley was fascinated with snowflakes, but his neighbors were not. In fact, family and friends considered studying snow downright foolish. Nevertheless, Bentley persevered. At first, he struggled to draw snowflakes because they always melted before he finished. Then, he read about a camera with its own microscope. His parents generously, and not without sacrifice, bought the camera to support his work. Finally, he succeeded at photographing snowflakes. He published his photographs in a book, *Snow Crystals*. Unfortunately, soon after publication Wilson Bentley died from pneumonia. His scientific discoveries changed the way we see snowflakes.

Figure 5.1 illustrates a Category Chart identifying and describing several important connections between these texts (see Harste & Short, with Burke, 1988; see also Short et al., 1995). These connections are represented as major categories.

Among others, five major categories connect these two texts. These categories include instruments and tools; challenging conventional thinking; thinking scientifically; publishing work posthumously; and demonstrating patience, perseverance, and passion. Individually and collectively, these categories have much power and potential for learning how scientists do science. In fact, they represent more than similarities and differences between *Starry Messenger* and *Snowflake Bentley*. Looking across these major categories, they represent major components for doing science and for learning about the characteristics of being a scientist.

For example, doing science often involves using instruments and tools, hopefully the best that are available at any given time. This was true for Galileo, who used a telescope, and Bentley, who used a camera. Today, scientists use the best instruments as well, including microscopes, lasers, computers, global positioning systems (GPS), ultrasounds, x-ray defractions, and imaging equipment. Doing science also involves thinking scientifically. Scientists pose problems, collect data systematically, analyze data rigorously, use trial and error, control for variables, and induce or deduce findings. Moreover, being a scientist often involves posing problems that challenge conventional thinking at a particular time. It also requires passion, patience, and perseverance, sometimes resulting in a lifetime of work, as in the case of Galileo and Bentley. Collectively, these categories represent important lessons for young scientists to learn about how to do science and how to be a scientist.

These, of course, are not the only connections that can be created from this paired text. Other connections and categories include:

- Both performed a variety of scientific inquiries.
- Both learned through trial and error.
- Both engaged in observational versus experimental inquiry.
- Both were criticized (Galileo was persecuted and Bentley was ridiculed).
- Both were perfectionists.
- Both lives involved irony (Galileo used his eyes to observe the heavens, but later went blind; Bentley developed pneumonia from a snow storm and later died).

BOOK TITLES	Instruments/Tools	Challenged Conventional Thinking	Thinking Scientifically	Publishing Work Posthumously	Patience, Perseverance, and Passion
Starry Messenger	Galileo built his own telescope out of glass. He was one of the first to use this instrument. He made it by putting two magnifying glasses in a tube. Some of the glass was colored to protect his eyes when he was observing the sun. The telescope represented the best technology for the time.	Based on his observations, Galileo challenged the popular wisdom of the time—that the earth was the center of the universe. Rather, he said that the sun was the center. This belief challenged the teachings of the church. As a result, he was tried, found guilty, and imprisoned by the pope. Later, the church said that he was indeed right.	Galileo thought like a scientist and engaged in scientific inquiry. He didn't do experimental design because he was observing the stars and planets. He did observational inquiry using a telescope. He stayed up at night collecting and recording data—the data were what he saw in the movement of stars.	Galileo published his observations in a book, *Starry Messenger*. This book was published after his death. In fact, Galileo became more popular after his death than during his life.	Galileo spent much of his life observing the stars and planets. Even though he was condemned to house arrest, he continued to share his discoveries. He was willing to pay a high price (imprisonment) because of believed he was right. Even after he went blind in prison, he still passed on his ideas.
Snowflake Bentley	Bentley used a camera with a microscope. He didn't make it; his parents bought it for him. Like Galileo's telescope, this camera was not common with people. It represented a new instrument that was very innovative for the time.	Unlike others, Bentley did not believe that snow in Vermont was common as dirt and not worth observing. Based on his observations, he believed that all ice crystals (snowflakes) were not the same, but rather each one was unique.	Bentley thought like a scientist, too. He collected and recorded in drawings and photographs ice crystals. He encountered problems in data collection in that the icy crystals he collected quickly melted or evaporated before he could draw or photograph them. So, he worked quickly in the cold and also found ways to preserve the ice crystals for longer periods of time.	Bentley published his observations in a book, *Ice Crystals*. This book was published after his death. Like Galileo, Bentley became more popular after his death than during his life.	Bentley spent much of his life studying ice crystals. He would wait for hours out in the cold and in the snow to find the right ice crystals to photograph. He also walked 6 miles through a blizzard to take pictures of snowflakes. He didn't give up because the snowflakes would melt. He found ways to preserve them long enough to photograph them.

FIGURE 5.1. Category Chart for *Starry Messenger* and *Snowflake Bentley*.

♦ Both were loners.

♦ Both spent their own, as well as others, meager financial resources on their work.

♦ Both were celebrated (extravaganzas were held for Galileo; a monument was built for Bentley).

♦ Galileo went against church teachings at the time; Bentley did not.

♦ Both discovered new knowledge (Galileo discovered four new moons; Bentley discovered that each snowflake is unique).

♦ Both were given nicknames (Galileo was "Starry Messenger" and Bentley was "Snowflake Man").

The CCSS Reading Standards for Literacy in Science

The CCSS call for using Reading Standards for Literacy in Science and Technical Subjects, grades 6–12. Here, I address reading standards for literacy in science, grades 6–8, across two categories: Key Ideas and Details, and Craft and Structure, because these standards are most conducive to paired text. These standards include:

Key Ideas and Details

1 Cite specific textual evidence to support analysis of science and technical texts.

2 Determine the central ideas or conclusions of text; provide an accurate summary of the text distinct from prior knowledge or opinions.

3 Follow precisely a multistep procedure when carrying out experiments, taking measurement, or performing technical tasks.

Craft and Structure

4 Analyze the structure an author uses to organize a text, including how the major sections contribute to the whole and to an understanding of the topic.

5 Analyze the author's purpose in providing an explanation, describing a procedure, or discussing an experiment in a text.

The Next Generation Science Standards

In addition to the CCSS Standards for Literacy in Science, I include the Next Generation Science Standards (NGSS). These standards are based on *A Framework for K–12 Science Education: Practices, Crosscutting Concepts, and Core Ideas* (National Research Council, 2012). This framework outlines three dimensions of science education: disciplinary core ideas, cross-cutting concepts, and science and engineering practices (NGSS Lead States, 2013, p. xv).

Disciplinary Core Ideas

This dimension focuses on the manageability of teaching and learning disciplinary-based scientific ideas. It states that a "limited set of ideas and practices in science and engineering should enable students to evaluate and select reliable sources of scientific information, and allow them to continue their development well beyond their K–12 school years as science learners, users of scientific knowledge, and perhaps also as producers of such knowledge" (NGSS Lead States, 2013, pp. xv–xvi). Disciplinary core ideas represent the progression of content that occurs at each grade band (i.e., K–2, 3–5, and 6–8) and is organized around four major domains: the physical sciences, the life sciences, the earth and space sciences, and engineering technology and application of science.

Cross-Cutting Concepts

This dimension unites disciplinary core ideas. They are designed to help students gain depth of understanding about important ideas and processes in science, as well as develop a scientifically informed and integrated view of the world. The seven cross-cutting ideas are:

1 Patterns.

2 Cause and effect.

3 Scale, proportion, and quantity.

4 Systems and system models.

5 Energy and matter.

6 Structure and function.

7 Stability and change.

Science and Engineering Practices

This dimension describes "the major practices that scientists employ as they investigate and build models and theories about the world, and a key set of engineering practices that engineers use as they design and build systems" (NGSS Lead States, 2013, p. xv). These practices reflect an inquiry-based approach to science teaching and learning and are used to emphasize that "engaging in scientific investigation requires not only skill but also knowledge that is specific to each practice" (NGSS Lead States, 2013, p. xv). These eight practices are:

1 Asking questions (for science) and defining problems (for engineering).

2 Developing and using models.

3 Planning and carrying out investigations.

4 Analyzing and interpreting data.

5 Using mathematics and computational thinking.

6 Constructing explanations (for science) and designing solutions (for engineering).

7 Engaging in argument from evidence.

8 Obtaining, evaluating, and communicating information.

Given this background, it is important to note the distinction between science and engineering. This distinction is admittedly slight, but nonetheless important. The best explanation I have heard is that "scientists ask and answers questions; engineers define and solve problems" (S. D. Moore, personal communication, September, 2013). This distinction is helpful and important to keep in mind. It is also important to note that, while here I describe the three dimensions of scientific education separately, the NGSS emphasize the integration of disciplinary core ideas, cross-cutting concepts, and science and engineering practices.

Theoretical Model

Figure 5.2 illustrates the relationships among the CCSS-ELA Reading Standards for Science and Technical Subjects, grades 6–8; the NGSS; and paired text.

The outer circle identifies the College and Career Readiness (CCR) Anchor Standards. CCR includes four major categories: Craft and Structure, Key Ideas and Details, Integration of Knowledge and Ideas, and Range of Reading and Level of Text Complexity. The inner circle identifies the specific ELA standards under each category to teach science and technical subjects. The three-circle Venn diagram in the middle identifies the NGSS three dimensions of science education and illustrates the emphasis on integration of these dimensions. The gold star illustrates how paired text can be used as a curricular resource and instructional strategy to address the CCR Anchor Standards and ELA Standards for Science and Technical Subjects, as well as integrating the three dimensions of science education. The star in the middle illustrates a paired text that addresses all three dimensions. However, the star can appear in the section of the Venn diagram that connects two dimensions: disciplinary core ideas and cross-cutting concepts, or disciplinary core ideas and science and engineering practices, or science and engineering practices and cross-cutting

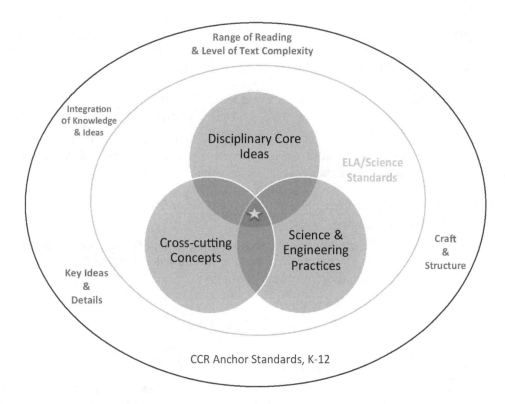

FIGURE 5.2. Theoretical model for science paired text.

concepts. Ideally, a paired text will integrate all three dimensions. At the same time, the model allows for additional flexibility.

Paired Text and the CCSS and NGSS

The NGSS are organized around four major domains: life science, earth space science, physical science, and science and engineering practices. In the following sections I identify paired text for specific disciplinary core ideas in each domain.

Life Science

Grades K–5

Structure and Function (K–5)

- *An Egg Is Quiet* by Diana Aston (RI)
- *Hunwick's Egg* by Mem Fox (RL)

Texts combine literary and informational text to introduce the science of eggs. One is a delightful story from Australia about a bandicoot that discovers what he thinks is an egg in the backyard a day after a storm. While others worry because the egg doesn't hatch, the bandicoot learns that it is actually a stone and decides to keep it as a friend. The other is an informational text introducing all kinds of eggs, little and big, soft and hard, oval and tubular, and discusses what makes an egg a real egg (and not a stone).

- *Chicken and Egg* by Christine Back and Jens Olesen (RI)
- *Chickens Aren't the Only Ones* by Ruth Heller (RL/RI)

Texts provide unique perspectives on chickens. One is an informational text detailing the life of a chicken, and the other is a literary text with rhymes and colorful illustrations that identify a variety of animals that lay eggs, including chickens.

- *Chicken and Egg* by Christine Back and Jens Olesen (RI)
- *First the Egg* by Laura V. Seeger

Texts focus on the relationship between the chicken and the egg. One is an informational text that details the life of a chicken, and the other is a delightful and colorful informational book introducing the concept of transformation.

Organization for Matter and Energy Flow in Organisms

- *Vultures* by Sandra Markle (RI)
- *Vulture View* by Steve Jenkins (RL)

Texts share two different perspectives on the vulture. One is a narrative that presents fascinating information about the vulture through figurative language, and the other is an informational text with rich, colorful illustrations about the life, behavior, and habitats of this creature.

Social Interactions and Group Behavior (3–5)

- *The Honey Makers* by Gail Gibbons (RI)
- *In the Trees, Honey Bees* by Lori Mortensen (RL/RI)

Texts address the importance of bees. One is an informational text about how bees are important insects and highlight vocabulary like *eggs, cells*, and *hives*, and the other is an informational text that describes how bees collaborate to make honey.

Interdependent Relationships in Ecosystems (K–5)

- *Who Eats What? Food Chains and Food Webs* by Patricia Lauber (RI)
- *Dory Story* by Jerry Pallotta (RL)

Texts present two different versions of food chains and food webs. One is an imaginative narrative about a young boy ostensibly taking a bath, but he is actually using toys, tub, and water to present a fascinating version of the food chain. The other is a colorful narrative showing how every link in the food chain is interdependent and necessary for survival.

- *Food Chain* by M. P. Robertson
- *Dory Story* by Jerry Pallotta (RL)

Texts highlight the importance of food chains and food webs. One is an imaginative narrative about a young boy ostensibly taking a bath, but he is actually using toys, tub, and water to present a fascinating version of the food chain. The other is a short, delightful story about a naughty, irresponsible young boy whose actions teach important concepts about the food chain and also that actions often have unintended consequences.

- *Dory Story* by Jerry Palotta (RL/RI)
- *Ocean Sunlight: How Tiny Plants Feed the Seas* by Molly Bang (RI)

Texts focus on the interrelationships among life cycles, food chains, and food webs. One is an imaginative narrative about a young boy ostensibly taking a bath, but he is actually using toys, tub, and water to present a fascinating version of the food chain. The other is a combined literary and informational text using rhythmic text and beautiful illustrations to focus on the interrelationship between things above and below the surface of the ocean.

- *Red Leaf, Yellow Leaf* (RI) and *Leaf Man* (RL/RI) by Lois Ehlert

Texts discuss the beauty of trees and leaves. One is an informational text about the life of a tree, and the other is a narrative that celebrates the beauty and diversity of leaves.

- *Jack's Garden* by Henry Cole (RL/RI)
- *My Backyard Garden* by Carol Lerner (Rl/RI)

Texts address the process of creating a garden. One is a narrative with rhyming text and an accumulative pattern describing how to create a garden step-by-step, and the other shares the steps needed to start a vegetable garden.

- *From Seed to Plant* by Gail Gibbons (RI)
- *The Dandelion Seed* by Joseph Anthony (RL/RI)

Texts deal with seeds and plants. One is a simple, straightforward, informative description of the relationship between seeds and plants, and the other is a narrative that gently tells the travels of a dandelion seed as it is blown around the world by the wind.

- *The Seasons of Arnold's Apple Tree* by Gail Gibbons (RL/RI)
- *How Do Apples Grow?* by Betsy Maestro (RI)

Texts provide interesting information about growing, using, and eating apples. One is a simple text about a young boy who loves an apple tree and how he uses apples throughout the seasons, and the other describes how apples grow.

- *Pumpkin Circle* by George Levenson (RL/RI)
- *How Many Seeds in a Pumpkin?* by Margaret McNamara (RL/RI)

Texts combine and use pumpkins to integrate math and science. One describes the cycle of growing pumpkins, from seed to garden to pumpkin and back to seed again, and the other is a narrative about a teacher using pumpkins to help students have fun with counting.

Information Processing

- *What Do You Do When Something Wants to Eat You?* by Steve Jenkins (RI)
- *Whose Sound Is This?* by Nancy Kelly Allen by (RI)

Texts address the unique sounds and behaviors that act as defense mechanisms for different animals.

■ *Raccoon Moon* by Nancy Carol Willis (RI)
■ *The Kissing Hand* by Audrey Penn (RL)

Texts combine to provide two different perspectives on the raccoon. One is an endearing narrative about a mother raccoon that soothes little raccoon's anxiety about starting school by sharing a family tradition. The other is a narrative following the life of a raccoon and including rich information about the lives and habits of raccoons.

■ *Just Us Two: Poems about Animal Dads* by Joyce Sidman (RL/RI)
■ *Animal Dads* by Sneed Collard (RI)

Texts focus on fathers as parents and caregivers. One is a collection of poems each highlighting a different father in the animal kingdom taking care of his young, and the other is an informational text describing the various different roles and responsibilities of fathers in the natural world.

■ *Just Us Two: Poems about Animal Dads* by Joyce Sidman (RL/RI)
■ *Hip-Pocket Papa* by Sandra Markle (RL/RI)

Texts highlight the role of fathers as caregivers. One is a collection of poems each highlighting a different father in the animal kingdom taking care of his young, and the other is a literary and informational text about a unique frog from Down Under that nurtures and cares for his offspring from birth.

■ *Never Smile at a Monkey* (RI) and *Slap, Squeak & Scatter* (RI) by Steve Jenkins

Texts present different perspectives on the unique characteristics of animals. One is an informational text with colorful collage illustrations about why and how different animals communicate with one another through cries, songs, dances, facial expressions, and many other interesting behaviors. The other is an informational text with colorful collage illustrations about dangerous creatures that use different body parts to warn others and protect themselves, and provides additional information about each creature.

■ *Living Color* (RI) and *What Do You Do with a Tail Like This?* (RI) by Steve Jenkins

Texts present different perspectives on the unique characteristics of animals. One is an informational text with large, colorful, collage illustration, which is organized by colors that describe how different animals use color to communicate with others, especially predators. It includes an extensive information about animals and colors., The other is an informational patterned text with colorful collage illustrations in a guessing game format about how animals use body parts (eyes, ears, mouths) for different reasons. It includes additional information about each animal at the end.

■ *Animal Defenses: How Animals Protect Themselves* by Etta Kaner (RI)
■ *Beaks!* by Sneed Collard (RI)

Texts provide unique perspectives on how animals protect themselves. One includes information about how animals cleverly and successfully (and sometimes unsuccessfully) protect themselves from predators, and the other presents information about different species of birds that use their beaks for all sorts of reasons, one of which is survival.

- *Hey, Daddy!* by Mary Batten
- *Animal Dads* by S. B. Collard

Texts focus on the role of fathers as nurturers and caregivers. One is an informational text describing the various roles and responsibilities of fathers in the natural world, and the other provides rich information about different species that participate in male parental behaviors.

- *Wolves* by Emily Gravett (RL)
- *Wolves* by Seymour Simon (RI)

Texts show two different images of wolves. One is an informational text detailing the life, behavior, and environment of wolves. The other is a delightfully humorous postmodern picture book about a young rabbit that reads about wolves so intently that he fails to see that he has encountered a real wolf, but fortunately includes an alternate ending.

- *Red Eyes or Blue Feathers: A Book about Animals* by Patricia Stockland and Todd Ouren (RI)
- *I See Animals Hiding* by Jim Arnosky (RL/RI)

Texts address the scientific topic of adaptation. One provides information about how animals adapt to their peculiar environment, and the other uses rhyming text to tell how animals adapt to protect themselves.

Growth and Development of Organisms (K–5)

- *Sea Turtles* by Gail Gibbons (RI)
- *Into the Sea* by Brenda Guiberson (RL)

Texts illuminate the beauty and mystery of sea turtles One is a narrative that tells the life cycle of a female sea turtle, and the other is a rich informational text that describes the different kinds of sea turtles.

- *The Dragons Are Singing Tonight* by Jack Prelutsky (RL)
- *Komodo!* by Peter Sis (RL)

Texts combine fact and fiction, and literature and informational text, on one of young children's favorite topics—dragons. One is a collection of poems that depict different kinds of dragons, some funny, most scary, and the other is an adventure narrated by a young boy who loves dragons so much that on a trip to Indonesia he actually meets a Komodo dragon.

- *Bats* by Gail Gibbons (RI)
- *Bats: Biggest! Littlest!* by Sandra Markle (RI)

Texts consist of two informational books describing different kinds of bats and bat features. One has amazing, up-close photographs and the other a concise and colorful account of fascinating facts about bats.

- *Bats* by Gail Gibbons (RI)
- *Big Brown Bat* by Rick Chrustowski (RI)

Texts show different ways informational books can provide information about bats. One includes a wide variety of factual information about bats, what they are, what they look like, and why they behave the way they do. The other also provides information but in narrative form.

■ *Mister Seahorse* by Eric Carle (RL)
■ *Seahorses* by T. C. George (RI)

Texts use different formats to introduce the beautiful and enigmatic seahorse. One is a brightly, multicolored illustrated narrative about a male seahorse entrusted by a female seahorse to protect and nurture her eggs, and the other is an informational text that provides glimpses into the undersea world of sea creatures, especially the beautiful seahorse.

■ *The Salamander Room* by Anne Mazer and Steve Johnson (RL)
■ *Salamander Rain: A Lake and Pond Journal* by K. J. Pratt-Serafini (RL/RI)

Texts combine literary and informational text on the life and attributes of salamanders. One is an imaginative story about a young boy who wants a pet, finds a salamander, and turns his bedroom into a place where he can properly take care of it. The other is a story of a boy who discovers a salamander and keeps a journal and scrapbook of what he learns.

■ *Daft Bat* by Jeannie Willis (RL)
■ *Bats* by Gail Gibbons (RI)

Texts combine literary and informational text to address the types, behaviors, and characteristics of bats. One is a humorous narrative about a group of animals that are convinced young Bat is looney because she likes to hang upside down, but learns from wise Owl that Bat is quite normal. The other is an informational text that includes a wide variety of factual information about bats, what they are, what they look like, and why they behave the way they do.

■ *Waiting for the Whales* by Sheryl McFarlane (RL)
■ *Whales Passing* by Eve Bunting (RL)

Texts provide unique perspectives on whales. One is a narrative about a young boy and his father who enjoy watching Orca whales passing by. The boy wonders if the whales talk about him as he talks about them with his dad. The other is a narrative about a grandfather who feels companionship with whales passing by each year and passes his love of these creatures to his daughter and granddaughter.

■ *Discovery of Dragons* by Graeme Base (RL)
■ *The Dragons Are Singing Tonight* by Jack Prelutsky (RL)

Texts share different perspectives on dragons. One is a collection of poems that depict different kinds of dragons, some funny, most scary, and the other is a collection of stunning illustrations and informative correspondences between a scientist and people around the world who have seen dragons.

■ *Home at Last: A Song of Migration* by April Pulley Sayre (RL/RI)
■ *Gotta Go, Gotta Go* by Sam Swope (RL/RI)

Texts address the topic of migration in two different ways. One is a story with lyrical and informational text about a variety of animals that migrate long distances, and the other is a delightful story of one migratory journey by a monarch butterfly that has to go to Mexico, but doesn't know why.

■ *Going Home: The Mystery of Animal Migration* by Marianne Berkes (RL/RI)
■ *Home at Last: A Song of Migration* by April Pulley Sayre (RL/RI)

Texts address the topic of migration in two different ways. One is a story with lyrical and informational text about a variety of animals that migrate long distances, and the other is a narrative that pays tribute to the many animals that travel long distances in the name of migration.

Growth and Development of Organisms (6–8)

■ *Cat on the Island* by Gary Crew (RL)
■ *Swan Song* by J. Patrick Lewis and Christopher Wormell (RL)

Texts address the topic of extinction and invasive species. One is a remarkable narrative with startling illustrations about a devastating consequence when humans introduce a single, feral cat to an island populated with beautiful birds, one of which is flightless. The other is a collection of poems that are reminders of the many animals made extinct over the years.

■ *Cat on the Island* by Gary Crew (RL
■ *I Said Nothing* by Gary Crew and Mark Wilson (RL)

Texts poignantly address the topic of extinction. One is a remarkable narrative with startling illustrations about a devastating consequence when humans introduce a single, feral cat to an island populated with beautiful birds, one of which is flightless. The other is a haunting narrative of how illegal trappers made the paradise parrot extinct.

■ *I Saw Nothing* (RL) and *I Said Nothing* by Gary Crew and Mark Wilson (RL)

Texts are companion pieces focused on the topic of the consequences of extinction. One is a gripping story of the extinction of the elusive Thulacine, or Tasmanian tiger, and the other is a haunting narrative of how illegal trappers made the paradise parrot extinct.

■ *Uno's Garden* by Graeme Base (RL)
■ *Gone Wild: An Endangered Animal Alphabet* by David McLimans (RI)

Texts address endangerment and extinction and the relationship between the two. One is a narrative about the critical importance of balancing the earth's resources with human wants and includes hidden and disguised images, mathematical problems and solutions, and captivating illustrations. The other is an innovative alphabet book with each letter identifying and describing a particular endangered species.

■ *The Story of Rosy Dock* by Jeannie Baker (RL/RI)
■ *Welcome to the River of Grass* by Jane Yolen (RI)

Texts address invasive species. One is a beautiful narrative with stunning, three-dimensional collage illustrations about the consequences of one invasive species, the plant Rosy Dock, in Australia. The other is a narrative describing the fragility of some ecosystems and the need to protect these environments from destruction and extinction.

■ *Aliens from Earth: When Animals and Plants Invade Other Ecosystems* by Mary Batten (RI)
■ *The Story of Rosy Dock* by Jeannie Baker (RL)

Texts address the topic of invasive species and the natural habitats of invasive species. One is an informational text describing the havoc and devastating effects invasive species can have on ecosystems, and the other is a beautiful narrative with stunning, three-dimensional collage illustration about the consequences of one invasive species, the plant Rosy Dock, in Australia.

Ecosystem Dynamics, Functioning, and Resilience (3–5)

■ *One Small Place by the Sea* by Barbara Brenner (RL/RI)
■ *In One Tidepool* by Anthony D. Fredericks (RL/RI)

Texts help explore two natural habitats. One is a narrative using lyrical prose to describe the habitat of a hole that functions as a home for many animals, and the other is about a tidepool that is a home to many crabs, snails, and other water creatures.

■ *In the Small, Small Pond* by Denise Fleming (RL/RI)
■ *Near One Cattail* by Anthony D. Fredericks (RL/RI)

Texts highlight the beauty of nature. One is a narrative about a pond and all the creatures that depend and live in and by it throughout the year, and the other is a simple narrative about all the creatures that live in wetland environments.

■ *The Ever-Living Tree: The Life and Times of a Coast Redwood* by Linda Vieira (RL/RI)
■ *The Tree* by Dana Lyons (RL/RI)

Texts address change over time by showcasing two ancient trees with narratives that unfold the many events that have occurred over the years in the life of a sequoia and a Douglas fir.

■ *Forest Bright* (RL/RI) and *Forest Night* (RL/RI) by Jennifer Ward

Texts are actually one text. One is a narrative about animals that live and are active in the forest during the day and, flipped over, the other is a narrative about animals that live and are active in the forest during the night.

■ *Song of the Water Boatmen and Other Pond Poems* (RL/RI) and *Butterfly Eyes and Other Secrets of the Meadow* (RL/RI) by Joyce Sidman

Texts use poems to present information about two unique habitats. One is a collection of poems with rhyming verse, colored woodcut illustrations, and informational text in the margins about unique pond creatures along with a rich glossary of pond terms. The other is a collection of prose and poems written as riddles with large, colorful illustrations about a diverse group of meadow creatures.

■ *Desert Giant* by Barbara Bash (RL/RI)
■ *Around One Cactus* by Anthony D. Fredericks (RL/RI)

Texts use different perspectives and formats to describe the vibrancy of the saguaro cactus. Both identify and describe all the animals that live on and around this majestic cactus in the desert.

■ *Rainforest* by Helen Cowcher (RL/RI)
■ *The Forest Forever* by Kristen Joy Pratt-Serafini (RL/RI)

Texts introduce rain forests as ecosystems. One is the inspiring story of dedication, commitment, and collaboration to create the Children's Eternal Rain Forest in Costa Rica, and the other is a brightly colored narrative that is a simple introduction to creatures in the rain forest and the need for conservation of these valuable habitats.

▪ *Pond Year* by Kathryn Lasky (RL/RI)
▪ *Edge of the Pond: Selected Haiku and Tanka of Darrell Lindsey* by Darrell Lindsey (RL/RI)

Texts are a unique combination of literary and informational text about ponds. One is a nicely illustrated narrative that describes the life of the pond throughout the year, and the other is a collection of haiku and tanka poetry about the natural beauty of the pond as an ecosysem.

▪ *One Small Place in a Tree* by Barbara Brenner (RL/RI)
▪ *Under One Rock* by Anthony D. Fredericks (RL/RI)

Texts focus on a common theme of seeing what is often unseen in the natural world. One involves lyrical prose that describes a hole in a tree that is much more than that, including a home for many animals. The other is a beautifully illustrated narrative showing that there is much more than dirt under a rock; there is a thriving community and ecosystem.

▪ *Weslandia* by Paul Fleischman (RL/RI)
▪ *Just a Dream* by Chris Van Allsburg (RL/RI)

Texts share a focus on the environment. One is a fantastic story of a boy who creates a new civilization for a summer project that hints at the value of maintaining sustainable environments, and the other is about a fantastic journey told with dream-like illustrations that raises issues over the need for people to be responsible with the environment.

▪ *Arrowhawk* by Lola M. Schaefer (RL)
▪ *Saving Samantha* by Robbyn Smith van Frankenhuyzen (RL)

Texts address the topic of animal survival. One is a beautifully illustrated narrative about a courageous red-tailed hawk, shot with a poacher's arrow, cared for and ultimately released back into the wild, and the other story is told in journal form about a young fox rescued from a hunter's trap, rehabilitated, and released to the wild.

▪ *Arrowhawk* by Lola M. Schaefer (RL)
▪ *Raptor! A Kid's Guide to Birds of Prey* by Christyna M. Laubach, Rene Laubach, and Charles W. G. Smith (RI)

Texts combine to present different perspectives on birds of prey. One is a beautifully illustrated narrative about a courageous red-tailed hawk, shot with a poacher's arrow, cared for and ultimately released back into the wild, and the other is an informational text that accurately illustrates and describes the life, characteristics, and behaviors of North American raptors.

▪ *Interrupted Journey* by Kathryn Lasky (RL)
▪ *Saving Samantha* by Robbyn S. van Frankenhuyzen (RL)

Texts address the topic of animal survival. One is a narrative about a sea turtle that unexpectedly washed up on the shore, was cared for, and returned to its rightful environment to prosper, and the other story is told in journal form about a young fox rescued from a hunter's trap, rehabilitated, and released to the wild.

Grades 6–8

Structure and Function

- ■ *Hear Your Heart* by Paul Showers (RL/RI)
- ■ *The Heart: Our Circulatory System* by Seymour Simon (RI)

Texts address the concept of the heart and how it works. One provides a simple introduction to the heart and what it takes to keep it healthy, and the other is an informational text that uses photography to teach the circulatory system and is a substantive extension to the first text.

- ■ *Bones: Our Skeletal System* (RI) and *Muscles: Our Muscular System* (RI) by Seymour Simon

Texts provide extraordinary illustrations and photographs about two important parts of human anatomy.

- ■ *The Brain: Our Nervous System* by Seymour Simon (RI)
- ■ *Big Head!: A Book about Your Brain and Your Head* by Dr. Pete Rowan (RI)

Texts provide different introductions to one of the most important parts of the human body.

Inheritance and Variation of Traits

- ■ *Cell Wars* (RI) and *Cells Are Us* (RI) by Fran Blakwill

Texts use colorful and informative illustrations to introduce the importance of human cells.

- ■ *Cells Are Us* by Fran Blakwill (RI)
- ■ *The Life of a Cell* by Andres llamas Ruiz (RI)

Texts provide two perspectives on what cells are and how they live.

- ■ *Cell Wars* by Fran Blakwill (RI)
- ■ *Atoms and Cells* by Lionel Bender (RI)

Texts provide different perspectives on what cells are and how they combat viruses and diseases in the human body.

- ■ *DNA Is Here to Stay* (RI) and *Amazing Schemes within Your Genes* (RI) by Fran Blakwill

Texts introduce the concept of DNA and discuss the structure and function of genes.

- ■ *DNA Is Here to Stay* by Fran Blakwill (RI)
- ■ *DNA Detectives* by Andrew Einspruch (RI)

Texts combine humor and information to introduce the complex concept of DNA.

- ■ *DNA Is Here to Stay* by Fran Blakwill (RI)
- ■ *Double Talking Helix Blues* by Joel Herskowitz (RL/RI)

Texts introduce the concept of DNA and focus on its relationship to the double helix.

- *Gregor Mendel: The Friar Who Grew Peas* by Cheryl Bardoe(RL/RI)
- *DNA and Genetic Engineering* by Robert Snedden (RI)

Texts introduce genetics, one is a biography of the man who is today considered the first geneticist and the other an informational text on genes and genetic engineering.

Natural Selection

- *Life on Earth: The Story of Evolution* by Steve Jenkins (RL/RI)
- *Our Family Tree: An Evolution Story* by Lisa Westberg Peters and Lauren Stringer (RL/RI)

Texts focus on the story of evolution with interesting text and intriguing illustrations. One explores the history of life on earth and the fascinating story of evolution. The other uses the metaphor of a family album to show connections between the evolution of life today and millions of years ago.

- *The Birth of the Earth* by Jacqui Bailey and Matthew Lilly (RL/RI)
- *Mammals Who Morph: The Universe Tells Our Evolution Story* by Jennifer Morgan (RL/RI)

Texts describe the story of the universe. One is an informative cartoon history and the other a beautifully illustrated description of the evolution filled with important science concepts, helpful timelines, and narrative language.

- *The Birth of the Earth* by Jacqui Bailey and Matthew Lilly (RL/RI)
- *Big Bang!: The Tongue Tickling Tale of a Speck That Became Spectacular* by Carolyn Cinami DeCristofano (RL/RI)

Texts describe the story of the universe and evolution. One is an informative cartoon history and the other uses alliterative verse to tell an entertaining story of a fascinating journey from speck to spectacular.

- *Life on Earth: The Story of Evolution* by Steve Jenkins (RL/RI)
- *The Tree of Life: A Book Depicting the Life of Charles Darwin* by Peter Sis (RL/RI)

Texts provides two different introductions to the concept of evolution. One uses very large, colorful, paper collage illustrations to provide an introduction to the basic principles of evolution, and the other is a beautifully illustrated narrative with abundant marginalia describing the life and times of Charles Darwin.

- *Charles Darwin and the Beagle Adventure* by A. J. Wood and Clint Twist (RL/RI)
- *Charles Darwin* by Alan Gibbons

Texts focus on the concept of evolution, one a biography of Charles Dawin and the other a narrative about Darwin's travels to the Gallapogos Islands.

- *Animals Charles Darwin Saw* by Sandra Markle (RL/RI)
- *The Mystery of Darwin's Frog* by Marty Crump (RL/RI)

Texts describe the mysteries behind all the things Darwin saw on his trip to the Gallopagos Islands.

- *Prehistoric Actual Size* by Steve Jenkins (RI)
- *Boy, Were We Wrong about Dinosaurs* by Kudlinski (RL/RI)

Texts address the topic about how scientists know about prehistoric life and how scientists' ideas change over time.

Earth Space Science

Grades K–5

Human Impacts on Earth Systems

- *Common Ground: The Water, Earth, and Air We Share* by Molly Bang (RL/RI)
- *The Earth Has Caught a Cold* by Roxane Marie Galliez (RL/RI)

Texts describe the devastating effects on the environment caused directly by humans.

- *A Warmer World* by Caroline Arnold (RI)
- *The Water Hole* by Graeme Base (RL/RI)

Texts provide two different perspectives on global warming, environmental change, and its affects on animals. One is a gorgeously illustrated story that integrates mathematics (counting), science (environment), and art (illustrations with hidden and shadowy images) that poses a dangerous possibility, namely, that as animals get thirstier around the world the water supply diminishes. The other is a collection of descriptions about particular animals around the world whose environments have and are being affected by global warming to the point that they face extinction.

- *Antarctica* by Helen Cowcher (RL/RI)
- *Loony Little* by Dianna Hutts Aston (RL/RI)

Texts provide informative glimpses into the mysterious world of Antarctica. One is a narrative that describes the frozen continent and the animals whose survival is threatened by humans. The other is a narrative based on the story of Chicken Little about a loon that notices that the ice is melting, a subtle reference to global warming, and that something must be done.

Weather and Climate

- *The Cloud Book* by Tomie DePaola (RL/RI)
- *Little Cloud* by Eric Carle (RL/RI)

Texts address the topic of clouds. One is a narrative with a surprising amount of information about clouds, and the other is an imaginative story about a little cloud that transforms itself into all kinds of shapes until other clouds join in the fun.

- *Cloud Dance* by Thomas Locker (RI)
- *Sector 7* by David Weisner (RL)

Texts provide both an introduction and extension to clouds. One is a delightful narrative with extraordinary illustrations about a boy on a field trip to the Empire State Building who makes friends with a small cloud hovering nearby and eventually with other clouds, as they also want to make friends. The other is a narrative with lyrical prose and paintings for illustrations that identify the different seasons in the course of a year and includes a section with interesting information about the science of clouds.

■ *The Man Who Named the Clouds* by Julie Hannah and Joan Holub (RL)
■ *Fluffy, Flat, and Wet: A Book about Clouds* by Dana Meachen Rau (RI)

Texts introduce clouds in two different ways. One is a wonderful biography of Luke Howard, an 18th-century meteorologist who spent his life studying and classifying clouds, and the other is a simple text with simple illustrations that identify clouds and discusses how they are formed.

The Roles of Water in Earth's Surface Processes

■ *A Drop around the World* by Barbara Shaw McKinney (RL/RI)
■ *A Raindrop's Journey* by Mark Graber (RL/RI)

Texts address the topic of how water behaves. One narrative follows one drop of water all around the world, illustrating different geographical locations and highlighting the water cycle, and the other narrative follows a raindrop on a similar adventure.

■ *The Drop in My Drink* by Marilyn Hooper and Chris Coady (RL/RI)
■ *The Incredible Water Show* by Debra Frasier (RL/RI)

Texts provide similar and different perspectives on water. One is a narrative with paintings as illustrations that provide a historical account of water on planet Earth, the water cycle, and many interesting facts about this important natural resource. The other is a narrative with colorful illustrations and a cast of characters who through a play describe the water cycle.

■ *Water Dance* by Thomas Locker (RL/RI)
■ *The Drop in My Drink* by Marilyn Hooper and Chris Coady (RL/RI)

Texts provide similar and different perspectives on water. One uses lyrical prose and stunning paintings to both describe and illustrate the water cycle. The other is a narrative also with stunning paintings that provides a historical account of water on planet Earth, the water cycle, and many interesting facts about this important natural resource.

■ *Wave* by Suzy Lee (RL)
■ *Tsunami!* by Kimiko Kajiikawa (RL/RI)

Texts focus on the beauty and power of water. One is a postmodern wordless picture book with artistic light blue and white watercolor illustrations that describes a little girl's day at the beach and imaginative play with waves. The other is a narrative of a rich rice farmer who first hears rumblings and warns villagers of a coming tsunami but also makes a great sacrifice to save others. Used together, both texts can help introduce the difference between a wave and a tsunami.

Earth and the Solar System

■ *How Do You Know What Time It Is?* by Robert E. Wells (RL/RI)
■ *On Time: From Seasons to Split Seconds* by Gloria Skurzynski (RL/RI)

Texts address time and the measurement of time from different perspectives. One is a short narrative introducing the concept of time and tracing the history of instruments created over time from the earliest sundials to contemporary atomic clocks. The other highlights the history of how humans have kept time.

■ *On the Same Day in March* by Marilyn Singer (RL/RI)
■ *Somewhere in the World Right Now* by Stacey Shuett (RL/RI)

Texts show two different ways to understand the concept of time in different geographical locations. One is a narrative that describes how time and weather on one day in March is so different for people depending on where they live around the world. The other shares the same topic by showing that on the same day and at the same time some people are getting up in the morning, some are going to bed at night, and others are enjoying the afternoon.

■ *Phases of the Moon* by Gillia M. Olson (RI)
■ *The Moon Book* by Gail Gibbons (RI)

Texts address the topic of the moon. One introduces different phases of the moon and how young moon gazers can recognize them, and the other gives a more detailed and historical account of the moon and how moon gazers, young and old, have observed it over time.

■ *Arctic Lights, Arctic Nights* by Debbie S. Miller (RL/RI)
■ *The Shortest Day: Celebrating the Winter Solstice* by Wendy Pfeffer (RI)

Texts introduce and explain what it is like to live in a place where the sun shines only a couple of hours a day on a winter's day. One is a narrative that provides a simple introduction to the solstice, the shortest day of the year, and how different cultures throughout history have observed and understood it. The other is a beautifully designed and illustrated narrative that extends basic understandings of the solstice by describing the fascinating relationship between time, light, and temperature in Fairbanks, Alaska, and the animals that live in this extreme environment.

■ *Roaring, Boring Alice: A Story of the Aurora Borealis* by Patricia K. Merski (RL/RI)
■ *Arctic Fives Arrive* by Elinor J. Pinczes (RL/RI)

Texts introduce the Northern Lights of the Arctic. One is a colorful, with no pun intended, narrative about a disagreeable young girl who is visited by someone who transforms her angry voice into a softer voice with vibrant colors like the Aurora Borealis. It also includes some fascinating information about the Northern Lights. The other integrates science and counting using rhyming text about a group of arctic animals that gather together five at a time to witness the beautiful Northern Lights.

■ *Stella Brite and the Dark Matter Mystery* by Sara L. Latta (RL/RI)
■ *Big Bang: The Tongue-Tickling Tale of a Speck That Became Spectacular* by Carolyn Cinami DeCristofano (RL/RI)

Texts provide an interesting relationship between the origin and mysteries of the universe. One is a narrative about a brother and sister who like to solve mysteries and this is one of the most mysterious of all mysteries, namely, dark matter in the universe. The other is a text that follows the history of the universe from Big Bang, formation, and expansion of the universe to how humans study this continuing history today.

Natural Resources

■ *The Deep-Sea Floor* by Sneed B. Collard (RL/RI)
■ *The Hidden Forest* by Jeannie Baker (RL/RI)

Texts deal with two different kinds of underwater habitats. One is an informational text about the mysterious deep sea habitat and all the plants and creatures that thrive there. The other is a narrative with stunning three-dimensional collage illustrations of blues and greens about a young boy and girl who pursue a mystery underwater only to discover a kelp forest and all the plants and creatures that thrive there.

- *Hidden Forest* by Jeannie Baker (RL/RI)
- *A Sea within a Sea* by Ruth Heller (RL/RI)

Texts deals with underwater habitats. One is a narrative with rhythmic and rhyming text and visually attractive and colorful illustrations. It is about the history and geography of a unique place called the Sargasso Sea, more popularly known as the Bermuda Triangle, and the unique creatures that make this sea home. The other is a narrative with stunning three-dimensional collage illustrations of blues and greens about a young boy and girl who pursue a mystery underwater only to discover a kelp forest and all the plants and creatures that thrive there.

The History of Planet Earth

- *Earthsteps: A Rock's Journey through Time* by Diane N. Spickert (RL/RI)
- *The Jupiter Stone* by Owen P. Lewis (RL/RL)

Texts use rock/stone journeys to introduce concepts about the history of the earth. One is a narrative that uses a historical timeline to follow a simple rock's journey and highlight the geologic cycle. The other is a thought-provoking narrative about a small, striped stone and ponders the journey the stone has been on from starting out somewhere in the universe, landing on earth, and returning to space once again.

- *The Pebble in My Pocket: A History of Our Earth* by Meredith Hooper (RL/RI)
- *Earthsteps: A Rock's Journey through Time* by Diane N. Spickert (RL/RI)

Texts use rocks to describe the history of the earth. One is a simple narrative that traces the way a single pebble is formed over time and includes an informative geologic timeline, and the other is a narrative that uses a historical timeline to follow a simple rock's journey and highlight the geologic cycle.

- *If You Find a Rock* by Peggy Christian (RL/RI)
- *Rocks: Hard, Soft, Smooth, and Rough* by Natalie M. Rosinsky (RL/RI)

Texts introduce the beauty of rocks. One is a simple text that uses black and white photographs to introduce kinds of rocks and places where rocks are usually found, especially rocks that young children like to play with. The other gives a simple explanation of different kinds and classification of rocks including igneous, metamorphic, and sedimentary.

- *Let's Go Rock Collecting* by Roman Gans (RL/RI)
- *The Rock Factory* by Jacqui Bailey (RL/RI)

Texts introduce the science of rocks and rock formation. One is a simple story about two rock lovers who travel around the world looking for rocks and learning how sedimentary, metamorphic, and igneous rocks are formed, and the other describes the rock cycle, identifies different kinds of rocks, and explains how rocks are formed.

- *When the Giant Stirred* by Celia Godkin (RL/RI)
- *Volcano Wakes Up!* by Lisa Westburg Peters (RL/RI)

Texts provide two different perspectives on the renewal of nature. One is a narrative, almost a mythological tale, about a Pacific island with a healthy ecosystem of plants, animals, and people. One day the giant stirred (a volcano occurred) causing villagers to leave the island. Life on the island was destroyed, but over time signs of life appear once again. The other is a lovely and informative collection of poems from different points of view that describe the causes and consequences of the volcanic process.

- *Starry Messenger* by Peter Sis (RL/RI)
- *The Fossil Girl: Mary Anning's Dinosaur Discovery* by Catherine Brighton (RL/RI)

Texts focus on the scientific topic of challenging conventional thinking. One is a striking biography of Galileo that describes his life and discoveries, and particularly highlights how and why he challenged conventional thinking at the time about the nature of the universe. The other is a beautiful narrative told in graphic novel format about a young girl whose family owns a fossil shop by the sea, but one day a storm destroys the stock of fossils. Mary then sets out to find more fossils to sell and sees a huge eye in a rock cliff and later learns that she has just discovered the first fossil of an Ichthyosaurus dinosaur.

- *The Dinosaurs of Waterhouse Hawkins* by Barbara Kerley (RL/RI)
- *Mary Anning: Fossil Hunter* by Sally M. Walker (RL/RI)

Texts focus on observational inquiry and discovery. One is a beautifully illustrated narrative and the other is an informative biography of Mary Anning, a self-taught paleontologist in 19th-century England, a little-known and little-recognized scientist who was the first to discover complete fossils.

- *Fossil* by Claire Ewart (RL/RI)
- *The Fossil Girl: Mary Anning's Dinosaur Discovery* by Catherine Brighton (RL/RI)

Texts focus on observational inquiry, fossils, and fossil formation. One is a narrative about a young girl who simply and innocently finds a rock, and then the narrative travels back millions of years to identify a Pterosaur and how it was formed. The other is a beautiful narrative told in graphic novel format about a young girl whose family owns a fossil shop by the sea, but one day a storm destroys the stock of fossils. Mary then sets out to find more fossils to sell and sees a huge eye in a rock cliff and later learns that she has just discovered the first fossil of an Ichthyosaurus dinosaur.

Plate Tectonics and Large-Scale System Interactions

- *Mountain Dance* by Thomas Locker (RL)
- *Mountains* by Seymour Simon (RI)

Texts present two different perspectives on mountains. One involves lyrical prose and colorful paintings for illustrations that beautifully uses dancing as a metaphor for how and why mountains move, and the other is a rich informational text about the beauty and majesty of mountains. Together these texts are a wonderful introduction to other related scientific concepts like plate tectonics and continental shift.

- *Mountain Dance* by Thomas Locker (RL/RI)
- *The Island That Moved: How Shifting Forces Shape Our Earth* by Meredith Hooper (RL/RI)

Texts present two different perspectives on mountains. One involves lyrical prose and colorful paintings for illustrations that beautifully uses dancing as a metaphor for how and why mountains move. The other is a beautifully illustrated narrative that unravels the history of one island while describing plate tectonics at the same time.

The Universe and Its Stars

- *Bright Star* by Gary Crew (RL/RI)
- *Look Up!* by Robert Burleigh (RL/RI)

Texts share inspiring stories of women astronomers. One is a biography but fictional account of a young girl in late 19th-century rural Australia who spends her days doing needlework and milking cows until she accidentally meets a famous astronomer who inspires her to look both at and beyond the stars. The other is an inspiring biography of Henrietta Leavitt, a young woman in 19th-century America who spends her days observing the stars at the Harvard College Observatory, and based on those observations helped other astronomers better understand and measure the vastness of the universe.

- *Maria's Comet* by Deborah Hopkinson (RL/RI)
- *Look Up!* by Robert Burleigh (RL/RI)

Texts introduce inspiring stories of women astronomers. One is a fictional account of the life of Maria Mitchell, America's first woman astronomer, and the other is an inspiring biography of Henrietta Leavitt, a young woman in 19th-century America who spends her days observing the stars at the Harvard College Observatory, and based on those observations helped other astronomers better understand and measure the vastness of the universe.

Earth's Materials and Systems

- *My Light* (RL/RI) and *Living Sunlight* (RL/RI) by Molly Bang

Texts introduces the power and wonder of the sun. One is a narrative and informational text that describes the importance of the sun by providing light and energy through its rays. The other is a narrative with lyrical text about ocean science that describes how the sun is a source of energy, all species on earth share energy, and photosynthesis connects all living things.

Physical Science

Forces and Motion

- *I Face the Wind* by Vicki Cobb (RI)
- *Feel the Wind* by Arthur Dorros (RL/RI)

Texts address in simple and understandable ways why wind behaves the way it does. One is a narrative that describes what wind is and what causes it, and the other is a narrative that identifies the properties and characteristics of wind, and includes practical, hands-on activities to try in class and at home.

- *Forces Make Things Move* by Kimberly Brubaker Bradley (RL/RI)
- *Forces around Us* by Sally Hewitt (RI)

Texts discuss the relationship between force and motion. One is an informational text that introduces force as something that pushes or pulls, and the other is a narrative that introduces the concept of forces and relevant vocabulary, and terms like *friction, inertia,* and *gravity.*

■ *Who Sank the Boat?* by Pamela Allen (RL/RI)
■ *Ducky* by Eve Bunting (RL/RI)

Texts address several scientific concepts, in particular, floating and sinking. One is a short, simple narrative about a group of animals that decide to go for a row in a boat in the bay, but as each steps into the boat it gets lower and lower in the water until finally a tiny mouse steps in and they all fall into the water. The other is a narrative based on a true story about a ship with a crate of yellow plastic ducks aboard that encounters stormy weather. The crate is washed overboard, but the ducks survive by floating and drifting in the water until they land on another shore far away from where they started.

■ *Moving Heavy Things* by Jan Adkins (RI)
■ *The New Way Things Work* (especially chapter 1, "The Mechanics of Movement") by David Macaulay (RL/RI)

Texts share a focus on physics. One is an informational text with detailed drawings introducing some principles of physics and celebrating the cleverness and ingenuity of people who developed tools to move very heavy things. The other is a highly informational text with visually appealing illustrations that explain the principles behind how machines work.

Conservation of Energy and Energy Transfer

■ *Pass the Energy, Please!* by Barbara Shaw McKinney (RL/RI)
■ *What Are Food Chains and Webs?* by Bobbie Kalman and Jacquelin Langille (RL/RI)

Texts share two different perspectives on the food chain. One is a rhyming story highlighting the importance of green plants, and the other includes both herbivores and carnivores.

■ *The Shocking Truth about Energy* by Loren Leedy (RL/RI)
■ *The Boy Who Harnessed the Wind* by William Kamkwamba and Bryan Mealer (RL)

Texts address the topic of energy. One is a narrative with funny characters that explain the simple basics of energy and how it can be harnessed in productive ways. The other is a narrative from Malawi about a young boy who responds to the loss of crops in his village from drought by teaching himself about windmills and how they harness the wind.

■ *The Boy Who Harnessed the Wind* by William Kamkwamba and Bryan Mealer (RL)
■ *Energy Island: How One Community Harnessed the Wind and Changed Their World* by Allan Drummond (RI)

Texts address the benefits of harnessing the wind. One is a narrative from Malawi about a young boy who responds to the loss of crops in his village from drought by teaching himself about windmills and how they harness the wind. The other is a narrative about a small town in Denmark that wisely and effectively harnessed the wind and in the process became completely energy independent.

■ *The Shocking Truth about Energy* by Loren Leedy (RL/RI)
■ *Energy Island: How One Community Harnessed the Wind and Changed Their World* by Allan Drummond (RI)

Texts address the topic of energy. One is a narrative with funny characters that explain the simple basics of energy and how it can be harnessed in productive ways. The other is a narrative about a small town in Denmark that wisely and effectively harnessed the wind and in the process became completely energy independent.

- *My Light* by Molly Bang (RL/RI)
- *Night Wonders* by Jane Ann Peddicord (RL/RI)

Texts share different perspectives on the concept of light. One is a narrative and informational text that describes the importance of the sun, which provides light and energy through its rays. The other is a narrative with wonderful information about light, light beams, and the speed of light as it travels through the universe.

- *Blackout* by John Rocco (RL)
- *Why Should I Save Energy?* by Jen Greene and M. Gordon (RI)

Texts teach lessons about energy conservation. One is a beautiful, award-winning narrative about a family that experiences a blackout. All the lights go off and cooking, using the computer, and watching television all stop, prompting the family to go up to the rooftop where they see light from the stars. When the electricity is restored lessons about energy have already been learned. The other is a delightful narrative based on the question "Why save energy?"

Structure of Matter (3–5)

- *Matter: See It, Touch It, Taste It, Smell It* by Darlene R. Stille (RI)
- *What's the Matter in Mr. Whiskers' Room?* by Michael Elsohn Ross (RL/RI)

Texts introduce the complex concept of matter. One is a simple but rich informational text about states of matter accompanied with experiments that explain each state in understandable ways. The other is a humorous but informational narrative about a teacher named Mr. Whiskers who teaches his students about matter through seven stations, each of which nicely explains and illustrates the principles of matter.

Structure of Matter (6–8)

- *Atoms and Molecules* by Phil Roxbee Cox (RI)
- *A Drop of Water: A Book of Science and Wonder* by Walter Wick (RI)

Texts address the relationship between water and molecules. One is a rich information text with colorful illustrations that provides a basic understanding of molecules (and atoms), and the other is an absolutely stunning collection of photographs with accompanying limited text, each one illustrating and describing why water behaves as it does.

Science and Engineering Practices

Asking Questions (for Science) and Defining Problems (for Engineering)

- *Counting on Frank* by Rod Clement (RL/RI)
- *If Frogs Made Weather* by Marion Dane Bauer (RL/RI)

Texts introduce the use of *if-then* statements and forming hypotheses in math and science. One is a thoroughly enjoyable series of situations involving a dog and his pet friend, Frank, as they go about solving lots of interesting problems. The other is a delightful collection of poems, phrased as if-then statements that depict what the weather would look like if it were up to animals.

- *The Crow and the Pitcher* illustrated and interpreted by Stephanie Gwyn Brown (RL/RI)
- *Mr. Archimedes' Bath* by Pamela Allen (RL/RI)

Texts focus on doing inquiry through experimental design. One is a delightful interpretation of an old Aesop fable about a crow that solves a problem by thinking scientifically, and the other is a delightful narrative about a man who designed an experiment to solve a mystery about water, and in the process discovered displacement.

- *June 29, 1999* by David Weisner (RL/RI)
- *Gregor Mendel: The Friar Who Grew Peas* by Cheryl Bardoe (RL/RI)

Texts show different versions of doing inquiry. One is a colorfully and whimsically illustrated story of a young girl who conducts a science experiment that in the beginning leaves her teacher and classmates speechless, but in the end realizes something has gone all wrong. The other is a beautifully illustrated biography of Gregor Mendel, a Friar, regarded as the world's first geneticist, who conducted an elaborate experiment on multiple generations of peas. He found that peas pass down traits through the same process and on the same principles as do animals, plants, and humans.

Developing and Using Models/Analyzing and Interpreting Data/Constructing Explanations (for Science) and Designing Solutions (for Engineering)

- *Nicolaus Copernicus: The Earth Is a Planet* by Dennis B. Fradin (RL/RI)
- *Anno's Medieval World* by Mitsumasa Anno (RL/RI)

Texts combine to provide rich historical accounts of people and times that radically changed how the universe was viewed. One is a fantastic and colorful biography of Copernicus, which includes an explanation of his heliocentric view of the universe, and the other is a striking narrative setting in Medieval times that describes how people viewed the universe at the time.

- *Nicolaus Copernicus: The Earth Is a Planet* by Dennis B. Fradin (RL/RI)
- *Starry Messenger* by Peter Sis (RL/RI)

Texts focus on famous scientists who challenged conventional thinking. One is a fantastic and colorful biography of Copernicus, which includes an explanation of his heliocentric view of the universe. The other is a striking biography of Galileo that describes his life and discoveries, which highlights how and why he challenged conventional thinking at the time about the nature of the universe.

- *Galileo's Journal 1609–1610* by Jeanne Pettenati (RL/RI)
- *Galileo's Treasure Box* by Catherine Brighton (RL/RI)

Texts use different formats to introduce the life and work of the famous scientist Galileo. One is a biography told by Galileo in the first person and in journal form over an 8-month period of time, giving insights into his interest in telescopes and new thinking about the universe. The other is a short but informative text about the relationship between Galileo and his daughter, and gives insights into his major discoveries as told by five objects in his treasure box.

Engaging in Argument from Evidence/Analyzing and Interpreting Data/Constructing Explanations (for Science) and Designing Solutions (for Engineering)

- *Come See the Earth Turn: The Story of Leon Foucault* by Lori Mortensen (RL/RI)
- *Mr. Archimedes' Bath* by Pamela Allen (RL/RI)

Texts focus on doing inquiry through experimental design. One is an intriguing biography of a young boy filled with curiosity and a passion for science who designed an experiment that proved what had never been proved before, namely, that the earth turns. The other is a delightful narrative about a man who designed an experiment to solve a mystery about water and in the process discovered displacement.

- *Gregor Mendel: The Man Who Grew Peas* by Cheryl Bardoe (RL/RI)
- *Theodoric's Rainbow* by Stephen P. Kramer (RL/RI)

Texts share the inquiries of two scientists and their amazing discoveries. One is a beautifully illustrated biography of Gregor Mendel, a Friar, regarded as the world's first geneticist, who conducted an elaborate experiment on multiple generations of peas. He found that peas pass down traits through the same process and on the same principles as do animals, plants, and humans. The other is an intriguing story of a 13th-century Monk who ingeniously experimented with light and water to understand rainbows.

Obtaining, Evaluating, and Communicating Information/Analyzing and Interpreting Data/ Constructing Explanations (for Science) and Designing Solutions (for Engineering)

- *Snowflake Bentley* by Jacqueline Briggs Martin (RL/RI)
- *In the Belly of an Ox: The Unexpected Photographic Adventures of Richard and Cherry Kearton* by Rebecca Bond (RL/RI)

Texts focus on doing inquiry through observational inquiry. One is a heartwarming story of little-known Wilson Bentley, who as a young man was fascinated with the intricacies of snowflakes. He used an innovative camera for the time to make a startling discovery about what was so common in Vermont. The other is a story about two brothers who captured the beauty of nature, especially birds, in photographs and in turn helped people see the need to appreciate and protect nature, particularly birds and their habitats.

- *Into the Deep: The Life of Naturalist and Explorer William Beebe* by David Sheldon (RL/ RI)
- *Snowflake Bentley* by Jacqueline Briggs Martin (RL/RI)

Texts focus on doing science through observational inquiry. One is a fascinating narrative of the adventurous life of a scientist and conservationist who was a pioneer in underwater exploration, and the other is a heartwarming story of little-known Wilson Bentley, who as a young man was fascinated with the intricacies of snowflakes. He used an innovative camera for the time to make a startling discovery about what was so common in Vermont.

- *John Muir: American's First Environmentalist* by Kathryn Lasky (RL/RI)
- *Rachel: The Story of Rachel Carson* by Amy Ehrlich (RL/RI)

Texts tell the inspiring stories of two famous American conservationists and environmentalists. One is a biography of John Muir, a naturalist who shared a deep commitment to establishing and preserving national parks, most notably Yosemite, and later founded the Sierra Club. The other is an insightful and informative biography of Rachel Carson who today is often credited with starting the environmental movement based on her groundbreaking work that exposed how pesticides killed wildlife.

- *Rachel Carson and Her Book That Changed the World* by Laurie Lawlor (RL/RI)
- *Rachel: The Story of Rachel Carson* by Amy Ehrlich (RL/RI)

Texts share different perspectives on the life and work of Rachel Carson. One is a simple narrative that introduces *Silent Spring*, the book that changed the way people looked at the environment. The other is an insightful and informative biography of Rachel Carson who today is often credited with starting the environmental movement based on her groundbreaking work that exposed how pesticides killed wildlife.

- *The Boy Who Drew Birds: The Story of John James Audubon* by Jacqueline Davies (RL)
- *For the Birds: The Life of Roger Tory Peterson* by Peggy Thomas (RL)

Texts tell the life and work of two environmentalists who both loved birds in different ways and different times. One is a lovely biography with exquisite illustrations of John James Audubon who studied birds outdoors in their natural environment and painted them in authentic ways. The other is a biography of Roger Tory Peterson who is loved by bird watchers around the world, especially for his now famous *Peterson Field Guides*.

Using Mathematics and Computational Thinking/Analyzing and Interpreting Data/ Constructing Explanations (for Science) and Designing Solutions (for Engineering)

- *On a Beam of Light: A Story of Albert Einstein* by Jennifer Berne (RL/RI)
- *Odd Boy Out: Young Albert Einstein* by Don Brown (RL/RI)

Texts share similar yet somewhat different versions of the life and times of Albert Einstein. Both narratives highlight the early struggles of the young scientist as well as his constant imagination, curiosity, and risk taking that led to discoveries that changed science and the world.

Planning and Carrying Out Investigations/Analyzing and Interpreting Data/Constructing Explanations (for Science) and Designing Solutions (for Engineering)

- *Me . . . Jane* by Patrick McDonnell (RL/RI)
- *The Watcher* by Jeannette Winter (RL/RI)

Texts present two different versions on observational inquiry through different biographies of the scientist Jane Goodall. One is a narrative that focuses on the early life of Goodall and highlights her early interest in the natural world. The other is a biography that describes Goodall's lifelong scientific work of observing and documenting the behaviors of chimpanzees in the Gombi forest and her attempts to protect these animals for all time.

- *Uncommon Traveler: Mary Kingsley in Africa* by Don Brown (RL/RI)
- *The Watcher* by Jeannette Winter (RL/RI)

Texts provide different biographies of women with unique similarities. One is a biography of Mary Kingsley, a heroine who in the late 19th century traveled and explored equatorial Africa, and later shared her observations and findings with the world. The other is a biography that describes Jane Goodall's lifelong scientific work of observing and documenting the behaviors of chimpanzees in the Gombi forest and her attempts to protect these animals for all time.

- *Manfish: A Story of Jacques Cousteau* by Jennifer Berne (RL/RI)
- *Life in the Ocean: The Story of Oceanographer Sylvia Earle* by Claire A. Nivola (RL/RI)

Texts introduce the adventurous lives and underwater discoveries of two underwater scientists. One is a biography of Jacques Cousteau, a man who was curious about the ocean throughout his life, and created equipment like swimming fins, masks, and scuba gear that helped him conduct his investigations. The other is a biography of Sylvia Earle, a woman who dedicated her life to ocean exploration and used her investigations to advocate for ocean protection.

- *Manfish: A Story of Jacques Cousteau* by Jennifer Berne (RL/RI)
- *The Fantastic Undersea Life of Jacques Cousteau* by Dan Yaccarino (RL/RI)

Texts introduce two different versions of the adventurous life and underwater discoveries of Jacques Cousteau, a man who was curious about the ocean throughout his life, and created equipment like swimming fins, masks, and scuba gear that helped him conduct his investigations.

- *Tracks in the Snow* by Wong Herbert Yee (RL/RI)
- *The Humblebee Hunter* by Deborah Hopkinson (RL/RI)

Texts provide multilayered stories to introduce observational inquiry. One is a simple rhyming text about a little girl who notices interesting tracks in the snow and hypothesizes who might have made them, only to discover later that she actually made them the day before. The other provides insight into the family life of Charles Darwin but through the voice of his daughter who, like her famous father, enjoys nothing more than to be outside during the year observing nature, asking questions, conducting experiments, and gaining new knowledge.

Additional Instructional Strategies

In addition to a Category Chart, other strategies can be used to help students make intertextual connections with paired text in science and other content areas. With the Connections Chart (see Appendix P at the end of this book) students record major connections or similarities between a paired text in the left-hand column and then describe in the middle and right columns how each text reflects that connection. Similarly, with the Connections Sheet (see Appendix Q at the end of this book) students record major connections in the middle column and then describe in the left and right columns how each text reflects that connection. Finally, with the Connections Wheel (see Appendix R at the end of this book) students record major connections or similarities in each section on the outer circle and describe in the corresponding section in the inner circle how they share these similarities.

PART SIX

Paired Text in Mathematics

> If teachers address isolated content areas, a school day will
> never have enough hours for them to teach both literacy and
> mathematics adequately and thoroughly. However, by creating
> connections between the two, teachers can help ensure that
> students have ample opportunity to develop both areas.
> —JENNIFER L. ALTIERI (2009, p. 346)

In Part Six, I introduce a paired text for mathematics that focuses on multiple ways to solve single problems. I describe a mini-lesson to introduce this paired text, provide background information for the mini-lesson, and use Interlocking Rectangles as a tool to illustrate intertextual connections (similarities and differences) between these two texts. Next, I describe several potentials for teaching mathematics with this paired text that were not necessarily intended by the authors, but can be taught successfully by teachers. Then, I identify the CCSS for Mathematics, highlighting important mathematical practices and mathematical content, connect paired text with CCSS in mathematics and organize these texts around mathematical content across 10 domains, and identify each paired text in terms of whether it represents reading literature (RL), reading informational text (RI), or both (RL/RI). I end with additional instructional strategies for helping students make intertextual connections across paired text in mathematics.

Mini-Lesson: Multiple Ways to Solve Single Problems

Materials

- Copy of paired text: *12 Ways to Get to 11* (Merriam, 1996) (RI) and *One Is a Snail, Ten Is a Crab* (Sayre & Sayre, 2006) (RI).
- Interlocking Rectangles (see Appendix S at the end of this book).

Procedure

- The teacher displays paired text and large Interlocking Rectangles to the whole class.

- The teacher invites students to infer how these two books are similar and how they are different, and records similarities and differences on the class Interlocking Rectangles.

- The teacher distributes Interlocking Rectangles to each student.

- The teacher reads aloud *12 Ways to Get to 11*, stopping at strategic places (e.g., how the text and illustrations show increasingly complex ways to get to 11), and inviting students to pause, ponder, and propose (PPP) to a partner ways the text shows how to get to 11, as well as other ways the text does not show. After reading, students share with the whole class some of the ways the text shows to get to 11 and some of the ways it doesn't.

- The teacher reads aloud *One Is a Snail, Ten Is a Crab*, tweaking the same procedure just a bit. After reading, students work in pairs and use Interlocking Rectangles to record some similarities and differences between these two books and share their Interlocking Rectangles with the whole class.

- The teacher uses a Three Addends and a Total sheet (see Appendix T at the end of this book) as a culminating strategy in which students reflect, record, and share three reflections. Adding them together equals a sum or new understanding about making connections between texts based on the whole experience.

Background for the Mini-Lesson

Eve Merriam was a poet, playwright, and prolific writer of picture books for young children. *12 Ways to Get to 11* (Merriam, 1996) is one of her most entertaining and informative picture books. At one level it is a simple mystery story. The sequence of numbers from 1 to 12 is mysteriously missing the number 11. Where is 11? And, like all mysteries, this one requires investigation. At another level this story is a clever and innovative mathematical investigation in addition. Each two-page spread provides a different solution to the mystery. For example, one page shows a little girl picking up nine pinecones and two acorns in the forest, showing one way to find the mysterious 11 (e.g., $9 + 2 = 11$). Another page shows a bouquet of flowers, a pitcher of water, five rabbits, and four banners pulled from a magician's hat, showing another way to find 11 (e.g., $1 + 1 + 5 + 4 = 11$). Another page shows six bites of an apple, an apple core, an apple stem, and three apple seeds, showing yet another way to find 11 (e.g., $6 + 1 + 1 + 3 = 11$). In essence, the story is a collection of different numerical ways to find 11 and invites readers to represent each of those ways mathematically. It is a delightful book that makes counting fun and creating and representing different combinations of 11 understandable.

One Is a Snail, Ten Is a Crab (Sayre & Sayre, 2003) is a delightful and playful counting book. What makes this book unique is that it is a counting-by-feet book. Readers use the different number of feet on a colorful cast of characters (animals and a person) to count from 1 to 100. These characters include a snail (1 foot), person (2 feet), dog (4 feet), insect (6 feet), spider (8 feet), and crab (10 feet). The book begins with counting from 1 to 10. Each character, except the snail, represents an even number. Odd numbers are included by adding a character with a snail. For example, 3 is a person and a snail, 5 is a dog and a snail, and so forth. After 1–10, numbers increase by 10's (e.g., 20, 30, 40). Each number is represented in two different ways on the same two-page spread (e.g., 30 is 3 crabs or 10 people and a crab). The book ends on a humorous note by showing that 100 is 10 crabs or 100 snails—but counting by snails is really, really slow.

Intertextual Connections

What intertextual connections, in terms of similarities and differences, can be created and represented between *12 Ways to Get to 11* (Merriam, 1996) and *One Is a Snail, Ten Is a Crab* (Sayre & Sayre, 2003)? Interlocking Rectangles is a variation of a traditional Venn diagram and can be used to represent some similarities and differences between these two texts. Figure 6.1 illustrates Interlocking Rectangles. Similarities are identified in the space where the two rectangles interlock (both texts), and differences are identified in the spaces where the rectangles do not interlock.

In terms of similarities, both are basically informational texts. They use fictional characters, situations, and outdoor settings to focus on addition, highlighting whole numbers and number combinations. Both texts use large, colorful, two-page illustrations. Each illustration includes a different number of familiar objects like feet, acorns, and pinecones, and uses these objects to represent numbers and number combinations.

In terms of differences, *12 Ways to Get to 11* is based on a question (Where's 11?), whereas *One Is a Snail, Ten Is a Crab* is based more on definitive statements or assertions (a snail has one foot, a person has two feet, three feet is a person and a snail, etc.). The largest number in the first text is 11; the largest number in the second text is 100. All combinations of numbers in the first text total 11 (e.g., 6 + 5 = 11). In the second text, combinations of numbers total different sums beyond 11 (e.g., combinations of numbers that total 20, 30, 50, 80). Moreover, in the first text multiple combinations of numbers are used to equal 11 (3 + 2 + 1 + 5 = 11), whereas in the second text mostly two numbers are used in each combination (1 snail plus 1 person equals 3 feet, or 1 + 2 = 3). Each illustration in *12 Ways to Get to 11* depicts a different setting, different objects, and a different combination that totals 11. Each illustration in *One Is a Snail, Ten Is a Crab* is based on the same setting, a beach, and a combination of two characters whose feet total a specific number. Finally, illustrations in the first text depict characters doing believable things and objects having accurate features. A little girl picks up pinecones and acorns in a forest, an elephant eats peanuts and popcorn at the circus, and a magician pulls objects out of a hat, as well as a house with two chimneys, a garage with two cars, an apple with one core, and a boat with four life preservers. However, illustrations in the second text depict characters in more unbelievable ways. Crabs are riding bikes, doing the

Text 1:
12 Ways to Get to 11

Both Texts

- Are informational texts
- Are counting books
- Focus on addition
- Highlight numbers and combinations of numbers
- Use large, colorful, two-page illustrations
- Illustrations include different numbers of objects for numbers and number combinations
- Take place in outdoor settings

- Largest number is 100
- Combinations of numbers total different sums
- Each page depicts same settings
- Each page depicts a different combination of number
- Depicts animals doing nonbelievable activities
- Book based on statements
- Only two numbers are used for combinations

- Large number used is 11
- All combinations of numbers total 11
- Each page depicts a different setting and a different combination of 11
- Depicts human characters doing believable activities
- Book is based on a question
- More than two numbers are used to find 11

Text 2:
One Is a Snail,
Ten Is a Crab

FIGURE 6.2. Theoretical model for mathematics paired text.

limbo, and playing volleyball on the beach, and dogs are lying on beach towels soaking up the sun and surf.

Nevertheless, this paired text clearly has much potential for helping young children to see that mathematics can be enjoyable and understandable. It invites them to play with numbers and see how numbers behave. More important, making mathematics enjoyable and understandable helps children develop a positive disposition toward mathematics. A positive disposition is essential for children, as well as for adolescents and adults. This disposition allows children to value mathematics, develop confidence in their ability to do mathematics, and encourage persistence to solve increasingly complex mathematical problems. It short, this paired text, and others like it, helps children understand that mathematics does not have to be scary; it can be just plain fun.

More Potentials

In addition to counting and number combinations, this paired text also has much potential to teach a variety of other important mathematical concepts. These concepts include problem solving, equality, value, and the commutative property. For example, this paired text beautifully illustrates the difference between solving problems and problem solving. Based on my experience as a teacher and parent, I have seen many activities and worksheets that ask young children to solve simple addition problems like:

Answer the following addition problems:

$$2 + 6 = \underline{\quad}$$
$$3 + 4 = \underline{\quad}$$
$$7 + 4 = \underline{\quad}$$

This activity, and others like it, is a process of solving problems, in this case, addition.

This paired text is an opportunity to shift from mathematics as solving problems to mathematics as problem solving. Instead of asking What does $7 + 4$ equal?, *12 Ways to Get to 11* (Merriam, 1996) at least on the surface asks "Where's 11?" But at a deeper level the text also asks "How many ways can we find 11?" Unlike solving problems, this question does not seek a single answer, but invites multiple answers. *One Is a Snail, Ten Is a Crab* (Sayre & Sayre, 2003) offers a similar opportunity. Using characters with different numbers of feet offer children the opportunity to problem solve, that is, to create a variety of different combinations to solve a problem. For example, here is a problem:

What combinations of feet from different characters will equal 30 feet?
There are many combinations, including:

3 crabs = 30 feet (each crab has 10 feet)

15 persons = 30 feet (each person has 2 feet)

6 dogs and 1 insect = 30 feet (each dog has 4 feet and one insect
    has 6 feet)

3 spiders and 1 dog and 1 person = 30 feet (each spider has
    8 feet, one dog has 4 feet, and one person has 2 feet)

30 snails = 30 feet (each snail has 1 foot)

More specifically, this paired text can introduce the concept of *equation*. In *12 Ways to Get to 11* a little girl found nine pinecones and two acorns. She found the missing 11! We can show students this can be represented by 9 + 2 = 11, and explain that this is an equation. It is an equation because it includes an *equal sign*. We can also explain that this equation shows *equality* and *value*. The combined value on the left side of the equation is equal to the single value on the right. Finally, we can build on this foundational knowledge to teach the commutative property. We can show: 9 + 2 = 2 + 9.

In sum, helping all students see mathematics as problem solving, not solving problems, is an important shift in teaching and learning mathematics. This paired text can help teachers and students make this shift, successfully and joyfully. Other text can also help. *Math-terpiecs: The Art of Problem-Solving* (Tang, 2003), *The Grapes of Math* (Tang, 2004), *The Best of Times* (Tang, 2002), *Two Ways to Count to Ten* (Dee, 1988), *Twelve Snails to One Lizard* (Hightower, 1997), *Mice Mischief: Math Facts in Action* (Stills, 2014), *My Full Moon Is Square* (Pinczes, 2002), *Ben Franklin and the Magic Squares* (Murphy, 2001), and *The Case of the Backyard Treasure* (Rocklin, 1998) are all examples of high-quality text that describe and illustrate clever problem solving. *Equal Shmequal* (Kroll, 2005) is a wonderful hybrid text (literature and informational) that helps students investigate meanings of equal. *Dinosaur Deals* (Murphy, 2001) and *Just a Little Bit* (Tompert, 1993) extend student understanding from equal numerical value to equivalent or comparative value. *Sea Sums* (Hulme, 1996) builds and broadens student understanding of mathematics (addition, subtraction, equations) and science (sea creatures living on an ocean coral reef).

The CCSS for Mathematics

The CCSS for mathematics consist of mathematical practices and mathematical content. There are eight mathematical practices:

1 Making sense of problems and persevere in solving them.

2 Reason abstractly and quantitatively.

3 Construct viable arguments and critique the reasoning of others.

4 Model with mathematics.

5 Use appropriate tools strategically.

6 Attend to precision.

7 Look for and make use of structure.

8 Look for and express regularity in repeated reading.

Basically, these practices are viewed as critical processes used in thinking mathematically and doing mathematics.

Mathematical content is organized by mathematical domains and represented in progressions (Institute for Mathematics and Education, 2011). For example, measurement and data is a mathematical domain. Standards in this domain are introduced in kindergarten and progress with increasing complexity and sophistication through grades K–5. Here, I focus on 10 domains:

1 Counting and Cardinality (K Only): "know number names and count sequence; count to tell the numbers of objects; compare numbers."

2 Measurement and Data (K–5): "emphasize common nature of all measurement as iterating by a unit; build understanding of linear spacing of numbers and support learning of number line; develop geometric measures; work with data to prepare for statistics and probability in middle school."

3 Numbers and Operations in Base 10 (K–5): "place value understanding; develop base-ten algorithms using place value and properties of operations; computation competencies (fluency, estimation)."

4 Operations and Algebraic Thinking (K–5): "concrete uses and meanings of basic operations (word problems); mathematical meaning and formal properties of the basic operations; prepare for later work with expressions and equations in middle school."

5 Geometry (K–8): "ascend through progressively higher levels of logical reasoning about shapes; reason spatially with shapes, leading to logical reasoning about transformation; connect geometry to number, operations, and measurement via notion of partitioning."

6 Number and Operations—Fractions (3–5): "enlarge concept of number beyond whole numbers to include fractions; use understanding of the four operations to extend arithmetic to fractions; solve word problems related to the equation $ax = b$ (a and b fractions)."

7 Ratio and Proportional Relationships (6–7): "extend work on multiplication and division; consolidate multiplicative reasoning; lay groundwork for linear functions in grade 8 by studying quantities that vary together; solve a wide variety of problems with ratios, rates, and percents."

8 The Number System (6–8): "build concepts of positive and negative numbers; work with the rational numbers as a system governed by properties of numbers; begin work with irrational numbers."

9 Statistics and Probability (6–8): "introduce concepts of central tendency, variability, and distribution; connect randomness with statistical inference; lay foundations from High School statistics and probability."

10 Expressions and Equations (6–8): "treat expressions as objects to reason about (not as instructions to complete an answer); transfer expressions using properties of operations; solve linear equations; use variables and equations as techniques to solve word problems."

Theoretical Model

Figure 6.2 is a theoretical model that illustrates the relationships among the CCR Anchor Standards, K–12; the CCSS Math Standards of Practice and Content, and paired text. The outer circle identifies four major categories of the CCR Anchor Standards (Craft and Structure, Key Ideas and Details, Integration of Knowledge

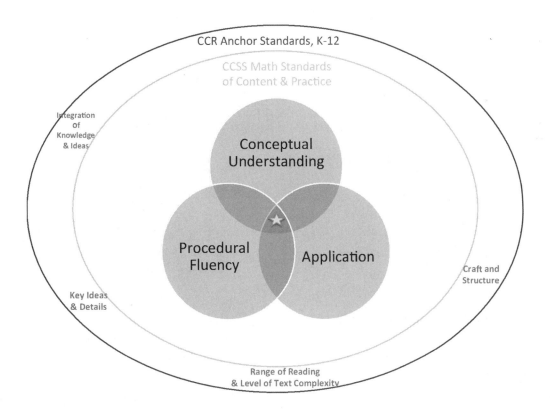

FIGURE 6.2. Theoretical model for mathematics paired text.

and Ideas, and Range of Reading and Level of Text Complexity). The inner circle refers to CCSS mathematical practices and mathematical domains. The three-circle Venn diagram identifies the interrelationship among the three elements of rigor in CCSS mathematics: Conceptual Understanding, Procedural Fluency, and Application. All three elements are needed in a balanced form to develop and implement a rigorous mathematics curriculum. It is not necessary to have all three elements in each mathematics lesson. The gold star symbolizes the function of paired text. When centered in the middle of the three elements of rigor, this positioning represents the idea that ideally a paired text can and should integrate all three elements. Alternatively, the gold star could be positioned in the overlapping space between Conceptual Understanding and Procedural Fluency to integrate these two elements, or in the overlapping space between Conceptual Understanding and Application, or between Application and Procedural Fluency. The emphasis on integration and the flexibility in positioning paired text are important features of this model. They allow for paired text to be used as a curricular resource and instructional tool to integrate all three (but at least two) of the elements of rigor.

Paired Text and Mathematical Content

Counting and Cardinality (K Only)

- *Counting Is for the Birds* by Frank Mazzola, Jr. (RL/RI)
- *One Less Fish* by Kim Michelle Toft and Allan Sheather (RL/RI)

Texts integrate mathematics and science. One is a beautifully illustrated information book with rhyming verse about a cat looking for food that waits by a feeder as birds from 1 to 20 stop by to eat. It ends with rich information about each species of bird and a picture of the cat still looking for food. The other is a colorfully illustrated information book with rhyming verse about different species of fish counted down from 12 to 0 to stress the fact that these species are threatened by extinction.

- *Even Steven and Odd Todd* by Kathryn Christaldi (RL/RI)
- *My Even Day* by Doris Fisher (RL/RI)

Texts introduce even and odd numbers. One is a simple story that introduces the difference between odd and even through two boys. Steven's world is filled with even things, and Todd's is filled with odd things The other is a humorous story about a boy who wakes up expecting an odd day but soon discovers an even day.

- *Underwater Counting* Jerry Pallotta (RI)
- *Among the Odd and Evens: A Tale of Adventure* by Priscilla Turner (RL/RI)

Texts integrate mathematics and science and extend understanding of odd and even numbers. One is a colorful information book that, while starting off counting with the number 1, shifts to counting by even numbers from 2 to 50, adding along the way interesting information about different species of fish living in the sea. The other is a delightful narrative about the letters X and Y that crash-land their aerocycle in a strange, uncharted land where the people are divided into two groups, evens and odds, and behave in strange and different ways. One group is wild and the other is orderly, but they learn to live harmoniously in the end.

■ *1 2 3: What Do You See?* by Arlene Alda (RI)
■ *City by Numbers* by Stephen J. Johnson (RI)

Texts introduce recognizing and counting numbers in nontraditional ways. One is a collection of photographs of everyday objects, each of which represents a specific number counting up from 1 to 10 and down from 10 to 1. The other is a collection of artful paintings of images in cities, each of which depicts a specific number counting from 1 to 21.

■ *1 2 3 to the Zoo* by Eric Carle (RL/RI)
■ *1 2 3: What Do You See?* by Arlene Alda (RI)

Texts share innovative techniques for counting. One is an informational book to introduce simple counting from 1 to 10 using large, bright illustrations of familiar animals as they board a train. The other is a collection of photographs of everyday objects, each of which represents a specific number counting up from 1 to 10 and down from 10 to 1.

■ *Blast Off! A Space Counting Book* by Norma Cole (RI)
■ *Over in the Ocean in a Coral Reef* by Marianne Berkes (RI)

Texts integrate mathematics and science above the earth and under the sea. One is an informational text that includes colorful illustrations and rich information about space while counting first from 0 to 20 and then by 10's to 100, until eventually it is time to return to earth while counting from 10 to 0. The other is an informational text based on the classic rhythmic song "Over in the Meadow" and presents interesting information about all kinds of sea creatures while counting from 1 to 10.

■ *Monster Math* by Grace Maccarone (RL/RI)
■ *Ten Sly Piranhas* by William Wise (RL/RI)

Texts highlight counting in reverse. One is a simple narrative with rhyming text about a group of 12 monsters that lose a member one by one until there are no more monsters, and the other is a colorful narrative with rhyming text about a school of 10 piranhas that lose a member one by one as they eat each other.

■ *Ten Rowdy Ravens* by Susan Ewing (RL/RI)
■ *Ten Sly Piranhas* by William Wise (RL/RI)

Texts highlight counting in reverse. One is a rollicking tale of 10 ravens that start with 10 but lose one with each shenanigan they do, and the other is a colorful narrative with rhyming text about a school of 10 piranhas that lose a member one by one as they eat each other.

■ *One Cow Coughs* by Christine Loomis (RL/RI)
■ *Mouse Count* by Ellen Stoll Walsh (RL/RI)

Texts provide different stories to understand counting up from 1 to 10 and down from 10 to 1. One is a narrative about a group of farm animals (1–10) that show symptoms of different ailments and illnesses but show how the (10–1) get better when they attend to their conditions. The other is a simple narrative with colorful illustrations about a group of mice that, while napping, get caught by a snake that puts them all in a jar (1–10), but in the end the mice outsmart the snake and tumble out of the jar (10–1).

- *A Shaker's Dozen* by Kathleen Thorne-Thomsen and Paul Rocheleau (RI)
- *Anno's Counting Book* by Mitsumasa Anno (RI)

Texts beautifully integrate mathematics and social studies. One is an informational text that uses photographs of authentic Shaker people and objects to teach counting from 1 to 12, adding historical information about the Shaker culture with each number. The other is an informational text that teaches counting from 1 to 12 with colorful illustrations that contain the number of objects corresponding to each number and ending with important information about the connection between this counting book and the history of numbers.

- *How Many, How Many, How Many* by Rick Walton (RL/RI)
- *1 Hunter* by Pat Hutchins (RI)

Texts integrate inquiry and counting. One is an informational book that uses guessing games with each number (1–10) to find the answers to questions about nursery rhymes, seasons, and so on. The other is an ingenious informational book that follows the adventures of one hunter walking through a forest and being watched by an increasing number of animals (1–10) and includes hints on each page about the type of animal that is watching next.

- *At the Edge of the Woods* by Cynthia Cotton (RI)
- *1 Hunter* by Pat Hutchins (RI)

Texts integrate mathematics and science. One is a rhyming, patterned text with a repeating refrain that counts animals in the woods from 1 to 10 and back from 10 to 1. The other is an ingenious informational book that follows the adventures of one hunter walking through a forest and being watched by an increasing number of animals (1–10) and includes hints on each page about the type of animal that is watching next.

- *One Wooly Wombat* by Rod Trinca and Kerry Argent (RI)
- *Ten Little Rabbits* by Virginia Grossman and Sylvia Long (RI)

Texts nicely integrate mathematics and social studies. One is a brightly colored counting book that uses rhyme to introduce 14 unique Australian animals (emus, magpies, platypuses, echidnas) as well as teach counting (1–14). The other is an informational counting book that depicts rabbits (1–10) dressed in Native American costumes engaged in a variety of traditional customs, and ends with rich information about different Native American Indian peoples.

- *Feast for 10* by Cathryn Falwell (RI)
- *Ten, Nine, Eight* by Molly Bang (RI)

Texts use the context of family to teach counting. One involves an African American family shopping at the grocery story buying items (1–10) for dinner and later arriving home where they go through the steps (1–10) to prepare the family meal. The other is a touching story about the relationship between an African American father and his daughter and the counting (1–10) that takes place as she gets ready to go to sleep for the night.

- *Arctic Fives Arrive* by Elinor J. Pinczes (RL/RI)
- *Count by Fives* by Jerry Pallotta (RI)

Texts highlight counting by fives. One integrates science and counting with rhyming text about a group of arctic animals that gather together five at a time to witness the beautiful

Northern Lights, and the other is an informational book that uses a favorite candy to teach counting by fives.

■ *Henry the Fourth* by Stuart J. Murphy (RL/RI)
■ *Where's Harley?* by Carol Felton and Amanda Felton (RL/RI)

Texts focus on ordinal numbers. One is a short narrative about a dog show and how different dogs are called up to perform first, second, third, and so forth. The other is a short narrative about a brother and sister who live on the sixth floor of an apartment building and take care of a pet rabbit but need to enlist the help of friends who live on other floors (first, second, third, etc.) to find their rabbit when he goes missing.

Measurement and Data (K–5)

■ *Who's Got Spots?* by Linda W. Aber (RL/RI)
■ *Bart's Amazing Charts* by Dianne Ochiltree (RL/RI)

Texts introduce the process of organizing and charting data. One is a simple story of a young boy who learns that some classmates have chicken pox and he collects and charts data from other classmates to determine if there will be enough students to perform in the holiday show. The other is a short narrative about a young boy who learns about the value and usefulness of charts from his mother and decides to create different kinds of charts about his life for a class project.

■ *Fair Is Fair* by Jennifer Dussling (RL/RI)
■ *Sir Cumference and the Off-the-Charts Dessert* by Cindy Neuschwander (RL/RI)

Texts focus on pie charts and bar graphs. One is a short narrative about a son who learns that creating bar graphs is a very convincing way to get his father to increase his allowance. The other is an entertaining narrative set in the time of King Arthur about how two bakers learn that using charts and graphs are successful ways to compete for the honor of baking all the sweets for the annual harvest.

■ *Lemonade for Sale* by Stuart Murphy (RL/RI)
■ *Graphs* by Bonnie Bader (RL/RI)

Texts introduce graphs. One is a colorful narrative about a group of young children who set up a lemonade stand to get enough money to fix their crumbling clubhouse, and they use a bar graph to keep track of profits. The other is a simple story about a young boy, bored at the family reunion and tired of being pinched by relatives, who goes outside to create different graphs for a homework project using relatives, food, and temperature as data sources.

■ *Tiger Math: Learning to Graph from a Baby Tiger* by Ann Whitehead Nagda and Cindy Bickel (RL/RI)
■ *The Great Graph Contest* by Loreen Leedy (RL/RI)

Texts provide different perspectives on the nature, function, and kinds of graphs. One is a hybrid text integrating a narrative about a Siberian tiger cub born at the Denver Zoo and the zookeepers who care for him. They keep track of the cub's healthy growth and development with different kinds of graphs. The other is an informational text with large, colorful illustrations about a frog and a lizard competing against each other to see who can make the best graphs.

■ *A Fly on the Ceiling* by Julie Glass (RL/RI)
■ *X Marks the Spot!* by Lucille Recht Penner (RL/RI)

Texts focus on coordinate graphs. One is an entertaining narrative about Rene Descartes, a French philosopher who is so messy he can't find anything in his apartment. With the help of an artist neighbor they paint a grid that helps him to easily locate anything, a grid known today as the Cartesian coordinate system. The other is a short story about two young boys who find a treasure map in their grandfather's attic and must learn how to read and interpret a coordinate graph chart in order to find the secret treasure.

■ *A Fly on the Ceiling* by Julie Glass (RL/RI)
■ *Sir Cumference and the Viking's Map* by Cindy Neuschwander (RL/RI)

Texts focus on coordinate graphs. One is an entertaining narrative about Rene Descartes, a French philosopher who is so messy he can't find anything in his apartment. With the help of an artist neighbor they paint a grid that helps him to easily locate anything, a grid known today as the Cartesian coordinate system. The other is a colorful narrative about two cousins who get lost while riding through the countryside of Angleland. They find a map and learn to successfully read, interpret, and follow the grid on the map in order to find a treasure and their way home.

■ *Chickens on the Move* by Pam Pollack and Meg Belviso (RI)
■ *Bigger, Better, Best* by Stuart J. Murphy (RL)

Texts provide a basic introduction to the concepts of area and perimeter. One is a colorful story about a grandfather who gives his three grandchildren some chickens so they can have fresh eggs. The three siblings learn about the important concept of perimeter as they all build a coop to house the chickens. The other is a story about a family moving to a new house and the children argue over who will have the largest room and the biggest windows, and learn to use principles of calculating area to solve the arguments.

■ *Racing Around* by Stuart J. Murphy (RL)
■ *Sir Cumference and the Isle of Immeter* by Cindy Neuschwander (RL)

Texts discuss the concept of perimeter. One is a colorful narrative with informational illustrations about a young boy whose older brother and sister warn against him entering a bike race on Perimeter Road, but with perseverance, determination, practice, and encouragement from his pet dog he made it all the way around. The other is a narrative set in King Arthur's time about a young girl, Pers, who learns an interesting game called Inners and Edges (area and perimeter), and uses her knowledge of the game to travel to the island of Immeter where she unlocks the secret to a mysterious castle.

■ *Spaghetti and Meatballs for All!* by Marilyn Burns (RL/RI)
■ *Perimeter, Area, and Volume: A Monster Book of Dimensions* by David A. Adler (RI)

Texts presents information about area and perimeter in different ways. One is a humorous narrative about Mr. and Mrs. Comfort who plan a family dinner for 32 people, but as more people unexpectedly arrive they have to rearrange the seating to accommodate all. The other is a rich informational book with colorful illustrations that introduce a variety of mathematical concepts including area and perimeter.

■ *Me and the Measure of Things* by Joan Sweeney (RL/RI)
■ *Measuring Penny* by Loreen Leedy (RL/RI)

Texts describe basic information about measurement. One is a colorful narrative told through the voice of a little girl who explains how and why she measures liquids and solids like milk and flour for pancakes, and what tools she also uses to measure all kinds of things. The other is a delightful story told through the voice of a young girl who decides to measure her dog in different ways and with different tools for a homework project on measurement.

■ *Keep Your Distance!* by Gail Herman (RL/RI)
■ *Carrie Measures Up* by Linda Williams Aber (RL/RI)

Texts present different stories about measurement. One is a simple narrative about a young girl who wants distance from her younger annoying sister. She threatens to first move out of their shared room to across the hall, next door, a friend's house a mile away, and finally to the moon (240,000 miles away), but in the end they reconcile and stay together because they are sisters. The other is a simple story about a young girl who receives a visit from her grandmother, a knitter, and is invited to be a measuring spy so that all the knitted gifts will fit the people on her list, even the pet dog.

■ *The Warlord's Puppeteers* by Virginia W. Pilegard (RL/RI)
■ *Beanstalk: The Measure of a Giant* by Ann McCallum (RL/RI)

Texts present different perspectives on the concepts of measurement, ratio, and proportion. One is a beautiful narrative about a young boy in long-ago China who travels to the warlord's palace. On the way he joins a troupe of puppeteers, meets bandits who steal all the troupe's puppets, and learns about an ancient rule in Chinese art about proportions that help him make new puppets. The other is a colorful narrative about Jack climbing a beanstalk high up in the sky only to meet and befriend Ray, a huge, sad, and lonely boy, by making toys and games for him that are proportionate to his size.

■ *Inch by Inch* by Leo Lionni (RL/RI)
■ *Inchworm and a Half* by Elinor J. Pinczes (RL/RI)

Texts highlight differences between whole numbers and fractional measurement. One is a lovely narrative about a clever and useful inchworm that measures different things inch by inch and as a result escapes danger. The other is a narrative with rhyming text about an inchworm that measures thing by inches and discovers that everything can't be measured in one-inch increments but requires fractional measurement.

■ *How Big Is a Foot?* by Rolf Muller (RL/RI)
■ *Measuring Penny* by Loreen Leedy (RI)

Texts present two different versions of and problems with measurement. One is a delightful story about a king who wants to give his queen something she doesn't have: a bed. The king is faced with a real problem because beds have not yet been invented so nobody knows how big a bed should be, but in the end an apprentice experiments with different measurements and successfully builds a bed for the queen. The other shows how a little girl uses measurement to solve real life problems in her house and neighborhood.

Numbers and Operations in Base 10 (K–5)

- *Counting with an Abacus* by Patricia J. Murphy (RI)
- *The Warlord's Beads* by Virginia Pilegard (RL/RI)

Texts focus on the concept of place value. One is an informational text that provides brief explanations on the history of an abacus, its relationship to place value, and how it was/is used for counting. The other is an engaging narrative about a young boy named Chuan in long-ago China who helps his father in the palace counting room keep track of the warlord's immense riches. They use different-colored beads on different branches to keep an accurate record, an earlier form of the ancient Chinese abacus.

- *The Blast-Off Kid* by Laura Driscoll (RL/RI)
- *Sir Cumference and All the King's Tens* by Cindy Neuschwander (RL/RI)

Texts focus on the concept of place value. One is a simple story of a young boy who needs to collect 10,000 wrappers of his favorite treat to win a trip to space camp. He has difficulty keeping count of all the wrappers until he learns to organize them by 1's, 10's, 100's, and 1,000's and wins a trip that is out of this world. The other tells the story of how the concept of tens is used to calculate the large number of unexpected guests for the king's birthday party

- *Zero the Hero* by Joan Holub (RL/RI)
- *A Place for Zero: A Math Adventure* by Angeline Sparagna LoPresti (RL/RI)

Texts focus on the concept of place value. One is a colorfully and comically illustrated narrative of the number 0. The other numbers felt zero didn't amount to anything or add anything to addition, subtraction, division, and multiplication, but in the end becomes their hero. The other is a humorous narrative with clever wordplay about zero who lives a lonely life in Digitaria because he had no place, unlike all the other numbers. Zero sets out on an adventurous journey and learns that he has a very special place.

- *Zero* by Kathryn Otoshi (RL)
- *Zero Is the Leaves on the Tree* by Betsy Franco (RL)

Texts provide different versions on the number 0. One is a charming concept book about how easy it is to count numbers but zero, while still a number, is not easy to count. The other is an imaginative concept book about how 0, like 1, 2, 3, 4, 5, . . ., is a number but unlike other numbers, it has no mathematical value but has great personal value.

- *Sir Cumference and All the King's Tens* by Cindy Neuschwander (RL)
- *One Riddle, One Answer* by Lauren Thompson (RL/RI)

Texts describe two different stories in different locations and times about place value. One is a delightful narrative about Sir Cumference and his wife, Lady Diameter, who plan a surprise party for King Arthur. Confusion results when guests kept appearing in unexpected numbers and counting guests becomes impossible until Lady Di finally finds a way to group the massive throng and count the total number of guests. The other is a beautiful and informative narrative set in Persia about Aziza, the daughter of a Sultan, who loves mathematics and riddles. With her father's permission and blessing, she creates a riddle and marries the suitor who solves it, which Ahmed eventually does because he knows the power of the number 1.

- *Little 1* by Ann Rand and Paul Rand (RL/RI)
- *Zero Is the Leaves on the Tree* by Betsy Franco (RL/RI)

Texts combine to teach the concept of place value. One is a simple story with clever wordplay about little 1 who seeks a friend to play with and have fun. Others like 2 pears, 3 bears, 4 bees, and so forth all reject him until at last he meets a bright red hoop that accepts him and they look like the number 10 standing side by side. The other is a charming concept book about how easy it is to count numbers but zero, while still a number, is not easy to count.

- *Blockhead: The Life of Fibonacci* by Joseph D'Agnese (RL/RI)
- *Math Curse* by Jon Scieszka and Lane Smith (RL/RI)

Texts identify two characters about Fibonacci, one historical and the other fictional. One is a biography and historical account of Leonardo Fibonacci who created the famous counting sequence. He dreamed about numbers day and night so many Italians at the time considered him a blockhead. The other is a humorous and clever story filled with mathematics about a young student who acquires math anxiety from his teacher, Mrs. Fibonacci, who says that everything can be thought of as a math problem.

- *The Rabbit Problem* by Emily Gravett (RL/RI)
- *Rabbits, Rabbits, Everywhere* by Ann McCallum (RL)

Texts show different versions of the Fibonacci problem. One is an innovative, beautifully designed and illustrated story of what happens when one rabbit plus one rabbit spend 1 year together and end up with 288 rabbits. Their time together represents the famous problem behind the Fibonacci sequence. The other is an entertaining but different tale about the same problem with rabbits.

- *Wild Fibonacci: Nature's Best Code Revealed* by Joy N. Hulme (RI)
- *Growing Numbers* by Sarah C. Campbell (RI)

Texts integrate mathematics and science. One is an interesting and informative introduction to the Fibonacci sequence as a code and numerical sequence found all throughout nature. The other is a collection of short, descriptive texts with stunning photographs of objects in nature that reflect the Fibonacci number sequence. It starts with a single seed, then a peace lily with one petal, a crown of thorns with two petals, a spiderwort with three petals, a quince with five petals, and so forth, and ends with a special spiral often seen in and formed by a sea nautilus.

- *How Much, How Many, How Far, How Heavy, How Long, How Tall Is 1000?* by Helen Nolan and Tracy Walker (RI)
- *Great Estimations* by B. Goldstone (RI)

Texts focus on the concept of estimation. One is a collection of situational problems with large colorful illustrations with answers to each problem requiring estimation. The other is a collection of visual images and questions based on those images that introduce the concept of estimation and specific strategies for estimating accurately.

- *The Long Wait* by Annie Cobb (RL/RI)
- *Betcha!* by Stuart J. Murphy (RL/RI)

Texts share two stories about the concept of estimation. One is about two boys who go to Thrillenium Park to ride on a popular ride. The line is long and they have to use estimation strategies to figure out how many people are in line and how long it will take for them to finally get on the ride. The other is a narrative about two boys who bet each other that they can guess the correct number of jelly beans in a jar and win a prize. They use different estimation skills until one wins the contest.

■ *Alice in Pastaland: A Math Adventure* by Alexandra Wright (RL/RI)
■ *Tyrannosaurus Math* by Michelle Mrkel (RL/RI)

Texts share different stories involving multiple mathematical operations. One is a spin-off of the classic tale of Alice in Wonderland in which a young girl named Alice is doodling with mathematics under an oak tree. She unexpectedly meets a white rabbit speaking about math that quickly disappears into a rabbit hole, the start of an imaginary trip through a place called Pastaland where Alice uses lots of operations to help the rabbit solve a math problem. The other is a colorful story about a family of dinosaurs, one of whom, T-Math, spends his day learning all kinds of math including addition, multiplication, and estimation.

■ *Arithme-Tickle: An Even Number of Odd Riddle-Rhymes* by J. Patrick Lewis (RL/RI)
■ *You Can, Toucan, Math* by David A. Adler (RI)

Texts use a collection of riddles and rhymes with a variety of math problems and mathematical operations to solve them.

Operations and Algebraic Thinking (K–5)

Addition

■ *One More Bunny: Adding from One to Ten* by Rick Walton (RI)
■ *The Mission of Addition* by Brian P. Cleary (RI)

Texts use different kinds of text to introduce simple addition. One is a story with large, colorful illustrations and rhyming text about increasing amounts of bunnies playing in a playground and introducing numbers 1–10. The accompanying illustrations show the basics of addition both numerically and symbolically. The other is a collection of episodes with colorful illustrations about an animal teacher that uses kid-friendly examples to teach her animal students the basics of addition.

■ *The M&M's Addition Book* by Barbara Barbieri McGrath (RI)
■ *Mission: Addition* by Loreen Leedy (RI)

Texts provide two different perspectives on the basics of addition. One is an informational text that uses the popular M&M's candy to present the definition of addition, ways to add, and important vocabulary like *addends, sum,* and *plus sign*. The other is a colorful story told in multiple episodes of an animal teacher that teaches her animal students the basics of addition by using real-world examples including important vocabulary like *add, column,* and *equal sign*.

■ *Dealing with Addition* by Lynette Long (RI)
■ *Hershey's Kisses Addition Book* by Jerry Pallotta (RI)

Texts focus on the concept of addition. One uses a deck of cards and the other uses Hershey's Kisses candy to teach the basic principles of addition.

Division

- *The Great Divide* by Dayle Ann Dodds (RL/RI)
- *Divide and Ride* by Stuart J. Murphy (RL/RI)

Texts introduce the basics of simple division. One is a large, colorful, two-page-spread narrative with rhyming text about 80 racers who start the Great Divide Race, but encounter challenges all along the way that keeps dividing the group in half until the end when one unexpected person crosses the finish line. The other is a patterned and colorful text about a group of 11 young friends who spend the day riding the rides at a carnival. They use division to make sure they have the right number of friends in seats and invite others to join them on the ride when they don't.

- *The Multiplying Menace Divides* by Pam Calvert (RL/RI)
- *Cheetah Math: Learning about Division from Baby Cheetahs* by Ann Whitehead Nagda (RL/RI)

Texts present different perspectives on division. One is a story about a young boy and a revengeful witch named Matilda who with the help of evil Rumpelstiltskin diabolically uses a magic great multiplier/great divider stick to turn people, young and old, into frogs. The boy ultimately outwits the witch by understanding the power of division. The other is a hybrid text that combines a heartwarming narrative with real photographs of two cheetah cubs that were raised by humans and paired with two dogs for friends at the San Diego Zoo. The informational text is accompanied by graphs charting the cubs' diet, growth, and development over time.

- *Bean Thirteen* by Matthew McEllicott (RL/RI)
- *A Remainder of One* by Elinor J. Pinczes (RL/RI)

Texts share different stories about the concept of remainder. One is a colorful and humorous story about two bugs picking 13 beans for dinner that soon realize that 13 is an unlucky number. Whichever way they divide them there is always a remainder of one bean. The other is a colorful narrative with rhyming text about a squadron of bugs proudly parading in front of the queen but no matter how they organize themselves in even rows there is always one bug left all alone.

- *Splitting the Herd: A Corral of Odds and Evens* by Trudy Harris (RL/RI)
- *Among the Odd and Evens: A Tale of Adventure* by Priscilla Turner (RL/RI)

Texts extends understanding of odd and even numbers. One is a nicely illustrated narrative with rhyming text about two neighbors who have a problem with wandering cattle going through the fence and onto the other's property. They try to solve the problem by separating the cows by odd and even numbers only to learn it does not work but knocking down the fence certainly does. The other is a delightful narrative about the letters *X* and *Y* that crash-land their aerocycle in a strange, uncharted land where the people are divided into two groups, evens and odds, and behave in strange and different ways. One group is wild and the other is orderly, but they learn to live harmoniously in the end.

- *The Lion's Share: A Tale of Halving Cake and Eating It, Too* by Matthew McElligott (RL/RI)
- *One Hundred Hungry Ants* by Elinor J. Pinczes (RL/RI)

Texts show different perspectives on the concept of division. One is a large, colorful story about an ant, along with other animals, that are invited to attend a dinner with Lion, the king of the jungle, but is shocked by the boorish manners of the animals, especially at dessert. The animals divide a cake continually in halves before passing the rest on until the final crumb, when ant makes a proposal that teaches all the animals a lesson in courtesy, generosity, and division. The other is a colorful, patterned story with rhyming text about 100 hungry ants on their way to a picnic that want to get there quickly. They rearrange themselves in different groups (2 rows of 50, 4 rows of 25, and so forth) but take too much time and in the end there is no food left to eat.

Multiplication

- *The Hershey's Milk Chocolate Multiplication Book* by Jerry Pallotta (RI)
- *Bunches and Bunches of Bunnies* by Louise Matthews (RI)

Texts introduce simple multiplication. One uses a popular candy to teach the principles of mathematics and introduces mathematical terms and vocabulary like *grid, array, equal sign, equations, factor, product*, and *multiplicand*. The other is a delightful, colorful, and simple counting book about a bunch of bunnies that introduce the basics of multiplication.

- *Ten Times Better* by Richard Michelson (RL/RI)
- *Too Many Kangaroo Things to Do!* by Stuart J. Murphy (RL)

Texts highlight multiplying by 10. One is a hybrid text telling a narrative with rhyming text about a collection of animals that introduce the numbers 1–10 by bragging about their special features. Other animals introduce the numbers 1–100 by bragging about their features multiplied by 10 and at the end the text includes detailed information about each animal. The other is a colorful and nicely illustrated narrative about a young kangaroo that is looking for friends to play with on his birthday but all the animals he asks already have multiple things to do. In fact, each animal has 10 times more things to do than the previous animal, but in the end, just when kangaroo thinks no one will play with him, all the animals throw him a happy birthday party.

- *Amanda Bean's Amazing Dream* by Cindy Neuschwander (RL/RI)
- *The Best of Times* by Greg Tang (RI)

Texts present different views on the concept of multiplication. One is a colorfully illustrated and humorous story about a young girl who loves math, especially counting, and starts to learn that multiplying is much faster and easier than counting. The other is a thoroughly entertaining and colorful informational text that highlights the concept of math as problem solving and provides strategies for learning multiplication.

- *Multiplying Menace: The Revenge of Rumpelstiltskin* by Pam Calvert (RL/RI)
- *2 × 2 = Boo!: A Set of Spooky Multiplication Stories* by Loreen Leedy (RL/RI)

Texts present different views on the concept of multiplication. One is a follow-up to *The Multiplying Menace Divides* in which the evil Rumpelstiltskin returns to steal Peter, the son of the king and queen. He uses his magical walking stick with the letter *X* on it to wreak havoc on the kingdom by multiplying things that should not be The other is a collection of very short stories involving witches, black cats, ghosts, and bats that highlight multiplication facts.

- *Breakfast at Danny's Diner: A Book about Multiplication* by Judith Bauer Stamper (RL/RI)
- *Corkscrew Counts: A Story about Multiplication* by Donna Jo Napoli and Richard Tchen (RL/RI)

Texts present simple stories and facts about multiplication. One is a short chapter book about two young children who help out at their uncle's diner when some of his employees are sick. They use multiplication to meet all the demands of preparing and serving food to the customers. The other is a story about a group of friends who throw a birthday party for a pet pig named Corkscrew, and organize themselves in different ways to play games while Corkscrew and a parrot, his new friend, try to join in on the fun.

Subtraction

- *Subtraction Action* by Loreen Leedy (RL/RI)
- *Math Curse* by Jon Scieszka (RL/RI)

Texts use teachers and their interesting names to introduce a variety of mathematical concepts. One, like *Mission: Addition*, is a collection of episodes with colorful illustrations about an animal teacher named Miss Prime that uses kid-friendly examples to teach her animal students the basics of subtraction. The other is a humorous narrative about a teacher named Miss Fibonacci who shows that everything can be a math problem and all math can be fun.

- *Elevator Magic* by Stuart J. Murphy (RL)
- *The Action of Subtraction* by Brian P. Cleary (RI)

Texts introduce the concept of subtraction. One is a colorful and humorous story with rhyming text about a young boy who meets his mother at work on the tenth floor of a building and uses subtraction skills and a wild imagination to help her do chores on different floors below. The other is a rhyming story about a humorous and colorful collection of animals that help define subtraction and describe how it works.

- *Sea Sums* (RI) and *Sea Squares* (RL/RI) by Joy N. Hulme

Texts integrate mathematics and science. One is a colorful adventure of creatures in an ocean coral reef. Interesting facts about each species are used to teach subtraction, addition, and equations. The other is a rhyming text with colorful illustrations of sea creatures that offer lots of opportunities to count, add, subtract, multiply, and divide.

Numbers and Operations—Fractions (3–5)

- *Apple Fractions* (RI) and *The Hershey's Milk Chocolate Fractions Book* (RI) by Jerry Pallotta (RI)

Texts use food to introduce the concept of fractions. One is an informational text that provides interesting information about different kinds, parts, and uses of apples, and illustrates these apples in different ways to show fractions. The other uses a popular candy, Hershey's Milk Chocolate, to define fraction and explain equivalent fractions, simplifying fractions, and a whole host of other fractions that make learning this concept fun and understandable.

- *Eating Fractions* by Bruce McMillan (RI)
- *Give Me Half!* by Stuart J. Murphy (RL/RI)

Texts use food to introduce the concept of fractions. One is an informational text that uses real photographs of food to illustrate wholes, halves, thirds, and fourths, and some of the author's delicious recipes at the end. The other is a simple story with rhyming text about a brother and sister who learn to share food while learning about the concept of halves.

- *Polar Bear Math: Learning about Fractions from Klondike and Snow* by Ann Whitehead Nagda and Cindy Bickel (RL/RI)
- *Fractions & Decimals* by Karen Bryant-Mole (RI)

Texts are rich informational books about fractions. One is a hybrid text that tells the story of two polar bear cubs, abandoned by their mother, and raised by humans at the Denver Zoo. It combines informational text and fractions to show the cubs' growth and development over time. The other is a story about a prehistoric family named the Og's who use fractions and decimals throughout their daily lives.

- *Go Fractions!* by Judith Bauer Stamper (RL)
- *Fraction Action* by Loreen Leedy (RL/RI)

Texts. provide an interesting and informative introduction to fractions. One is a short chapter book about a soccer team named the Fractions, coached by a math teacher who loves and uses fractions in try-outs, practices, and games. The other is a collection of episodes with colorful illustrations about an animal teacher that uses kid-friendly examples to teach her animal students the basics of fractions.

- *The Doorbell Rang* by Pat Hutchins (RL/RI)
- *Full House: An Invitation to Fractions* by Dayle Ann Dodds (RL/RI)

Texts. introduce fractions. One is a simple story about a mother who has made a batch of delicious cookies that, at first, her son and daughter plan to share equally. The doorbell rings over and over again with friends around the neighborhood, and the share for each person gets smaller and smaller. The doorbell rings again only this time it is grandma with another batch of cookies. The other is a delightful and patterned story with colorful illustrations and endearing characters about a woman who owns an inn with six rooms and accommodates all her guests one fraction at a time.

Geometry (K–8)

- *Three Pigs, One Wolf, and Seven Magic Shapes* by Grace Maccarone (RL/RI)
- *The Warlord's Puzzle* by Virginia Pilegard (RL/RI)

Texts address an ancient Chinese puzzle known as a tangram. One is a spin-off of the classic Three Little Pigs tale about three pigs that are given magic squares. Two pigs use the squares unwisely and the third pig uses them wisely, so much so that he meets another pig that also uses her squares wisely and they live happily ever after. The other is a narrative that takes place in long-ago China about an artist who accidentally drops a beautiful tile and it breaks into seven pieces. The artist is spared punishment when the warlord announces a contest and a prize to whoever can put the tile back together and an unexpected person does just that.

■ *Lost City: The Discovery of Machu Picchu* by Ted Lewin (RL)
■ *Patterns in Peru* by Cindy Neuschwander (RL/RI)

Texts integrate mathematics and social studies. One is a beautiful biography about a little-known historical figure who trekked through the thick and dangerous Peruvian jungle with the help of an indigenous boy to discover the now famous lost city of Machu Picchu. The other is a delightful story about a young boy and girl on a trip with their parents to Peru where they interpret many different patterns, each of which is an important clue to finding a lost city.

■ *Mummy Math: An Adventure in Geometry* (RL/RI) and *Sir Cumference and the Sword in the Cone* (RL/RI) by Cindy Neuschwander

Texts present different perspectives on three-dimensional geometric solids. One is a tale of adventure about a young brother and sister who get lost while on a family trip to an Egyptian pyramid. They use hieroglyphics, clues on pieces of papyrus, and pictures on the walls of geometric solids to solve unsolved mysteries, one of which is a map to exit the pyramid. The other, a spin-off of the famous tale of King Arthur and the knights of the round table, is an intriguing adventure of Radius, son of Sir Cumference and Lady Di of Ameter. Radius helps his friend Vertex solve the mystery of the missing sword, Edgecalibur, which has been hidden in a geometric solid so that Vertex will become the heir to the throne.

■ *Sir Cumference and the First Round Table* (RL/RI) and *Sir Cumference and the Great Knight of Angleland* (RL/RI) by Cindy Neuschwander

Texts introduce the basic concepts of geometry. One is a spin-off of the famous tale of King Arthur and the knights of the round table.It is a colorful narrative with wonderful wordplay about a knight who, with the help of his wife and son and the ability of two carpenters, designs and redesigns a table around which all knights can sit only to learn that the best design is based on the trunk of a fallen tree. The other is a sequel to the first text in this pair about a young squire named Radius who wants to be a knight but first must pass a test. He does so with the help of a special medallion in the shape of a circle that keeps him safe from a pair of dragons and helps him find a missing king.

■ *Palazzo Inverso* by D. B. Johnson (RL/RI)
■ *The Pop-Up Book of M. C. Escher* by M. C. Escher (RL/RI)

Texts present two innovative views of the artist M. C. Escher. One is a story about a young boy and an imaginary adventure in the building of a palazzo that pays tribute to the visual genius and artistry of a master artist. The other is an engaging and entertaining pop-up book showcasing some of the most popular images of Escher presented in 3-D.

■ *The Straight Line Wonder* by Mem Fox (RL)
■ *The Dot and the Line: A Romance in Lower Mathematics* by Norton Juster (RL/RI)

Texts share unusual and innovative perspectives on lines. One is a delightful and engaging tale of three straight lines. One line is bored with being straight so, despite disapproval from his fellow lines, he twists, swirls, and zigzags his way to be a great star and now his fellow lines are proud to know him. The other is an imaginative tale with a creative mixture of different types of illustrations. A straight line is in love with a dot but the dot prefers a wild, squiggly line until the line discovers angles and suddenly things change dramatically and romantically.

- *The Greedy Triangle* by Marilyn Burns (RL/RI)
- *Sigmund Square Finds His Family* by Jennifer Taylor-Cox (RL)

Texts show polygons and rectangles as one subset of geometric shapes/polygons. One is a colorful story with informational illustrations about a bored triangle. It transforms into different polygons by continually visiting a shape-shifter to get additional sides and angles but in the end happily returns to being a triangle. The other is a humorous narrative about a square that has difficulty finding a family until he realizes he belongs to the rectangle family and ultimately lives happily ever after.

- *Triangles: Shapes in Math, Science and Nature* by Catherine Sheldrick Ross (RI)
- *The Greedy Triangle* by Marilyn Burns (RL/RI)

Texts describe geometric shapes in the real world. One is an informational book that illustrates a variety of shapes in mathematics and science, and the other is a colorful story with informational illustrations about a bored triangle who transforms into different polygons. It continually visits a shape-shifter to get additional sides and angles but in the end happily returns to being a triangle.

- *Triangles* by David A. Adler
- *The Wing Wing Brothers Geometry Palooza!* by Ethan Long (RL/RI)

Texts address the concept of triangles. One uses two children and one robot to address important questions about all sorts of triangles. The other uses two hilarious brothers to introduce the basics of geometry, including triangles.

- *What's Your Angle, Pythagoras?* (RL/RI) and *Pythagoras and the Ratios* (RL/RI) by Julie Ellis

Texts share different but complementary versions of the life, times, and accomplishments of Pythagoras, and both use soft blue and green illustrations. One is the story of a curious young boy who learns about a special rope from a master builder, a rope that makes a right triangle. The boy makes a discovery known today as the Pythagorean theorem. The other is a narrative about how Pythagoras, instead of moving rocks as instructed, became distracted and used measurement to solve problems with different musical instruments by tuning them based on the ratio between the length and width of different pipes and strings.

- *Circles and Squares Everywhere!* by Max Grover (RI)
- *Round and Square* by Miriam Schlein (RL/RI)

Texts introduce basic geometric shapes. One is a simple, straightforward informational text with large colorful illustrations that introduces the concept of a circle and a square as they are commonly found almost everywhere. The other is a concept book with rhyming text and colorful illustrations that show the meaning and attributes of round and square.

- *A Triangle for Adaora: An African Book of Shapes* by Ifeoma Onyefulu (RL/RI)
- *The Village of Round and Square Houses* by Ann Grifalconi (RL)

Texts integrate mathematics and social studies. One is a richly colored hybrid text set in an African village and narrated about a young African girl who searches for a triangle because it is her cousin's favorite shape. After finding lots of other shapes in her village she finally finds one in the form of a headdress in the shape of a triangle. The other is a narrative with pastel illustrations about a young girl who eventually learns the history that explains why in her village men live in square houses and women live in round houses.

■ *Kitten Castle* by Mel Friedman and Ellen Weiss (RL/RI)
■ *The Incredibly Awesome Box: A Story about 3-D Shapes* by Joanne Rocklin (RL/RI)

Texts introduce the concept of three-dimensional shapes. One is a simple story about a family cat that has kittens that are so mischievous around the house it requires Anna to use a variety of 3-D shapes to build a kitty castle to keep them safe and out of people's way. The other is an e-mail conversation between a young girl to her friend about an unexpected, very big box delivered to her house. Before opening it they share guesses about the contents only to learn that the box contains a collection of 3-D shapes to build a wonderful birthday gift for grandma.

■ *Math Fair Blues* by Sue Kassirer (RL)
■ *Captain Invincible and the Space Shapes* by Stuart J. Murphy (RL)

Texts show the differences between 2-D and 3-D geometric shapes. One is a simple story of a group of friends who start a rock band and create their own costumes by using everyday objects to print colorful, 2-D shapes on T-shirts. The other is a colorful, cartoon-like story of a young boy, Captain Invincible, and his space dog, Comet, who on an imaginary adventure in space use a variety of 3-D objects to successfully return to earth.

■ *Shape Up!* by David A. Adler (RI)
■ *Changes, Changes* by Pat Hutchins (RL/RI)

Texts provide an interesting introduction to geometric shapes. One is an informational text with colorful illustrations that uses food to identify different kinds and attributes of triangles, quadrilaterals, and other polygons. The other is a wordless story of two wooden dolls that use a variety of colorful wooden blocks of different shapes to creatively build functional objects.

■ *Sea Shapes* by Suse MacDonald (RI)
■ *A Star in My Orange: Looking for Nature's Shapes* by Dana Meachen Rau (RI)

Texts highlight geometric shapes. One is a colorful informational text that identifies a variety of shapes found on all kinds of creatures living in the sea, and the other is an informational text with striking photographs of different objects that illustrate a variety of different shapes found in nature.

Ratios and Proportional Relationships (6–8)

■ *Big and Little* by Steve Jenkins (RI)
■ *Insects: Biggest! Littlest!* by Sandra Markle (RI)

Texts provide an introduction to the concept of comparative size and scale. One is an informational text with colorful collage illustrations about a collection of animals that are related but are very different sizes (e.g., a Siamese cat and a Siberian tiger). It includes information about each animal, mammal, fish, and so on at the end of the book. The other is an informational text with real-life photographs of insects, big and small, from around the world illustrating where these insects live. It explains how and why some insects are small and others are big, and offers important vocabulary words about insects at the end of the book.

■ *Beanstalk: The Measure of a Giant* by Ann McCallum (RL/RI)
■ *Jim and the Beanstalk* by Raymond Briggs (RL/RI)

Texts present different versions of the classic tale Jack and the Beanstalk and focuses on ratio and proportion. One is a colorful narrative about Jack climbing a beanstalk high up in the sky only to meet and befriend Ray, a huge, sad, and lonely boy. Jack makes toys and games for Ray that are proportionate to his size. The other is an innovative narrative, alternating colored with black and white illustrations, about Jim climbing a beanstalk through the clouds only to meet a very large and old giant who now has no teeth, poor vision, and no hair. Jim measures the giant for glasses, false teeth, and a wig, climbs down the beanstalk to purchase and return with all of the items, and narrowly escapes from the new and improved giant, only to find once again at home a handwritten thank-you note from the giant.

■ *Biggest, Strongest, Fastest* by Steve Jenkins (RI)
■ *What's Faster Than a Speeding Cheetah?* by Robert E. Wells (RI)

Texts present two different views on ratio, proportion, and scale. One is a substantive informational text with colorful collage illustrations about a collection of unique animals that are all world record holders for their size, strength, or speed. It includes small pictures to scale of each animal compared with characteristics of human beings. The other is a fascinating informational text with brightly colored pictures that compare the abilities of different animals in terms of speed with planes, rockets, meteoroids, and light beams.

■ *Is a Blue Whale the Biggest Thing There Is?* by Robert E. Wells (RI)
■ *Big Blue* by Shelley Gill (RL/RI)

Texts use a blue whale to introduce the concept of comparative size and scale on earth and in the universe. One is a narrative about a young girl who is knowledgeable about whales and dreams to swim with a blue whale. On a research trip with her mother and marine biologists her dream comes true and she learns firsthand the beauty and majesty of the big blue whale. The other is an informational text explaining how one blue whale is the largest creature on planet earth but compared with other things the blue whale is one the smallest, especially when compared with the universe.

■ *If You Hopped Like a Frog* by David M. Schwartz (RI)
■ *The Warlord's Puppeteers* by Virginia Pilegard (RL/RI)

Texts address ratio and proportion. One is a collection of humorous situations that depict what humans could do if they had the bodies and abilities of different animals, and the other is a beautiful narrative about a young boy in long-ago China who travels to the warlord's palace. On the way he joins a troupe of puppeteers, meets bandits who steal all the troupe's puppets, and learns about an ancient rule in Chinese art about proportions that help him make new puppets.

■ *The Warlord's Puppeteers* by Virginia Pilegard (RL)
■ *Gulliver in the South Seas* by Gary Crew (RL)

Texts provide a captivating introduction to ratio and proportion. One is a beautiful narrative about a young boy in long-ago China who travels to the warlord's palace. On the way he joins a troupe of puppeteers, meets bandits who steal all the troupe's puppets, and learns about an ancient rule in Chinese art about proportions that help him make new puppets.

The other presents a different perspective on the traditional story of *Gulliver's Travels* by Jonathan Swift by describing a new version that involves tiny inhabitants but takes place in the South Seas.

- *Cut Down to Size at High Noon* by Scott Sundby (RL/RI)
- *Leonardo's Horse* by Jean Fritz (RL/RI)

Texts integrate mathematics, science, and art related to drawing to scale. One is a narrative set in a frontier town named Cowlick about a creative haircutter and an expert at scale drawing who duels a barber new to the town. They both learn the value of working together. The other is a narrative about Leonardo Da Vinci who used his skills at drawing to scale to design and craft a horse for the Duke of Milan. The project was never finished until a man in 1977 set out to present posthumously the horse to Leonardo.

The Number System (6–8)

- *Infinity and Me* by Kate Hosford (RL/RI)
- *The Cat in Numberland* by Ivar Ekeland (RL)

Texts presents different perspectives on the concept of infinity. One is a narrative with beautiful and informative illustrations about a little girl who notices how small she is compared with the big night sky. She asks people at school how they imagine infinity, learning in the end that infinity for her is how much she loves her grandma. The other is a short chapter book with black and white line drawings about the Hotel Infinity in a place called Numberland that has an endless amount of rooms for numbers to live in.

- *Less Than Zero* by Stuart J. Murphy (RL/RI)
- *Zero* by Kathryn Otoshi (RL/RI)

Texts introduce the concept of negative numbers. One is a simple, straightforward story about a young penquin that wants to buy an ice scooter. He graphs his earnings and expenses and eventually has enough money for the scooter and also learns about negative numbers at the same time. The other introduces the importance of the number zero.

- *Of Numbers and Stars: The Story of Hypatia* by D. Anne Love (RL)
- *The Boy Who Loved Math: The Improbable Life of Paul Erdos* by Deborah Heiligman (RL)

Texts present short biographies of two historical figures who loved mathematics. One is a story set in ancient Egypt about Hypatia who learned a variety of subjects from her father. She later became a scholar and made numerous contributions to mathematics. The other is a colorful narrative about the legendary Paul Erdos, a man who possessed boundless curiosity for life and mathematics, and had a particular passion for prime numbers.

- *The Boy Who Loved Math: The Improbable Life of Paul Erdos* by Deborah Heiligman (RL)
- *You Can Count on Monsters* by Richar Evan Schwartz (RI)

Texts present different perspectives on the number system especially prime numbers and factoring. One is a colorful narrative about the legendary Paul Erdos, a man who possessed boundless curiosity for life and mathematics and had a particular passion for prime numbers. The other includes colorful, creative, and graphic illustrations to introduce multiplication, prime numbers, and factoring with the numbers 1–100.

■ *Little Numbers* (RI) and *Big Numbers* (RI) by Edward Packard

Texts show how little numbers become little and big numbers become big. One is a simple story with large, colorful illustrations about one large dinosaur that is depicted smaller and smaller as it moves from its original size to one-tenth, one-hundredth, one-thousandth, and so forth until it reaches one-trillionth and still isn't the smallest it can be. The other is a simple, companion story with large, colorful illustrations about one small pea on a plate that increases to 10, 100, 1,000, and so forth until it reaches a trillion and still isn't the largest it can be.

■ *A Million Dots* by Andrew Clements (RI)
■ *Millions of Cats* by Wanda Gag (RL)

Texts address the concept of million. One is a fascinating, visually appealing informational text that uses a series of illustrations of interesting and colorful images made up solely of single dots. It includes a dot number counter on each page showing an increasing number of dots ultimately adding up to a million dots. The other is a classic story and fairytale with a rhyming refrain about a man who sets out to find one cat so he and his wife will have company. He finds so many beautiful cats that he returns home with millions, all of whom soon disappear except for one little kitten who originally went unnoticed but now is the center of their lives.

■ *On Beyond a Million: An Amazing Math Journey* by David M. Schwartz (RI)
■ *Can You Count to a Googol?* by Robert E. Wells (RI)

Texts introduce very large numbers and powers of 10. One is a story about Professor X and his students who learn about easy and quick ways to count millions and trillions of popcorn kernels by learning about exponents and counting by powers of 10. The other is a colorful, informational text that introduces large numbers starting with 1, a very little number, and uses the powers of 10 to progress all the way up to a googol, a very big number.

■ *If You Made a Million* (RI) and *How Much Is a Million?* (RI) by David M. Schwartz

Texts introduce the concept of million. One is an informational text with bright, colorful illustrations and narrated by Marvelosissimo, the mathematical magician who congratulates different children for earning an increasing amount of money starting with one penny, one nickel, one dime, one quarter, and so forth all the way to a million. He explains along the way how each amount could be spent. The other is an informational text with bright, colorful illustrations that use a series of if-then situations to introduce very big numbers like million, billion, and trillion.

■ *One Grain of Rice: A Mathematical Folklore* (RL/RI) and *The King's Chessboard* (RL/RI) by David Birch Demi (RL/RI)

Texts provide a unique introduction how doubling can quickly produce very large numbers. One is a beautifully illustrated narrative set in India about a Raja who stored vast amounts of rice given to him by his people. One year they had no rice to give and the people went hungry until a young girl is rewarded by the Raja with a wish, only to learn that her wish to receive double amounts of rice for 1 month will teach him a lesson and feed his people. The other is a narrative also set in India about a king who grants the wish of a loyal servant to receive twice the number of grains of rice for each day represented by the 64 squares on a chessboard. He soon learns that granting this wish involves more grains of rice than he expected.

▪ *Two of Everything* by Lily Toy Hong (RL/RI)
▪ *The 512 Ants on Sullivan Street* by Carol A. Losi (RL/RI)

Texts introduce the concept of doubling. One is a Chinese folktale about a poor, elderly couple that grew and traded homegrown vegetables and discovered a brass pot that magically doubled any item placed in it. One coat turned into 2, 10 coins turned into 20, and so forth until the couple accidentally fell into the pot and suddenly discovered two other people just like them so now they are no longer lonely. The other is a simple, colorful story with a cumulative pattern and rhyming text about a father and daughter on a picnic. Increasing numbers of ants start stealing food from their basket, starting with one ant and one crumb, then two ants and two pieces of plum, four ants with chips, and so forth until finally 512 ants steal an entire cake and nothing is left for the little girl and her father.

▪ *Double Those Wheels* by Nancy Raines Day (RL/RI)
▪ *Two of Everything* by Lily Toy Hong (RL/RI)

Texts focus on the concept of doubling. One is a simple, colorful story about a little monkey that delivers pizza using different kinds of vehicles, ranging from a one-wheel unicycle, doubling to a two-wheel bicycle, to a four-wheel car, on up to a long train with 64 wheels and finally delivering a hot pizza to a birthday party. The other is a Chinese folktale about a poor, elderly couple that grew and traded homegrown vegetables and discovered a brass pot that magically doubled any item placed in it. One coat turned into 2, 10 coins turned into 20, and so forth until the couple accidentally fell into the pot and suddenly discovered two other people just like them so now they are no longer lonely

Statistics and Probability (6–8)

▪ *Bad Luck Brad* by Gail Herman (RL/RI)
▪ *Probably Pistachio* by Stuart J. Murphy (RL/RI)

Texts introduce the concept of probability. One is a short chapter book about a young boy who has a series of bad luck experiences on the last day of school at home, at school, at an arcade, and at the movies but believes that summer vacation will probably be different. The other is a charming story with colorful illustrations about a single unlucky day in the life of a young boy who thinks he is probably right about things at home, school, and soccer practice. He ends up being definitely wrong until he guesses right about his favorite ice cream.

▪ *That's a Possibility* by Bruce Goldstone (RL/RI)
▪ *A Very Improbable Story* by Edward Einhorn (RL/RI)

Texts help make probability interesting and understandable. One is a narrative about how a boy outwits his cat by winning a game of probability and the other describes how a young girl as part of her homework uses probability to solve real life problems.

▪ *It's Probably Penny* by Loreen Leedy (RL/RI)
▪ *Jumanji* by Chris Van Allsburg (RL)

Texts integrate and extend the concept of probability. One is a colorful narrative about an innovative teacher who teaches probability and the vocabulary of probability (*possible, might, equal and unequal chance*) by inviting students to do inquiry problems at school and real-life projects at home. One girl uese the family dog to complete her probability homework project. The other is an award-winning piece of literature with stunning black and white illustrations about a brother and sister who find and play a board game that they soon discover needs to end but that depends on whether they roll the right number on the dice.

- *The Sundae Scoop* by Stuart J. Murphy (RL/RI)
- *Anno's Mysterious Multiplying Jar* by Masaichiro Anno and Mitsumasa Anno (RI)

Texts introduce the mathematical concept of combinations and factorials. One is a simple, colorful story about a cafeteria lady and three children who operate an ice-cream booth at the school picnic. They explore possible combinations of tasty desserts using different kinds of ice cream, sauces, and toppings, and realize that there are more possible combinations than anticipated. The other is an attractive and imaginative story about the concept of factorials through the ever-increasing contents inside a mysterious blue jar.

Additional Instructional Strategies

In addition to Interlocking Rectangles, students can use other instructional strategies to record intertextual connections in mathematics and other content areas. With the Equal and Unequal Connections (see Appendix U at the end of this book) students record similarities between the paired text in and across the equal sign, and differences in the space cutting across the equal sign. With the Spiderweb (see Appendix V at the end of this book) students record similarities or differences between a paired text in the spaces provided.

Appendices

Venn Diagram

Problems and Pleasures

PROBLEMS

PLEASURES

Spokewheel

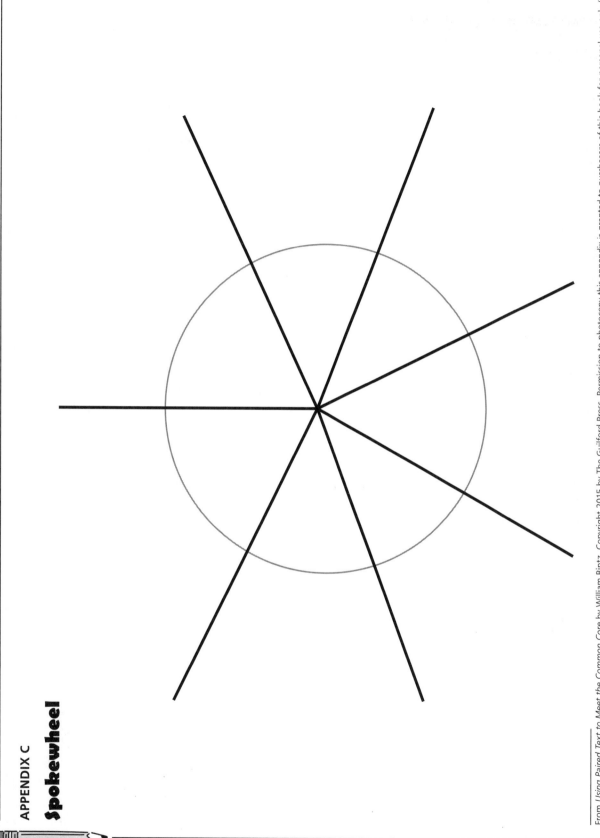

APPENDIX D

New Insights and New Questions

?

?

?

Listening and Connecting

Text 1	
Words, Phrases, Sentences, Quotes, etc.	Connections

Text 2	
Words, Phrases, Sentences, Quotes, etc.	Connections

Similarities and Differences

Text 1 and Text 2	
Similarities	Differences

H-Map

Swap Hypotheses

```
┌─────────────────┐
│                 │
│                 │
│                 │
└────────┐ ┌──────┘
         ▼ ▼
┌──────┐      ╭─────────╮      ┌──────┐
│      │ ──▶  │ Text 1  │ ◀── │      │
│      │      │   and   │      │      │
│      │      │ Text 2  │      │      │
└──────┘      ╰─────────╯      └──────┘
         ▲ ▲
┌────────┘ └──────┐
│                 │
│                 │
│                 │
└─────────────────┘
```

APPENDIX I

Aha! Sheet

Aha! 1

Aha! 2

Aha! 3

A-Map

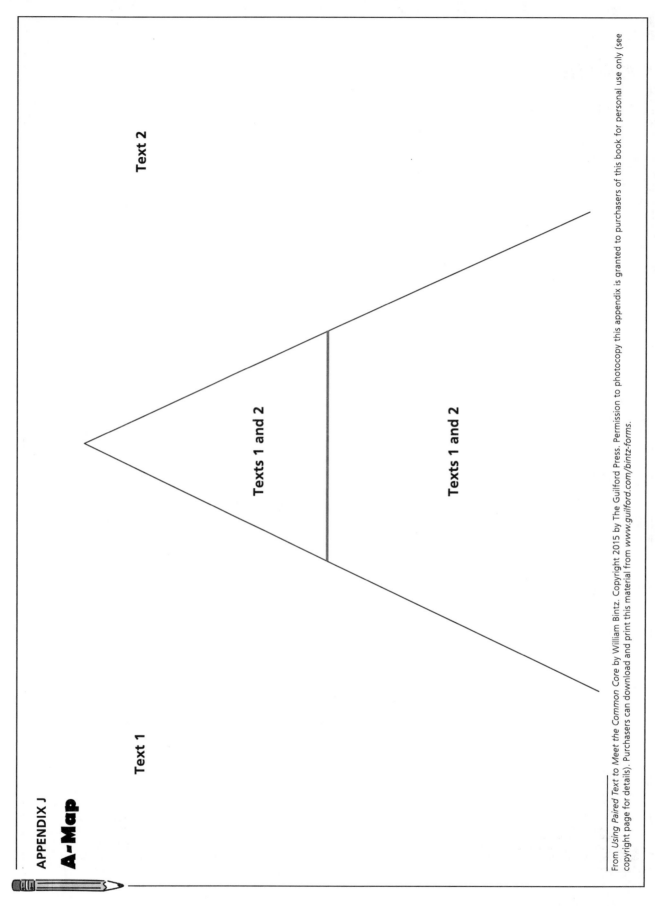

Text 1

Text 2

Texts 1 and 2

Texts 1 and 2

K-Map

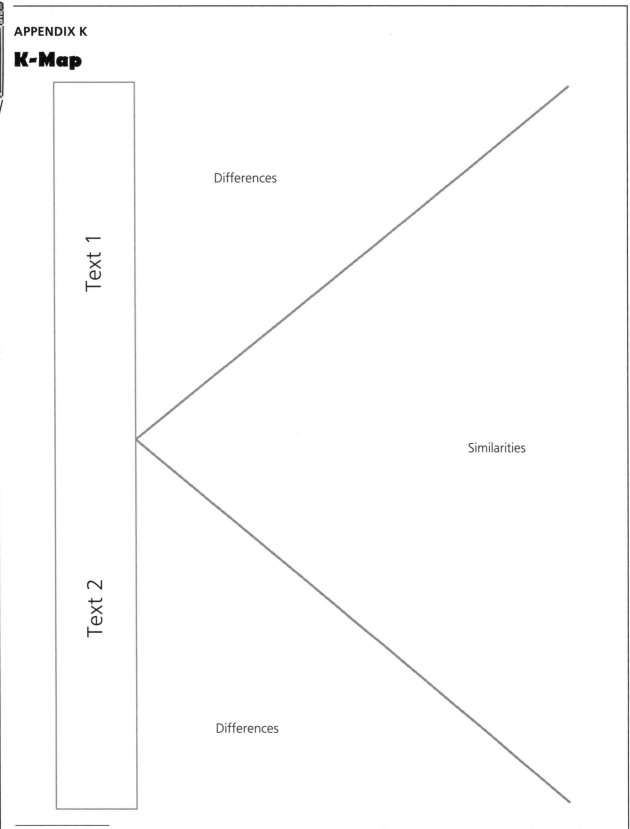

Differences

Text 1

Similarities

Text 2

Differences

M-Map

Text 1

Texts 1 and 2

Text 2

Z-Map

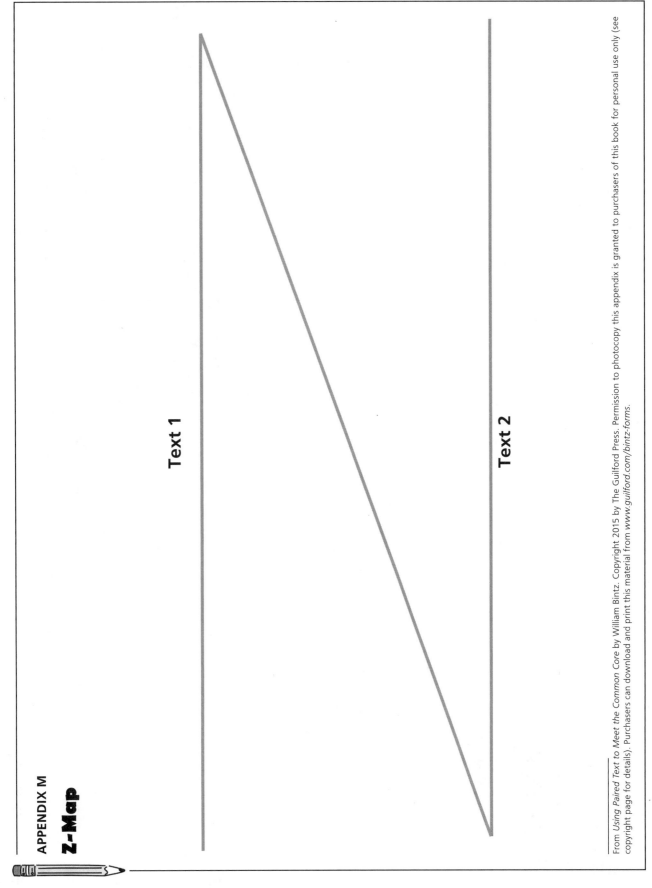

Text 1

Text 2

Category Chart

CATEGORIES

BOOK TITLES

Eureka! Sheet

Eureka! 1

Eureka! 2

Eureka! 3

Connections Chart

Connection	Text 1	Text 2

From *Using Paired Text to Meet the Common Core* by William Bintz. Copyright 2015 by The Guilford Press. Permission to photocopy this appendix is granted to purchasers of this book for personal use only (see copyright page for details). Purchasers can download and print this material from *www.guilford.com/bintz-forms*.

Connections Sheet

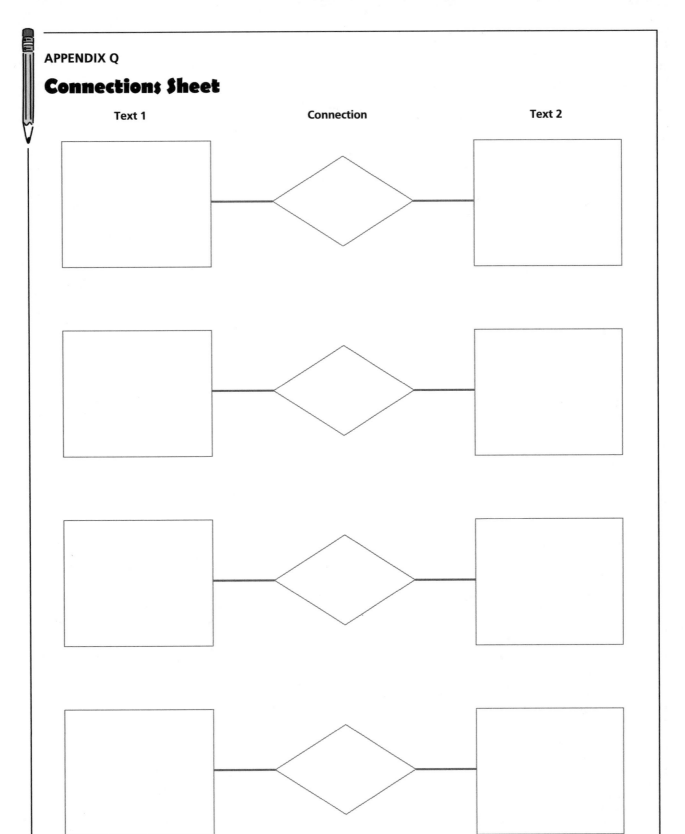

Text 1	Connection	Text 2

Connections Wheel

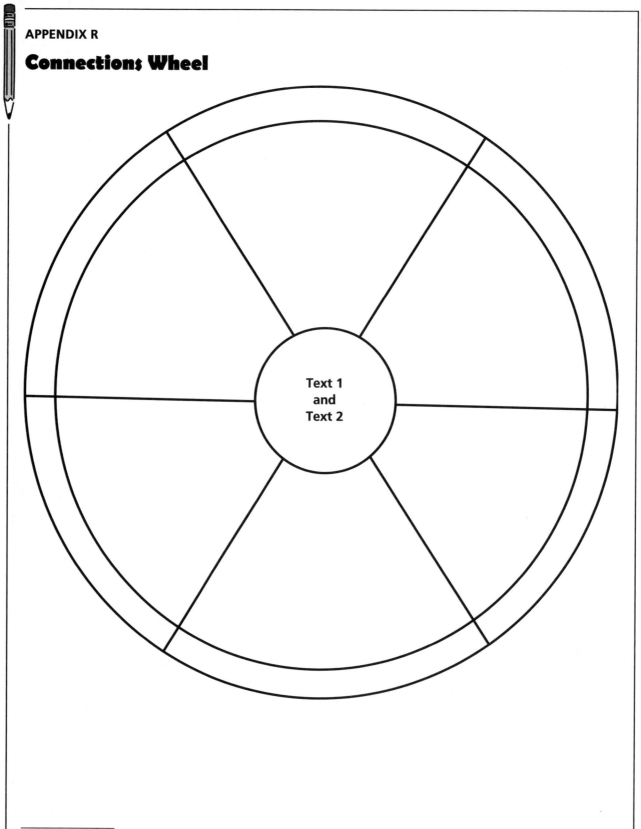

Interlocking Rectangles

Text 1:

Both Texts

Text 2:

Three Addends and a Total

$$+ \quad + \quad + \quad =$$

Equal and Unequal Connections

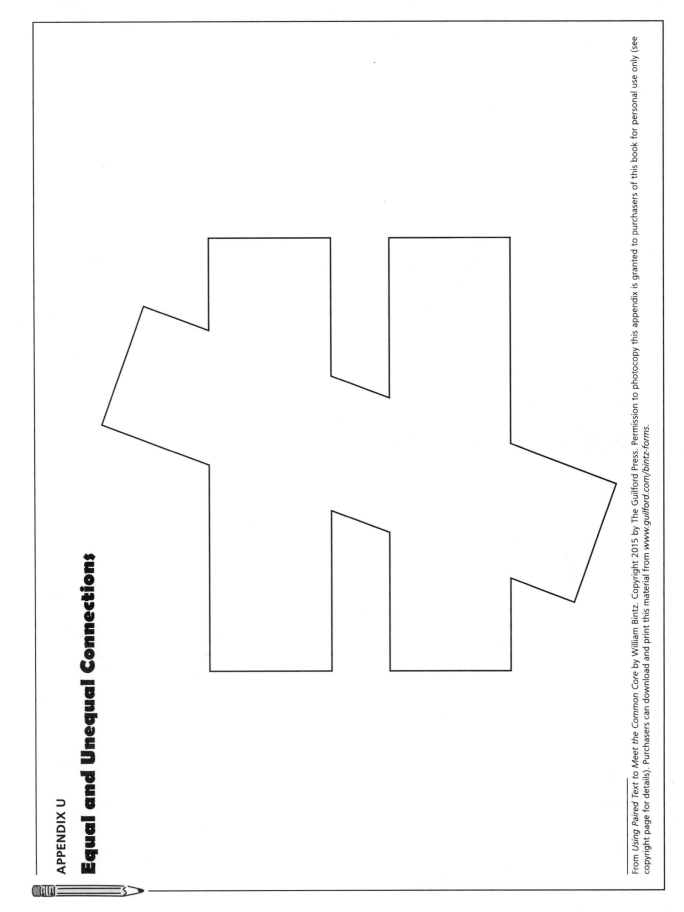

Spiderweb

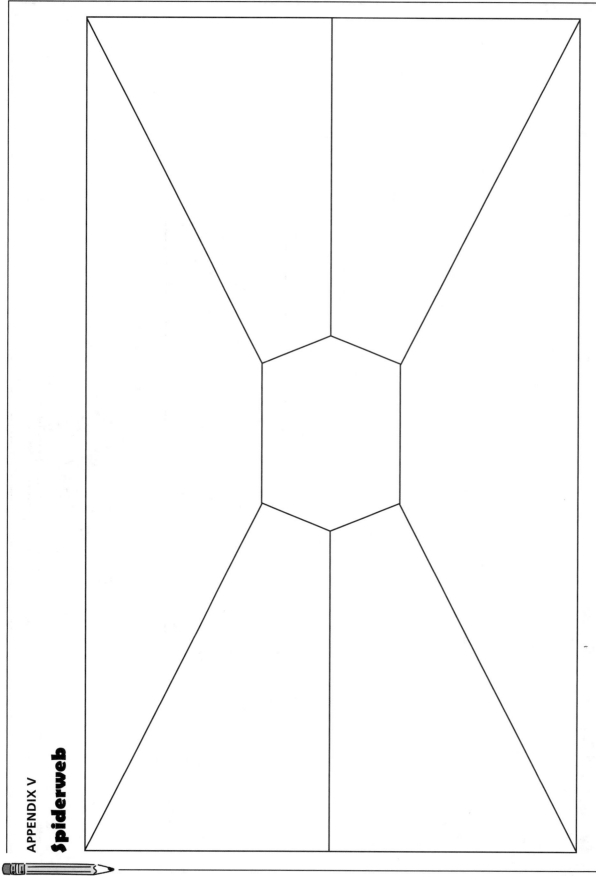

References

Allen, G. (2000). *Intertextuality*. London: Routledge.

Altieri, J. L. (2009). Strengthening connections between elementary classroom mathematics and literacy. *Teaching Children Mathematics, 15*(6), 346–351.

Apple, M. (2004). *Ideology and curriculum*. London: Routledge.

Baker, L., & Saul, W. (1994). Considering science and language arts connections: A study of teacher cognition. *Journal of Research in Science Teaching, 31*(9), 1023–1037.

Bakhtin, M. (1986). *The dialogic imagination: Four essays*. Austin: University of Texas Press.

Barnes, D. (1976). *From communication to curriculum*. Harmondsworth, UK: Penguin Books.

Barthes, R. (1975). *The pleasure of the text*. New York: Farrar, Straus & Giroux.

Barthes, R. (1979). From work to text. In J. V. Harari (Ed.), *Textual strategies: Perspectives in post-structuralist criticism* (pp. 73–81). New York: Cornell University Press.

Bateson, G. (1979). *Mind and nature: A necessary unity*. New York: Dutton.

Bay-Williams, J. M., & Martinie, S. L. (2004). *Math and literature, grades 6–8*. Sausalito, CA: Math Solutions.

Bintz, W. P., & Moore, S. D. (2003). Using literature to teach factorials. *Mathematics Teaching in the Middle School, 8*(9), 461–465.

Bintz, W. P., & Moore, S. D. (2004). Bands to books: Connecting literature to experimental design. *Science Scope, 28*(3), 16–19.

Bintz, W. P., & Moore, S. D. (2005a). To sink or not to sink: Using literature to support scientific inquiry. *Ohio Reading Teacher, 37*(1), 3–10.

Bintz, W. P., & Moore, S. D. (2005b). What's up with sinking? *Science and Children, 43*(1), 20–22.

Bintz, W. P., & Moore, S. D. (2006). Thinking interdisciplinary: John Harrison and longitude. *Kentucky Middle School Association Journal, 7*(1), 34–44.

Bintz, W. P., & Moore, S. D. (2007). The power and potential of art in literature to teach mathematics. In *Bridges donostia: Mathematics, music, architecture, and culture. 2007 Proceedings Yearbook* (pp. 31–33). Bridges Organization.

Bintz, W. P., & Moore, S. D. (2011/2012). Teaching measurement with literature. *Teaching Children Mathematics, 18*(5), 306–313.

Bintz, W. P., Moore, S. D., Adams, C., Pierce, R., Freer, T., Dutson, S., et al. (2008). Literacy across the curriculum: Using an interdisciplinary curricular framework and award-winning literature to learn about the man who solved one of the most important problems of the 19th century. In *2008 Hawaii International Conference on Education (HICE) Sixth Annual Conference Proceedings* (pp. 3512–3528). Honolulu: Hawaii International Conference on Education.

Bintz, W. P., Moore, S. D., Singleton, E., Tuttle, S., & Jones, R. (2006). Integrating literacy, math, and science to make learning come alive. *Middle School Journal, 37*(3), 30–37.

Bintz, W. P., & Wright, P. (2008). Balancing reading comprehension, phonemic awareness, and mathematics instruction. *Balanced Reading Instruction, 15*(1), 39–56.

Bintz, W. P., Wright, P., & Sheffer, J. (2010). Using copy change with trade books to teach earth science. *Reading Teacher, 64*(2), 106–119.

Bloome, D., & Egan-Robertson, A. (1993). The social construction of intertextuality in classroom reading and writing lessons. *Research Reading Quarterly, 28*(4), 304–333.

Bresser, R. (2004). *Math and literature, grades 4–6.* Sausalito, CA: Math Solutions.

Bright, A. (2011). Writing Homer, reading Riordan: Intertextual study in contemporary adolescent literature. *Journal of Children's Literature, 37*(1), 38–47.

Burns, M., & Sheffield, S. (2004a). *Math and literature, grades K–1.* Sausalito, CA: Math Solutions.

Burns, M., & Sheffield, S. (2004b). *Math and literature, grades 2–3.* Sausalito, CA: Math Solutions.

Cairney, T. (1990). Intertextuality: Infectious echoes from the past. *Reading Teacher, 43*, 478–484.

Cairney, T. H. (1992). Fostering and building students' intertextual histories. *Language Arts, 69*, 502–507.

Cambourne, B. (2001/2002). From conditions of learning to conditions of teaching, *Reading Teacher, 55*(4), 358–360.

Cambourne, B. (2002). The conditions of learning: Is learning natural? *Reading Teacher, 55*(8), 758–762.

Camp, D. (2000). It takes two: Teaching with twin texts of fact and fiction. *Reading Teacher, 53*(5), 400–408.

Cech, J. (1983/1984). Remembering Caldecott: The three jovial huntsmen and the art of the picture book. *Lion and the Unicorn, 7/8*, 110–119.

Chi, F. (2012). Searching for intertextual connections in small group text discussion. *Journal of Research in Reading, 35*, 251–266.

Columba, L., Kim, C. Y., & Moe, A. J. (2009). *The power of picture books in teaching math, science, and social studies: Grades PreK–8.* Scottsdale, AZ: Holcolb Hathaway.

Crafton, L. (1991). *Whole language: Getting started . . . moving forward.* Katonah, NY: Owen.

Cross, K. P. (1999, June). *Learning is about making connections* (Cross Papers, No. 3). League for Innovation in the Community College, Educational Testing Service.

Dean, D., & Grierson, S. (2005). Re-envisioning reading and writing through combined-text picture books. *Journal of Adolescent and Adult Literacy, 48*(6), 456–468.

Delbanco, A. (1981). *William Ellery Channing: An essay on the liberal spirit in America.* Boston: Harvard University Press.

DeStefano, J. S. (1981). Demonstrations, engagement and sensitivity: A revised approach to language learning—Frank Smith. *Language Arts, 58*(1), 103–112.

Dewey, J. (1963). *Experience and education.* New York: Collier Books.

Donovan, C. A., & Smokin, L. B. (2001). Genre and other factors influencing teachers' book selections for science instruction. *Reading Research Quarterly, 36*, 412–440.

Duke, N. K. (2000). 3.6 minutes per day: The scarcity of informational texts in first grade. *Reading Research Quarterly, 35*, 202–224.

Dunlap, J., & Lorbiecki, M. (2002). *Louisa May and Mr. Thoreau's flute.* New York: Dial Books for Young Readers.

Ebbers, M. (2002). Science text sets: Using various genres to promote literacy and inquiry. *Language Arts, 80*(1), 40–50.

Eisner, E. (1982). *Cognition and curriculum.* New York: Longman.

El-Hindi, A. E. (2003). Integrating literacy and science in the classroom: From ecomysteries to readers theatre. *Reading Teacher, 56*(6), 536–538.

Fairclough, N. (1992). Intertextuality in critical discourse analysis. *Linguistics and Education, 4*, 269–293.

Ferguson, M. (1997). On "thinking." In R. Maggio, *Quotations on education* (p. 108). Paramus, NJ: Prentice Hall.

Fox, M. (2008). *Reading magic: Why reading aloud to our children will change their lives forever.* New York: Mariner Books.

Freire, P. (2000). *Pedagogy of the oppressed.* New York: Bloomsbury Academic.

Gallagher, K. (2004). *Deeper reading: Comprehending challenging texts, 4–12.* Portland, ME: Stenhouse.

Giroux, H. (2001). *Theory and resistance in education: Towards a pedagogy for the opposition.* Santa Barbara, CA: Praeger.

Goodman, K. (1967). Reading: A psycholinguistic guessing game. *Journal of the Reading Specialist, 6*, 126–135.

Goodman, K. (1996). *On reading.* Portsmouth, NH: Heinemann.

Goodman, K. (2006). *What's whole in whole language* (20th anniversary ed). Muskegon, MI: RDR Books.

Goodman, Y. (1978). Gauging language development through "kid watching." *National Elementary Principal, 57*, 41–45.

Greenfield, E. (1988). *Nathaniel talking.* New York: Black Butterfly Children's Books.

Hadaway, N., & Young, T. (1994). Content literacy and language learning instruction. *The Reading Teacher, 47*(7), 522–527. Retrieved from *www.ira.org.*

Halliday, M. A. K. (1975). *Learning how to mean: Explorations in the development of language.* London: Edward Arnold.

Halliday, M. A. K. (1978). *Language as a social semiotic.* London: Edward Arnold.

Harris, T. L., & Hodges, R. E. (Eds.). (1995). *The literacy dictionary: The vocabulary of reading and writing.* Newark, DE: International Reading Association.

Harste, J., & Short, K., with Burke, C. (1988). *Creating classrooms for authors: The reading–writing connection.* Portsmouth, NH: Heinemann.

Harste, J., Woodward, V., & Burke, C. (1984). *Language stories and literacy lessons.* Portsmouth, NH: Heinemann.

Hartman, D. K. (1995). Eight readers reading: The intertextual links of proficient readers reading multiple passages. *Reading Research Quarterly, 30*, 520–561.

Harvey, S., & Goudvis, A. (2000). *Strategies that work.* Portland, ME: Stenhouse.

Harvey, S., & Goudvis, A. (2007). *Strategies that work* (2nd ed.). Portland, ME: Stenhouse.

Holdaway, D. (1979). *The foundations of literacy.* Syndey, Australia: Ashton Scholastic.

Institute for Mathematics and Education. (2011). CCSSM clickable map V2.0 [PowerPoint slide show]. Retrieved from *http://commoncoretools.me/tools.*

Jeffers, O. (2013, February 4). Maurice Sendak's jumper and me. *Guardian Books Blog.*

Keene, E. O., & Zimmerman, S. (1997). *Mosaic of thought: The power of comprehension strategy instruction.* Portsmouth, NH: Heinemann.

King-Shaver, B. (2005). *When text meets text: Helping high school readers make connections in literature.* Portsmouth, NH: Heinemann.

Kliebard, H. (1992). *Forging the American curriculum: Essays in curriculum history and theory.* New York: Routledge.

Konieck-Moran, R. (2013a). *Everyday life science mysteries: Stories for inquiry-based science instruction.* Arlington, VA: National Science Teachers Association.

Konieck-Moran, R. (2013b). *Everyday physical science mysteries: Stories for inquiry-based science instruction.* Arlington, VA: National Science Teachers Association.

Kristeva, J. (1980). *Desire in language: A semiotic approach to literature and art.* New York: Columbia University Press.

Lewis, C. S. in Winters, C. J., & Schmidt, G. D. (2001). *Edging the boundaries of children's literature.* Boston: Allyn & Bacon.

Lewison, M., Leland, C., & Harste, J. C. (2008). *Creating critical classrooms: K–8 reading and writing with an edge.* New York: Erlbaum.

Libresco, A. S., Balantic, J., & Kipling, J. C. (2011). *Every book is a social studies book.* Santa Barbara, CA: Libraries Unlimited.

Maloch, B., & Bomer, R. (2013). Teaching about and with informational texts: What does research teach us? *Language Arts, 90*(6), 441–448.

Mills, H., O'Keefe, T., & Whitin, D. (1996). *Mathematics in the making: Authoring ideas in primary classrooms.* Portsmouth, NH: Heinemann.

Moore, S. D., & Bintz, W. P. (2000, Fall). From bunches and bunches of bunnies to binary: Using literature to improve thinking about multiplication and exponents. *Kentucky Journal for Teachers of Mathematics.*

Moore, S. D., & Bintz, W. P. (2002a). From Galileo to Snowflake Bentley: Using literature to teach inquiry in middle school science. *Science Scope, 26*(1), 10–14.

Moore, S. D., & Bintz, W. P. (2002b, October). Teaching geometry and measurement through literature. *Mathematics Teaching in the Middle School, 8*(2).

Moore, S. D., & Bintz, W. P. (2002c, Winter). Using literature to teach forces and motion in middle school science. *Kentucky Middle School Association Journal, 4*(1).

Morgan, E., & Ansberry, K. (2010). *Picture-perfect science lessons: Using children's books to guide inquiry, 3–6.* Arlington, VA: National Science Teachers Association.

Morgan, E., & Ansberry, K. (2013). *Even more picture-perfect science lessons: Using children's books to guide inquiry, K–5.* Arlington, VA: National Science Teachers Association.

Murray, D. (1968). *A writer teaches writing; A practical method of teaching composition.* New York: Houghton Mifflin.

National Governors Association Center for Best Practices and Council of Chief State School Officers. (2010). *Common Core State Standards for English language arts and literacy in history/social studies, science, and technical subjects.* Washington, DC: Author. Available at *www.corestandards.org/ELA-Literacy.*

National Research Council. (2012). *A framework for K–12 science education: Practices, crosscutting concepts, and core ideas.* Washington, DC: National Academies Press.

Neufeld, P. (2005). Comprehension instruction in content area classes. *Reading Teacher, 59*(4), 302–312.

NGSS Lead States. (2013). *Next Generation Science Standards: For states, by states.* Washington, DC: National Academies Press.

Opitz, M., & Rasinski, T. (2008). *Good-bye round robin: 25 effective oral reading strategies.* Portsmouth, NH: Heinemann.

Orr, L. (1986). Intertextuality and the cultural text in recent semiotics. *College English, 48*(8), 811–823.

Pappas, C. C. (2006). The information book genre: Its role in integrated science literacy research and practice. *Reading Research Quarterly, 41*(2), 226–250.

Paretti, M. (1999). Intertextuality, genre, and beginning writers: Mining your own texts. In K. L. Weese, S. L. Fox, & S. Greene (Eds.), *Teaching academic literacy: The uses of teacher-research in developing a writing program* (pp. 110–134). Mahwah, NJ: Erlbaum.

Paterson, K. (1997). On "creativity." In R. Maggio, *Quotations on education* (p. 108). Paramus, NJ: Prentice Hall.

Porter, J. (1986). Intertextuality and the discourse community. *Rhetoric Review, 5*(1), 34–47.

Rhodes, L. (1981). I can read!: Predictable books as resources for reading and writing instruction. *Reading Teacher, 34*(5), 511–518.

Rosenblatt, L. (1994). *The reader, the text, the poem: The transactional theory of the literary work.* Carbondale: Southern Illinois University Press.

Royce, C. A., Morgan, E., & Ansberry, K. (2012). *Teaching science through trade books.* Arlington, VA: NSTA Press.

Saussure, F. D. (2012). *Course in general linguistics.* London, UK: Forgotten Books.

Shaughnessy, M. P. (1977). *Errors and expectations: A guide for the teacher of basic writing.* New York: Oxford University Press.

Sheffield, S., & Gallagher, K. (2004). *Math and nonfiction.* Sausalito, CA: Math Solutions.

Short, K., & Burke, C. (1991). *Creating curriculum: Teachers and students as a community of learners.* Portsmouth, NH: Heinemann.

Short, K., & Harste, J., with Burke, C. (1996). *Creating classrooms for authors and inquirers* (2nd ed.). Portsmouth, NH: Heinemann.

Sipe, L. (2000). Those two gingerbread boys could be brothers: How children use intertextual connections during storybook readalouds. *Children's Literature in Education, 31*(2), 73–90.

Sipe, L. R. (2001). Picturebooks as aesthetic objects. *Literacy Teaching and Learning, 6*(1), 23–42.

Sipe, L. R. (2011). The art of the picturebook. In S. Wolf, P. Encisco, K. Coats, & C. Jenkins (Eds.), *Handbook of research in children's literature* (pp. 238–251). New York: Routledge.

Sipe, L. R., & Bauer, J. (2001). Urban kindergartners' literary understanding of picture storybooks. *New Advocate, 14*(4), 329–342.

Smith, F. (1981). Demonstrations, engagement and sensitivity: The choice between people and programs. *Language Arts, 58*(6), 634–642.

Smith, F. (1998). *The book of learning and forgetting.* New York: Teachers College Press.

Smith, F. (2004). *Understanding reading: A psycholinguistic analysis of reading and learning to read.* New York: Routledge.

Smith, F. (2005). *Reading without nonsense.* New York: Teachers College Press.

Soalt, J. (2005). Bringing together fictional and informational texts to improve comprehension, *Reading Teacher, 58*(7), 680–683.

Trelease, J. (1990). *The new read-aloud handbook*. New York: Penguin.

Valencia, S. W., & Wixson, K. K. (2013). CCSS-ELA: Suggestions and cautions for implementing the reading standards. *Reading Teacher, 67*(3), 181–185.

Vygotsky, L. (1978). *Mind in society* (14th ed.). Cambridge, MA: Harvard Educational Press.

Weaver, C. (1994). *Reading process and practice: From socio-psycholinguistics to whole language* (2nd ed.). Portsmouth, NH: Heinemann.

Whitin, D., Mills, H., & O'Keefe, T. (1991). *Living and learning mathematics: Stories and strategies for supporting mathematical learning*. Portsmouth, NH: Heinemann.

Whitin, D., & Whitin, P. (2004). *New visions for linking literature and mathematics*. Reston, VA: National Council of Teachers of Mathematics.

Whitin, D., & Whitin, P. (2005). Pairing books for children's mathematical understanding. *Young Children, 60*(2), 42–48.

Whitin, D., & Wilde, S. (1992). *Read any good math lately?: Children's books for mathematical learning, K–6*. Portsmouth, NH: Heinemann.

Whitin, D., & Wilde, S. (1995). *It's the story that counts: More children's books for mathematical learning, K–6*. Portsmouth, NH: Heinemann.

Wilde, S. (2000). *Miscue analysis made easy: Building on student strengths*. Portsmouth, NH: Heinemann.

Winters, C. J., & Schmidt, G. D. (2001). *Edging the boundaries of children's literature*. Boston: Allyn & Bacon.

Picture Books Cited

Introduction

Adams, J. (1990). *Pigs and honey*. Adelaide, Australia: Omnibus Books.

Allen, P. (1990). *My cat Maisie*. Ringwood, Australia: Viking.

Baillie, A. (1989). *Drac and the gremlin*. New York: Dial Books for Young Readers.

Base, G. (1983). *My grandma lived in Gooligulch*. Melbourne, Australia: Nelson.

Bodsworth, N. (1991). *A nice walk in the jungle*. New York: Puffin Books.

Bunting, E. (1999). *Can you do this, old badger?* San Diego, CA: Harcourt.

Cohen, M. (1977). *When will I read?* New York: Dell.

Cohen, M. (1980). *First grade takes a test*. New York: Kane Press.

Cooney, B. (1991). *Roxaboxen*. New York: HarperCollins.

Cullum, A. (1976). *Murphy, Molly, Max and me*. New York: Delacorte Press

Daly, N. (2003). *Once upon a time*. New York: Farrar, Straus & Giroux.

Ernst, L. C. (1983). *Sam Johnson and the blue ribbon quilt*. New York: Lothrop, Lee & Shepard.

Fox, M. (1986). *Hattie and the fox*. New York: Scholastic.

Goss, J., & Harste, J. (1993). *It didn't frighten me*. Willowisp Press.

Gouldthorpe, P. J. (1991). *Hist!* Montville, Australia: McVitty Books.

Graham, B. (1987). *The wild*. New York: Bedrick/Blackie.

Grant, J. (2005). *Cat and fish*. Vancouver, BC: Simply Read Books.

Hamilton, M., & Weiss, M. (2008). *The ghost catcher*. Atlanta, GA: August House.

Haseley, D. (2002). *A story for bear*. San Diego, CA: Silver Whistle Harcourt.

Hilton, N. (1987). *The long red scarf*. Adelaide, Australia: Omnibus Books.

Hilton, N. (1990). *A proper little lady*. New York: Orchard Books.

Hoose, P., & Hoose, H. (1998). *Hey, little ant*. New York: Scholastic.

Ingpen, R. (1984). *Click go the shears*. Sydney, Australia: Fontana Picture Lions.

Lindbergh, R. (1994). *If I'd known then what I know now*. New York: Puffin Books.

Lionni, L. (1974). *Fish is fish*. Decorah, IA: Dragonfly Books.

Mahy, M. (1988). *The spider in the shower*. Crystal Lake, IL: Rigby.

McPhail, D. (1993). *Santa's book of names*. Boston: Little, Brown.

Morrison, T. (1997). *The Neptune fountain: The apprenticeship of a Renaissance sculptor.* New York: Holiday House.

O'Toole, M. (1987). *Kangaroo court.* Melbourne, Australia: Macmillan.

Paterson, A. B. (1991). *A bush christening.* Sydney, Australia: Angus & Robertson.

Pavey, P. (2009). *One dragon's dream.* Somerville, MA: Candlewick Press.

Polacco, P. (1998). *Thank you, Mr. Falker.* New York: Philomel.

Purdy, C. (1993). *Least of all.* New York: Aladdin Books.

Roughsey, D. (1973). *The giant devil-dingo.* New York: Macmillan.

Rowe, J. (1990). *Scallywag.* Gosford, Australia: Ashton Scholstic.

Rubinstein, G. (1991). *Dog in, cat out.* Norwood, South Australia: Omnibus Books.

Salmon, M. (1986). *The great Tasmanian tiger hunt.* Victoria, Australia: Lamont Books.

Stanley, D. (1983). *The conversation club.* New York: Aladdin Books.

Thomas, S., & Siegel, M. (1982). *No baths for Tabitha.* Willowisp Press.

Wild, M. (1988). *Mr. Nick's knitting.* San Diego, CA: Harcourt Brace Jovanovich.

Winch, J. (1996). *The old woman who loved to read.* New York: Holiday House.

Part One: Intertextuality

Asbjornsen, P. C., & Moe, J. E. (1957). *The three billy goats gruff.* San Diego: Harcourt Brace.

Browne, A. (2013). *A bear-y tale.* London: Walker Books.

Browne, A. (1998). *Voices in the park.* New York: DK.

Browne, A. (2004). *Into the forest.* London: Walker Books.

Dealey, E. (2002). *Goldie locks has chicken pox.* New York: Atheneum Books for Young Readers.

Donaldson, J. (2006). *Charlie Cook's favorite book.* New York: Dial Books.

Fleischman, P. (1993). *Bull run.* New York: Scholastic.

Fleischman, P. (1996). *Dateline: Troy.* Cambridge, MA: Candlewick Press.

Fleischman, P. (2007). *Glass slipper, gold sandal: A worldwide Cinderella.* New York: Henry Holt.

Galdone, P. (1984). *Henny penny.* New York: HMH Books for Young Readers.

Gerstein, M. (2009). *A book.* New York: Roaring Brook Press.

Gleeson, L., & Smith, C. (1992). *Where's mum?* Sydney, Australia: Omnibus Books.

Hoffman, E. T. A. (1996). *Nutcracker.* Mankato, MN: Creative Editions.

Innocenti, R., & Lewis, J. P. (2002). *The last resort.* Mankato, MN: Creative Editions.

Johnson, C. (2005). *Harold and the purple crayon.* New York: HarperCollins.

Johnson, D. B. (2000). *Henry hikes to Fitchburg.* Boston: Houghton Mifflin.

Johnson, D. B. (2002). *Henry builds a cabin.* Boston: Houghton Mifflin.

Johnson, D. B. (2003). *Henry climbs a mountain.* Boston: Houghton Mifflin.

Johnson, D. B. (2004). *Henry works.* Boston: Houghton Mifflin.

Johnson, D. B. (2009). *Henry's night.* Boston: Houghton Mifflin.

Lewis, J. P. (2005). *Please bury me in the library.* Orlando, FL: Gulliver Books.

Ludy, M. (2005). *The flower man.* Mifflin, PA: Green Pastures.

Macaulay, D. (1990). *Black and white.* Boston: Houghton Mifflin.

Macaulay, D. (1995). *Shortcut.* Boston: Houghton Mifflin.

Meltzer, M. (2006). *Henry David Thoreau.* Breckenridge, CO: Twenty First Century Books.

O'Neal, D., & Westengard, A. (2005). *The trouble with Henry*: *A tale of Walden Pond*. Cambridge, MA: Candlewick Press Press.

Schachner, J. B. (1998). *Mr. Emerson's cook*. New York: Dutton Children's Books.

Schmidt, G. (2002). *The wonders of Donal O'Donnell*. New York: Holt.

Schnur, S. (2002). *Henry David's house*. Watertown, MA: Charlesbridge.

Sunami, K. (2002). *How the fisherman tricked the genie*. New York: Atheneum Books for Young Readers.

Thoreau, H. D. (2009). *Walden and other writings: The works of Henry David Thoreau*. Houston, TX: Halcyon.

Walton, R. (1993). *How many, how many, how many*. Cambridge, MA: Candlewick Press Press.

Yolen, J. (2008). *Naming liberty*. New York: Philomel.

Yolen, J., & Dotlich, R. K. (2013). *Grumbles from the forest: Fairy-tale voices with a twist*. Honesdale, PA: Wordsong.

Part Two: Paired Text

Carle, E. (1996). *The grouchy ladybug*. New York: HarperCollins.

Charlip, R. (1993). *Fortunately*. New York: Aladdin.

Davies, N. (1997). *Big blue whale*. Cambridge, MA: Candlewick Press Press.

Marshall, J. (2000). *The three little pigs*. New York: Grosset & Dunlap.

Mayo, D. (2006). *The house that Jack built*. Concord, MA: Barefoot Books.

McNaughton, C. (2004). *Once upon an ordinary school day*. New York: Farrar, Straus & Giroux.

Miller, J. (1998). *If the earth . . . were a few feet in diameter*. Shelton, CT: Greenwich Workshop Press.

Nelson, M. (2005). *A wreath for Emmett Till*. New York: HMH Books for Young Readers

Pappas, T. (1993). *Fractals, googols, and other mathematical tales*. Concord, MA: Wide World.

Pappas, T. (1997a). *The adventures of Penrose the mathematical cat*. San Carlos, CA: Wide World.

Pappas, T. (1997b). *Math for kids and other people, too*. San Carlos, CA: Wide World.

Pappas, T. (2004). *Further adventures of Penrose the mathematical cat*. San Carlos, CA: Wide World.

Sayre, A. P. (2005). *The bumblebee queen*. Watertown, MA: Charlesbridge.

Thompson, L. (2001). *One riddle, one answer*. New York: Scholastic Press.

Wheatley, N. (2001). *Luke's way of looking*. La Jolla, CA: Kane/Miller.

Winter, J. (2012). *Just behave Pablo Picasso*. New York: Levine Books.

Wright, B. F. (1994). *The real mother goose*. New York: Scholastic.

Part Three: Paired Text in English Language Arts

Abercrombie, B. (1995). *Charlie Anderson*. New York: McElderry Books.

Alda, A. (2004). *ABC: What do you see?* Berkeley, CA: Tricycle Press.

Aliki. (1987). *The two of them*. New York: HarperCollins.

Aliki. (1997). *The gods and goddesses of Olympus.* New York: HarperCollins.

Aliki. (2000). *William Shakespeare and the globe.* New York: HarperCollins.

Allsburg, C. V. (1984). *Mysteries of Harris Burdick.* New York: HMH Books for Young Readers.

Allsburg, C. V. (1987). *The Z was zapped: A play in twenty-six acts.* New York: HMH Books for Young Readers.

Allsburg, C. V. (1988). *Two bad ants.* Boston: HMH Books for Young Readers.

Andersen, H. C. (2009). *The emperor's new clothes.* North Mankato, MN: Stone Arch Books.

Andersen, H. C. (2011). *The ugly duckling.* Toronto, Canada: Ripple Digital.

Appelt, K. (1997). *Elephants aloft.* New York: HMH Books for Young Readers.

Baker, J. (1979). *Grandmother.* New York: Dutton Children's Books.

Baker, J. (1988). *Where the forest meets the sea.* New York: Greenwillow Books.

Baker, J. (1991). *Window.* New York: Greenwillow Books.

Baker, J. (2000). *Hidden forest.* New York: Greenwillow Books.

Baker, J. (2001). *Home in the sky.* London: Walker Books.

Baker, J. (2004a). *Home.* New York: Greenwillow Books.

Baker, J. (2004b). *Millicent.* London: Walker Books.

Baker, J. (2010). *Mirror.* Somerville, MA: Candlewick Press Press.

Baretta, G. (2010). *Dear deer: A book of homophones.* New York: Square Fish.

Base, G. (1993). *Animalia.* New York: Abrams.

Beaumont, K. (2005). *I ain't gonna paint no more!* Boston: HMH Books for Young Readers.

Berne, J. (2013). *On a beam of light: A story of Albert Einstein.* San Francisco: Chronicle Books.

Binks, W. (2005). *Where's stripey?* Fremantle, Australia: Stunned Emu Press.

Bolin, F. S. (2008). *Poetry for young people: Carl Sandburg.* New York: Sterling.

Booth, P. (2013). *Crossing.* Somerville, MA: Candlewick Press.

Borden, L. (2001). *Lincoln and me.* New York: Scholastic.

Boynton, S. (1987). *A is for angry: An animal and adjective alphabet.* New York: Workman.

Brennan-Nelson, D. (2003). *My momma likes to say.* Chelsea, MI: Sleeping Bear Press.

Brenner, E. (2004). *On the first day of grade school.* New York: HarperCollins.

Brewster, H. (2006). *The other Mozart: The life of the famous Chevalier de Saint-George.* New York: Abrams.

Brown, D. (2008). *Odd boy out: Young Albert Einstein.* New York: HMH Books for Young Readers.

Brown, M. W. (2006). *The runaway bunny.* New York: HarperCollins.

Brown, S. G. (2003). *Aesop's the crow and the pitcher.* Berkeley, CA: Tricycle Press.

Browne, A. (2001). *Voices in the park.* New York: DK.

Browne, A. (2004). *Into the forest.* Somerville, MA: Candlewick Press.

Browne, A. (2010a). *Bear's magic pencil.* New York: HarperCollins.

Browne, A. (2010b). *Me and you.* London: Farrar, Straus & Giroux.

Browne, A. (2013). *A bear-y tale.* London: Walker Books.

Browne, A. (2013). *A walk in the park.* London: Walker Books.

Buchholz, Q. (1999). *The collector of moments.* London: Farrar, Straus & Giroux.

Burleigh, R. (1995). *Hercules.* New York: HMH Books for Young Readers.

Burleigh, R. (2004). *Langston's train ride.* New York: Orchard Books.

Cabrera, J. (2008). *Old Macdonald had a farm.* New York: Holiday House.

Calmenson, S. (1991). *The principal's new clothes.* New York: Scholastic.

Carle, E. (2013). *Friends.* New York: Philomel.

Carr, J. (2009). *Greedy apostrophe: A cautionary tale.* New York: Holiday House.

Catterwell, T. (2008) *Sebastian lives in a hat.* London: Omnibus Books.

Cheng, C. (2013). *Python.* Somerville, MA: Candlewick Press.

Cherry, L. (1999). *The armadillo from Amarillo.* New York: HMH Books for Young Readers.

Child, L. (2006). *The pea and the princess.* New York: Disney-Hyperion.

Christensen, B. (2012). *I, Galileo.* New York: Knopf Books for Young Readers.

Cleary, B. P. (1999). *A mink, a fink, a skating rink: What is a noun?* Minneapolis, MN: First Avenue Editions.

Cleary, B. P. (2001). *Hairy, scary, ordinary: What is an adjective?* Minneapolis, MN: Carolrhoda Books.

Cleary, B. P. (2003). *Under, over, by the clover.* Minneapolis, MN: First Avenue Editions.

Cleary, B. P. (2005). *Dearly, nearly, insincerely: What is an adverb?* Minneapolis, MN: First Avenue Editions.

Cleary, B. P. (2006). *I and you and don't forget who: What is a pronoun?* Minneapolis, MN: First Avenue Editions.

Cleary, B. P. (2007a). *How much can a bare bear bear? What are homonyms and homophones?* Minneapolis, MN: First Avenue Editions.

Cleary, B. P. (2007b). *Pitch and throw, grasp and know: What is a synonym?* Minneapolis, MN: First Avenue Editions.

Clements, A. (1997). *Double trouble in Walla Walla.* Minneapolis, MN: Carolrhoda Books.

Climo, S. (1992). *The Egyptian Cinderella.* New York: HarperCollins.

Climo, S. (1996). *The Korean Cinderella.* New York: HarperCollins.

Climo, S. (2001). *The Persian Cinderella.* New York: HarperCollins.

Coburn, J. R. (2000). *Domitila: A Cinderella story from the Mexican tradition.* Walnut Creek, CA: Shens Books.

Cohn, A. L., Schmidt, S., & Johnson, D. A. (2002). *Abraham Lincoln.* New York: Scholastic.

Cole, B. (1997) *Prince cinders.* New York: Puffin.

Collier, B. (2004). *Uptown.* New York: Square Fish.

Cooper, F. (1998). *Coming home from the life of Langston Hughes.* New York: Puffin.

Cowley, J. (2000). *The rusty, trusty tractor.* Honesdale, PA: Boyds Mills Press.

Crew, G. (2003a). *Troy Thompson's excellent poetry book.* La Jolla, CA: Kane/Miller.

Crew, G. (2003b). *The viewer.* Vancouver, Canada: Simply Read Books.

Crew, G. (2011). *The watertower.* Northampton, MA: Interlink.

Cronin, D. (2003). *Diary of a worm.* New York: HarperCollins.

Cronin, D. (2013a). *Click, clack, moo: Cows that type.* New York: Little Simon.

Cronin, D. (2013b). *Diary of a worm: Teacher's pet.* New York: HarperCollins.

Cronin, D. (2013c). *Giggle, giggle, quack.* New York: Atheneum Books for Young Readers.

Daywalt, D. (2013). *The day the crayons quit.* New York: Philomel.

Danneberg, J. (2000). *First day jitters.* Watertown, MA: Charlesbridge.

Danneburg, J. (2003). *First day letters.* Watertown, MA: Charlesbridge.

Dealey, E. (2005). *Goldie locks has chicken pox.* New York: Aladdin.

Demi. (1988). *Demi's reflective fables.* New York: Grosset & Dunlap.

Demi. (1997). *Buddha stories.* New York: Holt.

Demi. (2002). *King Midas: The golden touch.* New York: McElderry Books.

Dennis, C. J. (1989). *Hist!* Croydon, Australia: Child & Associates.

dePaola, T. (1984). *The popcorn book.* New York: Holiday House.

dePaola, T. (1996a). *The legend of the bluebonnet.* New York: Puffin.

dePaola, T. (1996b). *The legend of the Indian paintbrush.* New York: Putnam's Sons.

dePaolo, T. (1997). *The art lesson.* New York: Puffin.

dePaola, T. (2004). *Adelita.* New York: Puffin.

Donohue, M. R. (2010). *Alfie the apostrophe.* Park Ridge, IN: Whitman.

Early, M. (1991). *William Tell.* New York: Abrams.

Edwards, P. D. (1997). *Four famished foxes and Fosdyke.* New York: Tegen Books.

Edwards, P. D. (1998a). *Dinorella: A prehistoric fairy tale.* New York: Scholastic.

Edwards, P. D. (1998b). *Some smug slug.* New York: Tegen Books.

Edwards, P. D. (2003). *The worrywarts.* New York: HarperCollins.

Edwards, W. (2008). *Alphabeasts.* Tonawanda, NY: Kids Can Press.

Elting, M. (2005). *Q is for duck: An alphabet guessing game.* New York: HMH Books for Young Readers.

Emberley, R. (1998). *Three cool kids.* New York: Little, Brown.

Ernst, L. C. (1998). *Little red riding hood: A newfangled prairie tale.* New York: Simon & Schuster Books for Young Readers.

Everitt, B. (1995). *Mean soup.* Boston: HMH Books for Young Readers.

Faulkner, M. (2008). *A taste of colored water.* New York: Simon & Schuster Children's.

Feinstein, H. (2014). *The sissy duckling.* New York: Little Simon.

Flack, M. (2000). *Ping.* New York: Grosset & Dunlap.

Finchler, J. (2000a). *Miss Malarkey doesn't live in room 10.* New York: Walker Childrens.

Finchler, J. (2000b). *Miss Malarkey won't be in today.* New York: Walker Childrens.

Fisher, L. E. (1988). *Theseus and the minotaur.* New York: Holiday House.

Fisher, L. E. (1991). *Cyclops.* New York: Holiday House.

Fisher, L. E. (1996). *William Tell.* London: Farrar, Straus & Giroux.

Fox, M. (1997). *Sophie.* Orlando, FL: HMH Books for Young Readers.

Fox, M. (1998). *Tough Boris.* New York: HarperCollins.

Frasier, D. (2007). *Miss Alaineus: A vocabulary disaster.* New York: HMH Books for Young Readers.

French, J. (2009a). *Diary of a wombat.* Boston: HMH Books for Young Readers.

French, J. (2009b). *How to scratch a wombat.* New York: Clarion Books.

French, J. (2010). *Diary of a baby wombat.* New York: Clarion Books.

Frisch, A. (2012). *The girl in red.* Mankato, MN: Creative Editions.

Galdone, P. (1981). *The three billy goats gruff.* New York: HMH Books for Young Readers.

Gallaz, C. (2011). *Rose blanche.* Mankato, MN: Creative Editions.

Gibbons, G. (1988). *Trains.* New York: Holiday House.

Gibbons, G. (2002). *The berry book.* New York: Holiday House.

Gibertson, N. (2003). *Little red snapperhood,* Portland, OR: Westwinds Press.

Giovanni, N. (2007). *Rosa.* New York: Square Fish.

Goble, P. (1991). *Iktomi and the boulder.* New York: Orchard Books.

Goble, P. (1992). *Iktomi and the berries.* New York: Orchard Books.

Goble, P. (1993a). *Death of the iron horse.* New York: Aladdin.

Goble, P. (1993b). *The girl who loved wild horses.* New York: Aladdin.

Gomi, T. (2005). *My friends.* San Francisco: Chronicle Books.

Gray, L. M. (1994). *The little black truck.* New York: Simon & Schuster Children's.

Greenwood, M. (2008). *The donkey of Gallipoli: A true story of courage in World War I.* Somerville, MA: Candlewick Press.

Grey, M. (2011). *The very smart pea and the princess-to-be.* New York: Dragonfly Books.

Guillope, A. (2007). *One scary night.* New York: Milk and Cookies Press.

Gwynne, F. (1988a). *A chocolate moose.* New York: Aladdin.

Gwynne, F. (1988b). *The king who rained.* New York: Aladdin.

Harness, C. (2008). *Young Abe Lincoln.* Washington, DC: National Geographic Children's Books.

Hazen, B. S. (1983). *Tight times.* New York: Puffin.

Heller, R. (1998a). *A cache of jewels and other collective nouns.* New York: Puffin.

Heller, R. (1998b). *Kites sail high: A book of verbs.* New York: Puffin.

Heller, R. (1998c). *Many luscious lollipops: A book about adjectives.* New York: Puffin.

Heller, R. (1998d). *Merry-go-round: A book about nouns.* New York: Puffin.

Heller, R. (1998e). *Up, up and away: A book about adverbs.* New York: Puffin.

Heller, R. (1999). *Mine, all mine: A book about pronouns.* New York: Puffin.

Henkes, K. (1993). *Owen.* New York: Greenwillow Books.

Hesse, K. (2004). *The cats in Krasinski Square.* New York: Scholastic.

Hickox, R. (1999). *The golden sandal: A Middle Eastern Cinderella.* New York: Holiday House.

Hill, L. C. (2010). *Dave the potter: Artist, poet, slave.* New York: Little, Brown Books for Young Readers.

Hilton, N. (1990). *A proper little lady.* New York: Orchard Books.

Hoban, T. (2008). *Over, under and through.* New York: Aladdin.

Holub, J. (2013). *Little red writing.* San Francisco: Chronicle Books.

Hooks, W. (1990). *Moss gown.* New York: HMH Books for Young Readers.

Hopkinson, D. (1995). *Sweet Clara and the freedom quilt.* New York: Knopf.

Hubbard, P. (1999). *My crayons talk.* New York: Holt.

Huck, C. (1994). *Princess furball.* New York: Greenwillow Books.

Hughes, L. (2009). *The negro speaks of rivers.* New York: Jump at the Sun.

Hurwitz, J. (1993). *New shoes for Silvia.* New York: HarperCollins.

Hutchins, P. (1971). *Rosie's walk.* New York: Aladdin.

Hutton, W. (1989). *Theseus and the minotaur.* New York: McElderry Books.

Hutton, W. (1994). *Persephone.* New York: McElderry Books.

Hutton, W. (1995). *Odysseus and the cyclops.* New York: McElderry Books.

Innocenti, R. (2012). *The girl in red.* Mankato, MN: Creative Editions.

Jackson, E. (1998). *Cinder Edna.* New York: HarperCollins.

James, S. (1996). *Dear Mr. Blueberry.* New York: Aladdin.

James. S. (2008). *Dear Greenpeace.* London: Walker Books.

Jeffers, O. (2007). *The incredible book eating boy.* New York: Philomel.

Johnson, A. (2003). *I dream of trains.* New York: Simon & Schuster Children's.

Johnson, A. (2007). *A sweet smell of roses.* New York: Simon & Schuster Children's.

Johnson-Davies, D. (2005). *Goha the wise fool.* New York: Philomel.

Johnson, S. T. (1999). *Alphabet city.* New York: Puffin.

Jonas, A. (1997). *Watch William walk.* New York: Greenwillow Books.

Joosse, B. M. (1998). *Mama, do you love me?* San Francisco: Chronicle Books.

Joosse, B. M. (2005). *Papa, do you love me?* San Francisco: Chronicle Books.

Kaler, R. (1995). *Blueberry bear.* Bloomington, IN: Inquiring Voices Press.

Karlin, B. (2001). *James Marshall's Cinderella*. New York: Puffin.

Katz, A. (2007). *Don't say that word*. New York: McElderry Books.

Keats, E. J. (1998). *Peter's chair*. New York: Puffin.

Keller, H. (1988). *Geraldine's blanket*. New York: Greenwillow Books.

Kellogg, S. (1988). *Johnny Appleseed*. New York: HarperCollins.

Kellogg, S. (1992a). *Aster aardvark's alphabet adventure*. New York: HarperCollins.

Kellogg, S. (1992b). *Pecos Bill*. New York: HarperCollins.

Kellogg, S. (1995). *Sally Ann Thunder Ann Whirlwind Crockett*. New York: HarperCollins.

Kellogg, S. (1997). *Jack and the beanstalk*. New York: HarperCollins.

Kellogg, S. (1998). *Mike Fink*. New York: HarperCollins.

Kellogg, S. (2004). *Paul Bunyan*. New York: HarperCollins.

Kerley, B. (2004). *Walt Whitman: Words for America*. New York: Scholastic.

Kimmel, E. A. (1991). *Don Quixote and the windmills*. New York: Farrar, Straus & Giroux.

Kitamura, S. (2006). *Pablo the artist*. London: Farrar, Straus & Giroux.

Klassen, J. (2011). *I want my hat back*. Somerville, MA: Candlewick Press.

Klassen, J. (2012). *This is not my hat*. Somerville, MA: Candlewick Press.

Kline, S. (1995). *Mary Marony and the snake*. New York: Yearling.

Kloske, G. (2005). *Once upon a time, the end (asleep in 60 seconds)*. New York: Atheneum Books for Young Readers.

Knowles, S. (1997). *Edwina the emu*. New York: HarperCollins.

Kraus, R. (1997). *Fables Aesop never wrote*. New York: Puffin.

Krensky, S. (2002). *Paul Revere's midnight ride*. New York: HarperCollins.

Lamug, K. K. (2012). *A box story*. Las Vegas, NV: Rabble Box.

Lasky, K. (1997). *Hercules: The man, the myth, the hero*. New York: Disney-Hyperion.

Lawlor, L. (2011). *Muddy as a duck puddle and other American similes*. New York: Holiday House.

Lawson, H. (1984). *Andy's gone with cattle*. Australia: HarperCollins.

Lechner, J. (2009). *The clever stick*. Somerville, MA: Candlewick Press.

Leedy, L. (1994). *Messages in the mailbox: How to write a letter*. New York: Holiday House.

Leedy, L. (2009). *Crazy like a fox: A simile story*. New York: Holiday House.

Lee, S. (2007). *The zoo*. La Jolla, CA: Kane/Miller.

Lee, S. (2008). *Wave*. San Francisco: Chronicle Books.

Lee, S. (2010a). *Mirror*. New York: Seven Footer Press.

Lee, S. (2010b). *Shadows*. San Francisco: Chronicle Books.

Lester, H. (2002). *Hooway for Wodney wat*. Boston: HMH Books for Young Readers.

Levin, J. E., & Levin, M. R. (2010). *Abraham Lincoln's Gettysburg address*. New York: Threshold Editions.

Lewin, T. (1998). *The storytellers*. New York: HarperCollins.

Lewis, J. P. (2003). *The last resort*. Mankato, MN: Creative Editions.

Lewis, J. P. (2009). *The house*. Mankato, MN: Creative Editions.

Lewis, P. O. (2001a). *Frog girl*. Berkeley, CA: Tricycle Press.

Lewis, P. O. (2001b). *Storm boy*. Berkeley, CA: Tricycle Press.

Lionni, L. (1995). *Little blue and little yellow*. New York: HarperCollins.

Lobel, A. (1983). *Fables*. New York: HarperCollins.

Loewen, N. (2011). *Believe me, Goldilocks rocks!: The story of the three bears as told by baby bear*. North Mankato, MN: Picture Window Books.

Long, M. (2007). *Pirates don't change diapers*. New York: HarperCollins.

Longfellow, H. W. (2001). *The midnight ride of Paul Revere*. San Francisco: Chronicle Books.

Louie, A. (1996). *Yeh-Shen: A Cinderella story from China*. New York: Puffin.

Lowell, S. (1992). *The three little javelinas*. Flagstaff, AZ: Cooper Square.

Macauley, D. (1999). *Shortcut*. Boston: HMH Books for Young Readers.

Macauley, D. (2005). *Black and white*. Boston: HMH Books for Young Readers.

Mandell, M. (2011). *A donkey reads*. New York: Star Bright Books.

Manna, A. (2011). *The orphan: A Cinderella story from Greece*. New York: Schwartz & Wade.

Marshall, J. (2002). *Goldilocks and the three bears*. Greensboro, NC: Brighter Child.

Martin, B., Jr. (1996). *Brown bear, brown bear: What do you see?* New York: Holt.

Martin, B., Jr. (1997a). *Knots on a counting rope*. New York: Square Fish.

Martin, B., Jr. (1997b). *Polar bear, polar bear: What do you hear?* New York: Holt.

Martin, J. B. (2009). *Snowflake Bentley*. New York: HMH Books for Young Readers.

Martin, R. (1998). *The rough-face girl*. New York: Puffin.

Massachusetts St. Mary's Catholic School. (2005). *Haiku hike*. New York: Scholastic.

McCully, E. A. (1997). *Popcorn at the palace*. New York: HMH Books for Young Readers.

McDonnell, P. (2011). *Me, Jane*. New York: Little, Brown Books for Young Readers.

McNaughton, C. (1997). *Oops! A Preston pig story*. Boston: HMH Books for Young Readers.

McNaughton, C. (1998). *Suddenly! A Preston pig story*. Boston: HMH Books for Young Readers.

Merriam, E. (1990). *How to eat a poem*. New York: HarperCollins.

Miller, M. L. (1994). *Those bottles!* New York: Putnam Juvenile.

Monnar, A. (2008). *Adelaida: A Cuban Cinderella*. Miami, FL: Readers Are Leaders, USA.

Moore, I. (1993). *Six-dinner Sid*. New York: Aladdin.

Moore, N. D. (2006). *Kiernan's jam*. London: Ingledew Press.

Morris, J. (1997). *The wombat who talked to the stars*. Maleny, Australia: Greater Glider.

Morris, J. (2004). *Koala number one*. Maleny, Australia: Greater Glider.

Most, B. (1981). *There's an ape behind the drape*. New York: Morrow.

Most, B. (1992). *There's an ant behind Anthony*. New York: HarperCollins.

Muth, J. J. (2002). *The three questions*. New York: Scholastic.

Muth, J. J. (2003). *Stone soup*. New York: Scholastic.

Muth, J. J. (2005). *Zen shorts*. New York: Scholastic.

Muth, J. J. (2008). *Zen ties*. New York: Scholastic.

Myers, B. (1990). *It happens to everyone*. Decatur, GA: Trumpet.

Myers, W. D. (2012). *Harlem*. New York: Scholastic.

Nelson, M. (2009). *A wreath for Emmett Till*. New York: HMH Books for Young Readers.

Nikola-Lish, W. (2007). *Magic in the margins*. New York: Houghton Mifflin.

Niland, D. (1987) *Drovers dream*. New York: HarperCollins.

Niven, P. (2003). *Carl Sandburg: Adventures of a poet*. New York: HMH Books for Young Readers.

Odgers, S. F. (1989). *Dreadful David*. New York: Scholastic.

Okimoto, J. D. (1996). *A place for Grace*. Seattle, WA: Sasquatch Books.

O'Malley, K. (2005). *Mount Olympus basketball*. New York: Walker Childrens.

O'Neill, A. (2002). *The recess queen*. New York: Scholastic.

Parlotto, S. (2008). *The world that loved books*. Vancouver, Canada: Simply Read Books.

Paterson, A. B. (1981). *The man from ironbark.* New York: HarperCollins.

Paterson, A. B. (1993). *Mulga Bill's bicycle.* Australia: Angus & Robertson Childrens.

Paterson, A. B. (1998). *Waltzing Matilda.* New York: HarperCollins.

Paterson, A. B. (2014). *The man from snowy river.* Seattle, WA: CreateSpace.

Peake, M. (2003). *Figures of speech.* Somerville, MA: Candlewick Press.

Pelletier, D. (1996). *The graphic alphabet.* New York: Scholastic.

Perdomo, W. (2005). *Visiting Langston.* New York: Square Fish.

Pettenati, J. K. (2006). *Galileo's journal: 1609–1610.* Watertown, MA: Charlesbridge.

Pichon, L. (2010). *The three horrid little pigs.* Wilton, CT: Tiger Tales.

Pinkney, A. D. (2006). *Duke Ellington.* New York: Hyperion.

Pinkney, J. (2009). *The lion and the mouse.* New York: Little, Brown Books for Young Readers.

Pinkney, J. (2013). *The tortoise and the hare.* New York: Little, Brown Books for Young Readers.

Pinkwater, D. (1993). *The big orange splot.* New York: Scholastic.

Pollock, P. (1996). *The Turkey girl: A Zuni Cinderella story.* New York: Little, Brown Books for Young Readers.

Portis, A. (2007). *Not a stick.* New York: HarperCollins.

Portis, A. (2012). *Not a box.* New York: HarperCollins.

Prelutsky, J. (2004). *If not for the cat.* New York: Greenwillow Books.

Pulver, R. (2007a). *Nouns and verbs have a field day.* New York: Holiday House.

Pulver, R. (2007b). *Punctuation take a vacation.* New York: Holiday House.

Ramsey, C. A. (2010). *Ruth and the green book.* Minneapolis, MN: Carolrhoda Books.

Rappaport, D. (2008). *Abe's honest words: The life of Abraham Lincoln.* New York: Disney-Hyperion.

Raschka, C. (2000). *Ring! Yo?* New York: DK.

Raschka, C. (2007). *Yo! Yes?* New York: Scholastic.

Rathmann, P. (1995). *Officer Buckle and Gloria.* New York: Putnam Juvenile.

Rayevsky, K., & Rayevsky, R. (2006). *Antonyms, synonyms & homonyms.* New York: Holiday House.

Reynolds, P. (2004a). *The dot.* Somerville, MA: Candlewick Press.

Reynolds, P. (2004b). *Ish.* Somerville, MA: Candlewick Press.

Rinck, M. (2008). *I feel a foot.* Honesdale, PA: Lemniscaat USA.

Roennfeldt, M. (1992). *What's that noise?* New York: Orchard Books.

Rogers, G. (2004). *The boy, the bear, the baron, the bard.* New Milford, CT: Roaring Brook Press.

Rosenthal, A. K., & Lichtenheld, T. (2009). *Duck! Rabbit!* San Francisco, CA: Chronicle Books.

Roughsey, D. (1973). *The giant devil-dingo.* New York: Atheneum.

Roughsey, D. (1994). *The rainbow serpent.* New York: HarperCollins.

Ryan, P. M. (1999). *Amelia and Eleanor go for a ride.* New York: Scholastic.

Ryan, P. M. (2002). *When Marian sang.* New York: Scholastic.

Rylant, C. (1991). *Night in the country.* New York: Atheneum Books for Young Readers.

Rylant, C. (1993). *Night in the country.* New York: Puffin.

Rylant, C. (1994a). *All I see.* New York: Scholastic.

Rylant, C. (1994b). *Something permanent.* New York: HarperCollins.

Say, A. (2005). *Kamishibai man.* New York: HMH Books for Young Readers.

Scieszka, J. (1992). *The stinky cheese man and other fairly stupid tales*. New York: Viking Juvenile.

Scieszka, J. (2003). *Squids will be squids*. New York: Puffin.

Seymour, T. (1996). *The gulls of the Edmund Fitzgerald*. New York: Orchard Books.

Shange, N. (2004). *Ellington was not a street*. New York: Simon & Schuster Children's.

Shannon, D. (1998). *No, David*! New York: Blue Sky Press.

Shannon, D. (2002). *David gets in trouble!* New York: Blue Sky Press.

Shaskan, T. S. (2011). *Honestly, red riding hood was rotten: The story of little red riding hood as told by the wolf*. North Mankato, MN: Picture Window Books.

Shulman, L. (2004). *Old Macdonald had a workshop*. New York: Puffin.

Siebert, D. (1993). *Train song*. New York: HarperCollins.

Sis, P. (2000). *Starry messenger: Galileo Galilei* . New York: Square Fish.

Smith, I. (2008). *Mei Ling in China city*. Manhattan Beach, CA: East West Discovery Press.

Stanley, D. (2001). *Saving sweetness*. New York: Puffin.

Stanley, D. (2002). *Raising sweetness*. New York: Puffin.

Stewig, J. W. (1999). *King Midas: A golden tale*. New York: Holiday House.

Still, J. (1996). *Jack and the wonder beans*. Lexington: University Press of Kentucky.

Sweet, M. (2005). *Carmine: A little more red*. New York: HMH Books for Young Readers.

Swinburne, S. R. (2009). *Armadillo trail: The northward journey of the Armadillo*. Honesdale, PA: Boyds Mills Press.

Teague, M. (2011). *Dear Mrs. LaRue: Letters from obedience school*. New York: Scholastic.

Tolhurst, M. (1995). *Somebody and the three Blairs*. New York: Scholastic.

Trivizas, E. (1997). *The three little wolves and the big bad pig*. New York: McElderry Books.

Truss, L. (2007). *The girl's like spaghetti: Why you can't manage without apostrophes!* New York: Putnam Juvenile.

Truss, L. (2008). *Twenty-odd ducks: Why every punctuation mark counts!* New York: Putnam Juvenile.

Turkle, B. (1992). *Deep in the forest*. New York: Puffin.

Turner, A. (1999). *Red flower goes west*. New York: Hyperion.

Turner, A. (2003). *Abe Lincoln remembers*. New York: HarperCollins.

Turner, P. (1999). *The war between the vowels and consonants*. New York: Square Fish.

Vautier, C. (1989a). *The shinning stars: Greek legends of the zodiac*. New York: Cambridge University Press.

Vautier, C. (1989b). *The way of the stars: Greek legends of the constellations*. New York: Cambridge University Press.

Waldherr, K. (1993). *Persephone and the pomegranate*. New York: Dial.

Walker, S. M. (2008). *The vowel family: A tale of lost letters*. Minneapolis, MN: Carolrhoda Books.

Wargin, K. (2003). *The Edmund Fitzgerald: The song of the bell*. Chelsea, MI: Sleeping Bear Press.

Watson, J. (1989). *Grandpa's slippers*. New York: Scholastic.

Weisner, D. (1995). *June 29, 1999*. New York: HMH Books for Young Readers.

Weisner, D. (2001). *The three pigs*. New York: Clarion Books.

Weisner, D. (2006). *Flotsam*. New York: Clarion Books.

Whitman, W. (2004). *When I heard the learned astronomer and nothing but miracles*. New York: Simon & Schuster Children's.

Wild, M. (1996). *Let the celebrations begin*. New York: Orchard Books.

Wild, M. (1998). *Our granny*. Boston: HMH Books for Young Readers.

Willems, M. (2003). *Don't let the pigeon drive the bus*. New York: Hyperion.

Willems, M. (2004). *Knuffle bunny: A cautionary tale*. New York: Hyperion.

Willems, M. (2006). *Don't let the pigeon stay up late!* New York: Hyperion.

Willems, M. (2007). *Knuffle bunny too: A case of mistaken identity*. New York: Hyperion.

Williams, M. (2011a). *Miguel de Cervantes's Don Quixote*. Somerville, MA: Candlewick Press.

Williams, M. (2011b). *Greek myths*. Somerville, MA: Candlewick Press.

Williams, S. (1996). *I went walking*. Boston: HMH Books for Young Readers.

Williams, S. (2000). *Let's go visiting*. Boston: HMH Books for Young Readers.

Willis, J., & Ross, T. (2008). *Daft bat*. New York: Sterling.

Wing, N. (2005). *The night before first grade*. New York: Grosset & Dunlap.

Winter, J. (1992). *Follow the drinking gourd*. New York: Dragonfly Books.

Winter, J. (2011). *The watcher*. New York: Schwartz & Wade.

Wood, A. (2006). *The Bunyans*. New York: Scholastic.

Woodson, J. (2001). *The other side*. New York: Putnam Juvenile.

Yolen, J. (1991). *Wings*. New York: HMH Books for Young Readers.

Yolen, J. (2009). *The seeing stick*. Philadelphia: Running Press.

Yolen, J., & Dotlich, R. K. (2013). *Grumbles forest: Fairy-tale voices with a twist*. Honesdale, PA: Worldsong.

Yoo, T. (2007). *The little red fish*. New York: Dial.

Young, E. (1996). *Lon Po Po: A red riding hood story from China*. New York: Puffin.

Young, E. (2002). *Seven blind mice*. New York: Puffin.

Youngquist, C. V. (2002). *The three billygoats gruff and mean calypso Joe*. New York: Atheneum Books for Young Readers.

Zee, R. V. (2003). *Erika's story*. Mankato, MN: Creative Editions.

Zelinsky, P. (1996). *Hansel and Gretel*. New York: Puffin.

Part Four: Paired Text in History/Social Studies

Addy, S. H. (1999). *Right here on this spot*. New York: HMH Books for Young Readers.

Adler, D. A. (2004). *The babe and I*. New York: HMH Books for Young Readers.

Adoff, A. (2004). *Black is brown is tan*. New York: Amistad.

Anno, M. (1990). *Anno's medieval world*. New York: Philomel.

Anzaldua, G. (1997). *Friends from the other side*. New York: Children's Book Press.

Bailer, D. (1996). *Wanted: A few bold riders: The story of the Pony Express*. Norfolk, CT: Soundprints.

Baillie, A. (1994). *Rebel*. New York: HMH Books for Young Readers.

Bair, S. (2006). *Rock, brock, and the savings shock*. Morton Grove, IN: Whitman.

Baker, J. (1991). *Window*. New York: Greenwillow Books.

Bandy, M. S., & Stein, E. (2011). *White water*. Somerville, MA: Candlewick Press.

Banks, S. H.(1996). *A net to catch time*. New York: Knopf Books for Young Readers.

Bearden, R. (2003). *Lil Dan, the drummer boy: A Civil War story*. New York: Simon & Schuster Children's.

Bircher, W. (1999). *A Civil War drummer boy: The diary of William Bircher, 1861–1865 (diaries, letters, memoirs)*. Mankato, MN: Blue Earth Books.

Birtha, B. (2005). *Grandmama's pride*. Park Ridge, IN: Whitman.

Brewster, H. (2006). *Before Mozart: The life of the famous Chevalier de Saint-George*. New York: Abrams.

Bridges, R. (1999). *Through my eyes*. New York: Scholastic.

Brighton, C. (1990). *Mozart: Scenes from the childhood of a great composer by Catherine*. New York: Doubleday Books for Young Readers.

Brill, M. T. (2000). *Diary of a drummer boy*. Minneapolis, MN: Millbrook Press.

Brown, D. (2006). *Bright path: Young Jim Thorpe*. New Milford, CT: Roaring Brook Press.

Brown, M. (1993). *Arthur's pet business*. New York: Little, Brown Books for Young Readers.

Browne, A. (1986). *A walk in the park*. New York: Macmillan.

Browne, A. (2010). *Me and you*. New York: Farrar, Straus & Giroux.

Bruchas, J. (2007). *Squanto's journey*. New York: HMH Books for Young Readers.

Bruchac, J. (2008). *Jim Thorpe's bright path*. New York: Lee & Low Books.

Bunting, E. (1989a). *Terrible things*. Philadelphia: Jewish Publication Society.

Bunting, E. (1989b). *The Wednesday surprise*. New York: HMH Books for Young Readers.

Bunting, E. (1993). *Fly away home*. New York: HMH Books for Young Readers.

Bunting, E. (1997). *A day's work*. New York: HMH Books for Young Readers.

Bunting, E. (1998a). *Going home*. New York: HarperCollins.

Bunting, E. (1998b). *So far from the sea*. New York: Clarion Books.

Bunting, E. (1998c). *Your move*. New York: HMH Books for Young Readers.

Bunting, E. (1999). *Smoky night*. New York: HMH Books for Young Readers.

Bunting, E. (2000a). *Dreaming of America: An Ellis Island story*. Mahwah, NJ: Troll Communications.

Bunting, E. (2000b). *The memory string*. New York: Clarion Books.

Bunting, E. (2000c). *Train to somewhere*. New York: HMH Books for Young Readers.

Bunting, E. (2002). *Cheyenne again*. New York: HMH Books for Young Readers.

Bunting, E. (2005). *Gleam and glow*. New York: HMH Books for Young Readers.

Bunting, E. (2006a). *One green apple*. New York: Clarion Books.

Bunting, E. (2006b). *Pop's bridge*. New York: HMH Books for Young Readers.

Burton, V. L. (2009). *The little house*. New York: HMH Books for Young Readers.

Carle, E. (1998). *Pancakes, pancakes*. New York: Aladdin.

Carlson, L. (1998). *Boss of the plains*. New York: DK.

Caselli, G. (1988). *The middle ages*. New York: Bedrick Books.

Castaneda, O. S. (1995). *Abuela's weave*. New York: Lee & Low Books.

Catrow, D. (2005). *We the kids*. New York: Puffin.

Cha, D. (1996). *Dia's story cloth*. New York: Lee & Low Books.

Cheng, A. (2003). *Grandfather counts*. New York: Lee & Low Books.

Choi, Y. (2003). *The name jar*. New York: Dragonfly Books.

Christensen, B. (2009). *Django: World's greatest jazz guitarist*. New York: Square Fish.

Cline-Ransome, L. (2000). *Sachel Paige*. New York: Aladdin.

Cline-Ransome, L. (2004). *Major Taylor, champion cyclist*. New York: Atheneum Books for Young Readers.

Cline-Ransome, L. (2011). *Before there was Mozart: The story of Joseph Boulogne Chevalier de Saint-George*. New York: Schwartz & Wade.

Cline-Ransome, L. (2012). *Words set me free: The story of young Frederick Douglass*. New York: Simon & Schuster Children's.

Clinton, C. (2005). *Hold the flag high*. New York: Tegen Books.

Cohn, D. (2005). *Si, se puede! Yes we can!* El Paso, TX: Cinco Puntos Press.

Coleman, E. (1996). *White socks only.* Morton Grove, IN: Whitman.

Coles, R. (2010). *The story of Ruby Bridges.* New York: Scholastic.

Colon, E. (2011). *Good-bye Havana! Hola New York!* New York: Simon & Schuster Children's.

Condra, E. (2006). *Come see the ocean.* Nashville, TN: Ideal's Children's Books.

Cooney, B. (1999). *Basket moon.* New York: Little, Brown Books for Young Readers.

Cooper, F. (2000). *Mandela: From the life of the South African statesman.* New York: Puffin.

Cooper, M. (2000). *Gettin' through Thursday.* New York: Lee & Low Books.

Corey, S. (2003). *Players in pigtails.* New York: Scholastic.

Cristaldi, K. (1992). *Baseball ballerina.* New York: Random House.

Cronin, D. (2004). *Duck for president.* New York: Atheneum Books for Young Readers.

Curtis, G. (2001). *The bat boy and his violin.* New York: Aladdin.

Decker, T. (2005). *The letter home.* Honesdale, PA: Front Street.

Deedy, C. A. (2000). *The yellow star: The legend of king Christian X of Denmark.* Atlanta: Peachtree.

Demi. (1998). *The Dalai Lama.* New York: Holt.

Demi. (2001). *Ghandi.* New York: McElderry Books.

Demi. (2008). *Marco Polo.* Allentown, PA: Two Lions.

dePaola, T. (1979). *Oliver Button is a sissy.* New York: HMH Books for Young Readers.

dePaola, T. (1982). *Charlie needs a cloak.* New York: Aladdin.

Driscoll, L. (2002). *Negro leagues all-black baseball.* New York: Grosset & Dunlap.

Drummond, A. (2011). *Energy Island: How one community harnessed the world and changed their world.* New York: Farrar, Straus & Giroux.

Edwards, B. (1999). *My brother Sammy.* Minneapolis, MN: Millbrook Press.

Egan, T. (2000). *The drover boy.* Melbourne, Australia: Lothian.

Erdrick, L. (2003). *Sacagawea.* Minneapolis, MN: Carolrhoda Books.

Eubank, P. R. (2002). *Seaman's journal: On the trail with Lewis and Clark.* Nashville, TN: Ideals Children's Books.

Faulkner, M. (2008). *A taste of colored water.* New York: Simon & Schuster Children's.

Fisher, L. E. (1995a). *Ghandi.* New York: Atheneum Books for Young Readers.

Fisher, L. E. (1995b). *The great wall of China.* New York: Aladdin.

Fleischman, P. (2013). *The matchbox diaries.* Somerville, MA: Candlewick Press.

Fox, M. (1992). *Wilfred Gordon McDonald Partridge.* New York: Puffin.

Fraser, M. A. (1996). *Ten mile day: And the building of the continental railroad.* New York: Square Fish.

Fraustino, L. R. (2001). *The hickory chair.* New York: Levine Books.

Freidrich, E. (1999). *Leah's pony.* Honesdale, PA: Boyds Mills Press.

Garland, S. (1994). *I never knew your name.* New York: HMH Books for Young Readers.

Gerstein, M. (2007). *The man who walked between the towers.* New York: Square Fish.

Gibbons, G. (1986). *Up goes the skyscraper!* New York: Atheneum Books for Young Readers.

Gill, S. (2002). *The big buck adventure.* Watertown, MA: Charlesbridge.

Giovanni, N. (2007). *Rosa.* New York: Square Fish.

Glaser, L. (2013). *Emma's poem.* New York: HMH Books for Young Readers.

Goble, P. (1993). *Death of the iron horse.* New York: Aladdin.

Golenbeck, P. (1992). *Teammates.* New York: HMH Books for Young Readers.

Granfield, L. (2005). *Where poppies grow: A World War I companion.* Markham, Canada: Fitzhenry & Whiteside.

Harris, R. (1997). *Who taught you about money?* Newburyport, MA: Hampton Roads.

Hathorn, L. (2003). *Way home.* London: Andersen Press.

Hausfater, R. (2006). *The little boy star: An allegory of the Holocaust.* New York: Milk & Cookies Press.

Hazen, B. S. (1983). *Tight times.* New York: Puffin.

Heide, F. P., & Gilliland, J. H. (1995). *Sami and the time of the troubles.* New York: HMH Books for Young Readers.

Hest, K. (2003). *When Jessie came across the sea.* Somerville, MA: Candlewick Press.

Hoffman, M. (1998). *Amazing Grace.* New York: Dramatic.

Holman, S. L. (1998). *Grandpa, is everything black bad?* Davis, CA: Culture Co-Op.

Holman, S. L. (2002). *We all have a heritage.* Davis, CA: Culture Co-Op.

Homan, L. (2002). *The Tuskegge airmen story.* Gretna, LA: Pelican.

Hopkinson, D. (2002). *A band of angels.* New York: Aladdin.

Hopkinson, D. (2006). *Girl wonder.* New York: Aladdin.

Hopkinson, D. (2012). *Sky boys: How they built the Empire State Building.* New York: Dragonfly Books.

Igus, T. (2001). *Two Mrs. Gibsons.* New York: Children's Book Press.

Isadora, R. (1984). *Max.* New York: Aladdin.

Jacobs, W. J. (1990). *Ellis Island: New hope in a new land.* New York: Atheneum Books for Young Readers.

Johnson, A. (2001). *Those building men.* New York: Blue Sky Press.

Johnson, A. (2007). *Wind flyers.* New York: Simon & Schuster Children's.

Johnson, D. B. (2003). *Henry climbs a mountain.* New York: HMH Books for Young Readers.

Johnston, T. (2011). *Levi Strauss gets a bright idea: A fairly fabricated story of a pair of pants.* New York: HMH Books for Young Readers.

Jones, C. (1997) *Daffy duck for president.* Burbank, CA: Warner Bros. Worldwide.

Jukes, M. (2005). *Like Jake and me.* New York: Yearling.

Juster, N. (2005). *The hello-goodbye window.* New York: Hyperion.

Kalman, M. (2014). *Thomas Jefferson: Life, liberty and the pursuit of everything.* New York: Paulsen Books.

Kamkwamba, W., & Mealer, B. (2010). *The boy who harnessed the wind.* New York: Morrow.

Kay, V. (2003). *The orphan train.* New York: Putnam Juvenile.

Kay, V. (2007). *Rough, tough Charley.* Berkeley, CA: Tricycle Press.

Kay, V. (2012). *Civil War drummer boy.* New York: Putnam Juvenile.

King, M. L. (2012). *I have a dream.* New York: Schwartz & Wade.

Knight, M. B. (1995). *Talking walls.* Gardiner, ME: Tilbury House.

Kroll, S. (1996). *Pony Express!* New York: Scholastic.

Kroll, S. (1999). *Robert Fulton: From submarine to steamboat.* New York: Holiday House.

Kroll, S. (2000). *The Boston tea party.* New York: Holiday House.

Kroll, V. (1997). *Masai and I.* New York: Aladdin.

Krull, K. (2000). *Wilma unlimited.* New York: HMH Books for Young Readers.

Krull, K. (2003). *Harvesting hope.* New York: HMH Books for Young Readers.

Laminack, L. (1998). *The sunsets of Miss Oliva Wiggins*. Atlanta, GA: Peachtree.

Lang, H. (2012). *Queen of the track: Alice Coachmen, Olympic high-jump champion*. Honesdale, PA: Boyds Mills Press.

Lanthier, J. (2012). *The stamp collector*. Markham, Canada: Fitzhenry & Whiteside.

Lasky, K. (2003). *The man who made time travel*. New York: Farrar, Straus & Giroux.

Lee, M. (2006). *Landed*. New York: Farrar, Straus & Giroux.

Lee-Tai, A. (2006). *A place where sunflowers grow*. San Francisco: Children's Book Press.

Lewin, T. (1993). *Amazon boy*. New York: Simon & Schuster Children's.

Lewin, T. (1995). *Sacred river*. New York: HMH Books for Young Readers.

Lewin, T. (2001). *Red legs: A drummer boy of the Civil War*. New York: HarperCollins.

Lewis, T. (2003). *My piggy bank*. Chelsea, MI: Sleeping Bear Press.

Lincoln, A. (1998). *The emancipation proclamation*. Bedford, MA: Applewood Books.

Lindsey, K. D. (2008). *Sweet potato pie*. New York: Lee & Low Books.

Lipp, F. (2001). *The caged birds of Phnom Penh*. New York: Holiday House.

Littlesugar, A. (2001). *Freedom school, yes!* New York: Philomel.

Lofthouse, L. (2007). *Ziba came on a boat*. La Jolla, CA: Kane/Miller.

Lorbiecki, M. (1996). *Just one flick of a finger*. New York: Dial.

Lorbiecki, M. (2000). *Sister Anne's hands*. New York: Puffin.

Lumpkin, B. (1991). *Senefer: A young genius in old Egypt*. Trenton, NJ: Africa World Press.

Lyon, G. L. (1996a). *Dreamplace*. New York: Scholastic.

Lyon, G. L. (1996b). *Who came down that road?* New York: Orchard Books.

Maestro, B. (1989). *The story of the statue of liberty*. New York: HarperCollins.

Maestro, B. (1996). *Coming to America*. New York: Scholastic.

Malone, P. (2007). *Close to the wind: The Beauport scale*. New York: Putnam Juvenile.

Markel, M. (2013). *Brave girl: Clara and the shirtwaist makers' strike of 1909*. New York: Balzer & Bray.

Markle, S. (2009). *Animals Charles Darwin saw*. San Francisco: Chronicle Books.

Markle, S. (2009). *Animals Marco Polo saw*. San Francisco: Chronicle Books.

Marsden, J. (2008). *Home and away*. Melbourne, Australia: Lothian Books.

Mason, M. H. (2011). *These hands*. New York: HMH Books for Young Readers.

McGill, A. (2009). *Molly Bannaky*. New York: HMH Books for Young Readers.

McKay, L., Jr. (1998). *Journey home*. New York: Lee & Low Books.

McKee, D. (2005). *The conquerors*. London: Andersen Press.

Mellage, N. (2001). *Coming home*. New York: Scholastic.

Merrill, J. (1992). *The girl who loved caterpillars*. New York: Philomel.

Michelson, R. (2006). *Across the alley*. New York: Putnam Juvenile.

Miller, M. L. (1994). *Those bottles!* New York: Putnam Juvenile.

Milway, K. S. (2008). *One hen: How one small loan made a big difference*. Tonawanda, NY: Kids Can Press.

Mitchell, M. K. (1998). *Granddaddy's gift*. Mahwah, NJ: Troll Communications.

Mitchell, M. K. (1998). *Uncle Jed's barbershop*. New York: Aladdin.

Mitchell, P. (2005). *Petar's song*. London: Lincoln Children's Books.

Mitchell, R. P. (2013). *Hue boy*. London: Lincoln Children's Books.

Mochizuki, K. (1995). *Baseball saved us*. New York: Lee & Low Books.

Mochizuki, K. (1997). *Heroes*. New York: Lee & Low Books.

Mochizuki, K. (2003). *Passage to freedom: The Sugihara story*. New York: Perfection Learning.

Moss, M. (2000). *Amelia works it out*. Middletown, WI: American Girl.

Moss, M. (2001). *Brave Harriett*. New York: HMH Books for Young Readers.

Moss, M. (2004). *Mighty Jackie*. New York: Simon & Schuster Children's.

Moss, M. (2009). *Sky high: The true story of Maggie Gee*. Berkeley, CA: Tricycle Press.

Moss, M. (2011). *Nurse, soldier, spy: The story of Sarah Edmonds, a Civil War hero*. New York: Abrams.

Myers, W. D. (1996). *Toussaint l'ouverture: The fight for Haiti's freedom*. New York: Simon & Schuster Children's.

Nagel, K. B. (1996). *The lunch line*. New York: Scholastic.

Nelson, K. (2008). *We are the ship: The story of the baseball*. New York: Jump at the Sun.

Nelson, K. (2013). *Nelson Mandela*. New York: Tegen Books.

Noble, T. H. (2006). *The last brother: A Civil War tale*. Chelsea, MI: Sleeping Bear Press.

O'Brien, P. (2005). *The great ships*. New York: Walker Childrens.

O'Brien, P. (2007). *Duel of the ironclads: The* Monitor *vs. the* Virginia. New York: Walker Childrens.

Olson, N. (2006). *Levi Strauss and blue jeans*. North Mankato, MN: Graphic Library.

Peacock, L. (2007). *At Ellis Island: A history of many voices*. New York: Atheneum Books for Young Readers.

Perez, L. K. (2002). *First day in grapes*. New York: Lee & Low Books.

Pinkney, A. D. (1998). *Dear Benjamin Banneker*. New York: HMH Books for Young Readers.

Pinkney, A. D. (2003). *Fishing day*. New York: Jump at the Sun.

Pinkwater, D. M. (1993). *The big orange splot*. New York: Scholastic.

Polacco, P. (2009). *The butterfly*. New York: Puffin.

Ramsey, C. A., & Stoud, B. (2011). *Belle, the last mule at Gees Bend: A civil rights story*. Somerville, MA: Candlewick Press.

Rappaport, D. (1990). *The Boston coffee party*. New York: HarperCollins.

Rappaport, D. (2000). *Dirt on their skirts: The story of the young women who won the world championship*. New York: Dial.

Raven, M. T. (1997). *Angels in the dust*. Mahwah, NJ: Troll Communications.

Raven, M. T. (2005a). *America's white table*. Chelsea, MI: Sleeping Bear Press.

Raven, M. T. (2005b). *Let them play*. Chelsea, MI: Sleeping Bear Press.

Raven, M. T. (2007). *Circle unbroken*. New York: Square Fish.

Reynolds, J. (2009). *Cycle of rice, cycle of life: A story of sustainable farming*. New York: Lee & Low Books.

Ringgold, F. (2003). *If a bus could talk: The story of Rosa Parks*. New York: Aladdin.

Ritter, L. (1995). *Leagues apart: The men and times of the negro baseball league*. Darby, PA: Diane.

Robinson, S. (2009). *Testing the ice*. New York: Scholastic.

Rockwell, A. (2006). *They called her Molly Pitcher*. New York: Dragonfly Books.

Rodriguez, L. J. (2004). *It doesn't have to be this way*. New York: Lee & Low Books.

Rosenberg, L. (1999). *The silence in the mountains*. New York: Orchard Books.

Rosenstock, B. (2013). *Thomas Jefferson builds a library*. Honesdale, PA: Calkins Creek.

Sakai, K. (1997). *Sachiko means happiness*. New York: Children's Book Press.

Santiago, C. (1998). *Home to Medicine Mountain*. San Francisco: Children's Books Press.

Say, A. (2002). *Home of the brave*. New York: HMH Books for Young Readers.

Say, A. (2004). *Music for Alice*. New York: HMH Books for Young Readers.

Say, A. (2008). *Grandfather's journey*. New York: HMH Books for Young Readers.

Say, A. (2009). *Tea with milk*. New York: Orchard Books.

Schanzer, R. (2002). *How we crossed the west: The adventures of Lewis and Clark*. Washington, DC: National Geographic Children's Books.

Schmandt-Besserat, D. (1999). *The history of counting*. New York: HarperCollins.

Sendak, M. (1993). *We are all in the dumps with Jack and Guy: Two nursery rhymes with pictures*. New York: HarperCollins.

Seymour, T. (1998). *We played marbles*. New York: Orchard Books.

Seymour, T. (2005). *Auction!* Somerville, MA: Candlewick Press.

Shea, P. D. (1995). *The whispering cloth: A refugee's story*. Honesdale, PA: Boyds Mills Press.

Sherman, P. (2009). *Ben and the emancipation proclamation*. Grand Rapids, MI: Eerdmans Books for Young Readers.

Shriver, M. (2001). *What's wrong with Timmy?* New York: Little, Brown Books for Young Readers.

Silverman, E. (2011). *Liberty's voice: The Emma Lazarus story*. New York: Dutton Juvenile.

Sis, P. (1998). *Tibet: Through the red box*. New York: Farrar, Straus & Giroux.

Skarmeta, A. (2003). *The composition*. Toronto, Canada: Groundwood Books.

Smith, C. R., Jr. (2012). *Brick by brick*. New York: Amistad.

Smith, L. (2011). *Grandpa Green*. New Milford, CT: Roaring Brook Press.

Steenwyk, E. V. (2000). *My name is York*. Flagstaff, AZ: Cooper Square.

Stone, T. L. (2010). *Elizabeth leads the way*. New York: Square Fish.

Tan, S. (2007) *The arrival*. New York: Levine Books.

Turner, A. W. (1998). *Drummer boy: Marching to the Civil War*. New York: HarperCollins.

Uchida, Y. (1996). *The bracelet*. New York: Puffin.

Vaughn, M. (2009). *Up the learning tree*. New York: Lee & Low Books.

Viorst, J. (1978) *Alexander, who used to be rich last Sunday*. New York: Aladdin.

Walsh, B. (2012). *The poppy lady: Moina Belle Michael and her tribute to veterans*. Honesdale, PA: Calkins Creek.

Walter, P. (2005). *Alec's primer*. Lebanon, NH: Vermont Folklife Center.

Warren, S. (2012). *Dolores Huerta: A hero to migrant workers*. New York: Two Lions.

Watkins, A. F. (2010). *My Uncle Martin's big heart*. New York: Abrams Books for Young Readers.

Watson, R. (2012). *Harlem's little blackbird*. New York: Random House.

Weatherford, C. B. (2007). *Freedom on the menu*. New York: Puffin.

Wells, R. (2002). *Wingwalker*. New York: Disney-Hyperion.

Whelan, G. (2011). *Megan's year: An Irish traveler's story*. Chelsea, MI: Sleeping Bear Press.

Wild, M. (2007). *Woolvs in the sitee*. Honesdale, PA: Boyds Mills Press.

Wiles, D. (2005). *Freedom summer*. New York: Aladdin.

Williams, K. L. (2007). *Two sandals, four feet*. Cambridge, UK: Eerdmans.

Williams, V. B. (2007). *A chair for my mother*. New York: Greenwillow Books.

Winter, J. (2009). *Nasreen's secret school: A true story from Afghanistan*. New York: Beach Lane Books.

Wiviott, M. (2010). *Benno and the night of broken glass*. Minneapolis, MN: Kar-Ben.

Woodruff, E. (1999). *A memory coat*. New York: Scholastic.

Woodruff, E. (2014). *Small beauties*. New York: Knopf Books for Young Readers.

Woodson, J. (2001). *The other side*. New York: Putnam Juvenile.

Woodson, J. (2001). *Each kindness*. New York: Paulsen Books.

Yaccarino, D. (2011). *All the way to America*. New York: Knopf Books for Young Readers.

Yang, B. (2004). *Hannah is my name*. Somerville, MA: Candlewick Press.

Yashima, T. (1976). *The crow boy*. New York: Puffin.

Yim, S. (2002). *Ruby's wish*. San Francisco: Chronicle Books.

Yin. (2003). *Coolies*. New York: Puffin.

Yolen, J. (1996). *Encounter*. New York: HMH Books for Young Readers.

Yolen, J. (2008). *Naming liberty*. New York: Philomel.

Yoo, P. (2010). *Sixteen years in sixteen seconds: The Sammy Lee story*. New York: Lee & Low Books.

Zee, R. V. (2008). *Always with you*. Grand Rapids, MI: Eerdmans Books for Young Readers.

Zimelman, N. (1992). *How the second grade got $8,205.50 to visit the Statue of Liberty*. Morton Grove, IN: Whitman.

Zimelman, N. (2000). *Sold! A mathematics adventure*. Watertown, MA: Charlesbridge.

Zolotow, C. (1985). *William's doll*. New York: Harper & Row.

Part Five: Paired Text in Science

Adkins, J. (2004). *Moving heavy things*. Brooklyn, MA: Wooden Boat.

Allen, N. K. (2004). *Whose sound is this?* New York: Nonfiction Picture Books.

Allen, P. (1994). *Mr. Archimedes' bath*. New York: Puffin.

Allen, P. (1996). *Who sank the boat?* New York: Puffin.

Allsburg, C. V. (2011). *Just a dream*. New York: HMH Books for Young Readers.

Anno, M. (1990). *Anno's medieval world*. New York: Philomel.

Anthony, J. P., & Arbo, C. (1997). *The dandelion seed*. Nevada City, CA: Dawn.

Arnold, C. (2012). *A warmer world*. Watertown, MA: Charlesbridge.

Arnosky, J. (2000). *I see animals hiding*. New York: Scholastic.

Aston, D. H. (2006). *An egg is quiet*. San Francisco: Chronicle Books.

Aston, D. H. (2007). *Loony little*. Somerville, MA: Candlewick Press.

Back, C., & Olesen, J. (1992). *Chicken and egg*. London: Black.

Bailey, J. (2001). *The birth of the earth*. Tonawanda, NY: Kids Can Press.

Bailey, J. (2006). *The rock factory*. North Mankato, MN: Picture Window Books.

Baker, J. (2000). *Rosy dock*. New York: Greenwillow Books.

Baker, J. (2003). *The hidden forest*. New York: Greenwillow Books.

Balkwill, F. (1992). *Cell wars*. Minneapolis, MN: Carolrhoda Books.

Balkwill, F. (1993a). *Amazing schemes within your genes*. Minneapolis, MN: First Avenue Editions.

Balkwill, F. (1993b). *Cell are us*. Minneapolis, MN: Carolrhoda Books.

Balkwill, F. (1993c). *DNA is here to stay*. Minneapolis, MN: Carolrhoda Books.

Bang, M. (1997). *Common ground: The water, earth, and air we share*. New York: Blue Sky Press.

Bang, M. (2004). *My light*. New York: Blue Sky Press.

Bang, M. (2009). *Living sunlight*. New York: Blue Sky Press.

Bang, M., & Chisholm, P. (2012). *Ocean sunlight: How tiny plants feed the seas*. New York: Blue Sky Press.

Bardoe, C. (2006). *Gregor Mendel: The friar who grew peas*. New York: Abrams.

Base, G. (1996). *Discovery of dragons*. New York: Abrams.

Base, G. (2001). *The water hole*. New York: Abrams.

Base, G. (2006). *Uno's garden.* New York: Abrams.

Bash, B. (2002). *Desert giant.* San Francisco: Sierra Club Books for Children.

Batten, M. (2002). *Hey, daddy!* Atlanta, GA: Peachtree.

Batten, M. (2008). *Aliens from earth: When animals and plants invade other ecosystems.* Atlanta: Peachtree.

Bauer, M. D. (2005). *If frogs made weather.* New York: Holiday House.

Bender, L. (1989). *Atoms and cells.* New York: Scholastic.

Berkes, M. (2010). *Going home: The mystery of animal migration.* Nevada City, CA: Dawn.

Berne, J. (2008). *Manfish: A story of Jacques Cousteau.* San Francisco: Chronicle Books.

Berne, J. (2013). *On a beam of light: A story of Albert Einstein.* San Francisco: Chronicle Books.

Bond, R. (2009). *In the belly of an ox: The unexpected photographic adventures of Richard and Cherry Kearton.* New York: HMH Books for Young Readers.

Bradley, K. B. (2005). *Forces make things move.* New York: HarperCollins.

Brenner, B. (2004). *One small place by the sea.* New York: HarperCollins.

Brighton, C. (2007). *The fossil girl: Mary Anning's dinosaur discovery.* London: Lincoln Children's Books.

Brighton, C. (2009). *Galileo's treasure box.* New York: Walker.

Brown, D. (2003). *Uncommon traveler: Mary Kingsley in Africa.* New York: HMH Books for Young Readers.

Brown, D. (2008). *Odd boy out: Young Albert Einstein.* New York: HMH Books for Young Readers.

Brown, S. G. (2003). *The crow and the pitcher.* Berkeley, CA: Tricycle Press.

Bunting, E. (2003). *Whales passing.* New York: Blue Sky Press.

Bunting, E. (2004). *Ducky.* New York: HMH Books for Young Readers.

Burleigh, R. (2013). *Look up!* New York: Simon & Schuster Children's.

Carle, E. (1997). *Little cloud.* New York: Philomel.

Carle, E. (2011). *Mister seahorse.* New York: Philomel.

Christian, P. (2008). *If you find a rock.* New York: HMH Books for Young Readers.

Chrustowski, R. (2008). *Big brown bat.* New York: Holt.

Clement, R. (1999). *Counting on Frank.* New York: Stevens.

Cobb, V. (2003). *I face the wind.* New York: HarperCollins.

Cole, H. (1997). *Jack's garden.* New York: Greenwillow Books.

Collard, S. B., III. (2000). *Animal dads.* New York: HMH Books for Young Readers.

Collard, S. B., III. (2002). *Beaks!* Watertown, MA: Charlesbridge.

Collard, S. B., III. (2003). *The deep-sea floor.* Watertown, MA: Charlesbridge.

Cowcher, H. (1997). *Rainforest.* Chicago: Milet.

Cowcher, H. (2009). *Antarctica.* New York: Square Fish.

Cox, P. R. (1993). *Atoms and molecules.* Tulsa, OK: E.D.C.

Crew, G. (1997). *Bright star.* La Jolla, CA: Kane/Miller.

Crew, G. (2008). *Cat on the island.* New York: HarperCollins.

Crew, G., & Wilson, M. (2003a). *I said nothing.* Melbourne, Australia: Lothian Books.

Crew, G., & Wilson, M. (2003b). *I saw nothing.* Melbourne, Australia: Lothian Books.

Crump, M. (2013). *The mystery of Darwin's frog.* Honesdale, PA: Boyds Mills Press.

Davies, J. (2004). *The boy who drew birds: The story of John James Audubon.* New York: HMH Books for Young Readers.

DeCristofano, C. C. (2005). *Big bang!: The tongue tickling tale of a speck that became spectacular.* Watertown, MA: Charlesbridge.

dePaola, T. (1984). *The cloud book*. New York: Holiday House.

Drummond, A. (2011). *Energy island: How one community harnessed the world and changed their world*. New York: Farrar, Straus & Giroux.

Ehlert, L. (1991). *Red leaf, yellow leaf*. New York: HMH Books for Young Readers.

Ehlert, L. (2005). *Leaf man*. New York: Harcourt.

Ehrlich, A. (2008). *Rachel: The story of Rachel Carson*. New York: HMH Books for Young Readers.

Einspruch, A. (2012). *DNA detectives*. New York: Powerkids Press.

Ewart, C. (2014). *Fossil*. New York: Walker Childrens.

Fleischman, P. (2002). *Weslandia*. Somerville, MA: Candlewick Press.

Fleming, D. (1998). *In the small, small pond*. New York: Holt.

Fox, M. (2005). *Hunwick's egg*. New York: HMH Books for Young Readers.

Fradin, D. B. (2004). *Nicolaus Copernicus: The earth is a planet*. New York: Mondo.

Frasier, D. (2004). *The incredible water show*. New York: HMH Books for Young Readers.

Fredericks, A. D. (2001). *Under one rock*. Nevada City, CA: Dawn.

Fredericks, A. D. (2002). *In one tidepool*. Nevada City, CA: Dawn.

Fredericks, A. D. (2003). *Around one cactus*. Nevada City, CA: Dawn.

Fredericks, A. D. (2005). *Near one cattail*. Nevada City, CA: Dawn.

Galliez, R. M. (2009). *The earth has caught a cold*. Mount Morris, MI: Hammond.

Gans, R. (1997). *Let's go rock collecting*. New York: HarperCollins.

George, T. C. (2005). *Seahorses*. Minneapolis, MN: Millbrook Press.

Gibbons, A. (2011). *Charles Darwin*. New York: Kingfisher.

Gibbons, G. (1988). *The seasons of Arnold's apple tree*. New York: HMH Books for Young Readers.

Gibbons, G. (1993). *From seed to plant*. New York: Holiday House.

Gibbons, G. (1998a). *The moon book*. New York: Holiday House.

Gibbons, G. (1998b). *Sea turtles*. New York: Holiday House.

Gibbons, G. (2000a). *Bats*. New York: Holiday House.

Gibbons, G. (2000b). *The honey makers*. New York: HarperCollins.

Godkin, C. (2005). *When the giant stirred*. Markham, Canada: Fitzhenry & Whiteside.

Graber, M. (1994). *A raindrop's journey*. Mankato, MN: Creative Advantages.

Gravett, E. (2006). *Wolves*. New York: Simon & Schuster Children's.

Greene, J., & Gordon, M. (2005). *Why should I save energy?* Hauppauge, NY: Barron's Educational Series.

Guiberson, B. Z. (2000). *Into the sea*. New York: Square Fish.

Hannah, J., & Holub, J. (2006). *The man who named the clouds*. Morton Grove, IN: Whitman.

Heller, R. (1999). *Chickens aren't the only ones*. New York: Puffin.

Heller, R. (2000). *A sea within a sea*. New York: Grosset & Dunlap.

Herskowitz, J. (1993). *Double talking helix blues*. Cold Spring Harbor, NY: Cold Spring Harbor Laboratory Press.

Hewitt, S. (2000). *Forces around us*. Danbury, CT: Watts.

Hooper, M. (2004). *The island that moved: How shifting forces shape our earth*. New York: Viking Juvenile.

Hooper, M. (2012). *The drop in my drink*. New York: Lincoln Children's Books.

Hopkinson, D. (2007). *Maria's comet*. Westport, CT: Libraries Unlimited.

Hopkinson, D. (2010). *The humblebee hunter*. New York: Hyperion.

Hosler, J. (2011). *Evolution: The story of how life developed on earth.* New York: Hill and Wang.

Jenkins, S. (2001a). *Slap, squeak, and scatter.* New York: HMH Books for Young Readers.

Jenkins, S. (2001b). *What do you do when something wants to eat you?* New York: HMH Books for Young Readers.

Jenkins, S. (2002). *Life on earth: The story of evolution.* New York: HMH Books for Young Readers.

Jenkins, S. (2005). *Prehistoric actual size.* New York: HMH Books for Young Readers.

Jenkins, S. (2008). *What do you do with a tail like this?* New York: HMH Books for Young Readers.

Jenkins, S. (2009). *Never smile at a monkey.* New York: HMH Books for Young Readers.

Jenkins, S. (2012). *Living color.* New York: HMH Books for Young Readers.

Kajiikawa, K. (2009). *Tsunami!* New York: Philomel.

Kalman, B., & Langille, J. (1998). *What are food chains and webs?* New York: Crabtree.

Kamkwamba, W., & Mealer, B. (2012). *The boy who harnessed the wind.* New York: Dial.

Kaner, E. (1999). *Animal defenses: How animals protect themselves.* Tonawanda, NY: Kids Can Press.

Kerley, B. (2001). *The dinosaurs of Waterhouse Hawkins.* New York: Scholastic.

Kramer, S. P. (1995). *Theodoric's rainbow.* New York: Freeman.

Kudlinski, K. V. (2008). *Boy, were we wrong about dinosaurs!* New York: HMH Books for Young Readers.

Lasky, K. (1997). *Pond year.* Somerville, MA: Candlewick Press.

Lasky, K. (2006). *Interrupted journey.* Somerville, MA: Candlewick Press.

Lasky, K. (2008). *John Muir: American's first environmentalist.* Somerville, MA: Candlewick Press.

Latta, S. L. (2006). *Stella Brite and the dark matter mystery.* Watertown, MA: Charlesbridge.

Laubach, C. M., Laubach, R., & Smith, C. W. G. (2002). *Raptor!: A kid's guide to birds of prey.* North Adams, MA: Storey.

Lauber, P. (1994). *Who eats what?: Food chains and food webs.* New York: HarperCollins.

Lawlor, L. (2012). *Rachel Carson and her book that changed the world.* New York: Holiday House.

Lee, S. (2008). *Wave.* San Francisco: Chronicle Books.

Leedy, L. (2011). *The shocking truth about energy.* New York: Holiday House.

Lerner, C. (1998). *My backyard garden.* New York: HarperCollins.

Levenson, G. (2002). *Pumpkin circle.* Berkeley, CA: Tricycle Press.

Lewis, J. P. (2003). *Swan song.* Mankato, MN: Creative Editions.

Lewis, O. P. (2003). *The jupiter stone.* Berkeley, CA: Tricycle Press.

Lindsey, D. (2012). *Edge of the pond: Selected haiku and tanka of Darrell Lindsey.* Seattle, WA: CreateSpace.

Locker, T. (2001). *Mountain dance.* New York: HMH Books for Young Readers.

Locker, T. (2002). *Water dance.* New York: HMH Books for Young Readers.

Locker, T. (2003). *Cloud dance.* New York: HMH Books for Young Readers.

Lyons, D. (2002). *The tree.* Bellevue, WA: Illumination Arts.

Macaulay, D. (1988). *The new way things work.* New York: Lorraine Books.

Maestro, B. (2000). *How do apples grow?* New York: HMH Books for Young Readers.

Markle, S. (2005). *Vultures.* Minneapolis, MN: Lerner.

Markle, S. (2009). *Animals Charles Darwin saw.* San Francisco: Chronicle Books.

Markle, S. (2010). *Hip-pocket papa*. Watertown, MA: Charlesbridge.

Markle, S. (2013). *Bats: Biggest! Littlest!* Honesdale, PA: Boyds Mills Press.

Martin, J. B. (2009). *Snowflake Bentley*. New York: HMH Books for Young Readers.

Mazer, A. (1994). *The salamander room*. New York: Dragonfly Books.

McDonnell, P. (2011). *Me . . Jane*. New York: Little, Brown Books for Young Readers.

McFarlane, S. (2002). *Waiting for the whales*. Custer, WA: Orca.

McKinney, B. S. (1998). *A drop around the world*. Nevada City, CA: Dawn.

McLimans, D. (2006). *Gone wild: An endangered animal alphabet*. New York: Walker Books.

McNamara, M. (2007). *How many seeds in a pumpkin?* New York: Schwartz & Wade.

Merski, P. K. (2004). *Roaring, boring Alice: A story of the Aurora Borealis*. Erie, PA: Skeezel Press.

Miller, D. S. (2007). *Arctic lights, arctic nights*. New York: Walker Childrens.

Morgan, J. (2006). *Mammals who morph: The universe tells our evolution story*. Nevada City, CA: Dawn.

Mortensen, L. (2009). *In the trees, honey bees*. Nevada City, CA: Dawn.

Mortensen, L. (2010). *Come see the earth turn: The story of Leon Foucault*. Berkeley, CA: Tricycle Press.

Nivola, C. A. (2012). *Life in the ocean: The story of oceanographer Sylvia Earle*. New York: Farrar, Straus & Giroux.

Olson, G. M. (1987). *Phases of the moon*. New York: HarperCollins.

Pallotta, J. (2006). *Dory story*. Watertown, MA: Charlesbridge.

Peddicord, J. A. (2005). *Night wonders*. Watertown, MA: Charlesbridge.

Penn, A. (1993). *The kissing hand*. Terre Haute, IN: Tanglewood Press.

Peters, L. W. (2010). *Volcano wakes up!* New York: Holt.

Peters, L. W., & Stringer, L. (2003). *Our family tree: An evolution story*. New York: HMH Books for Young Readers.

Pettenati, J. (2006). *Galileo's journal, 1609–1610*. Watertown, MA: Charlesbridge.

Pfeffer, W. (2003). *The shortest day: Celebrating the winter solstice*. New York: Dutton Juvenile.

Pinczes, E. J. (1998). *Arctic fives arrive*. New York: Scholastic.

Pratt-Serafini, K. J. (2008). *The forest forever*. Nevada City, CA: Dawn.

Pratt-Serafini, K. J. (2001). *Salamander rain: A lake and pond journal*. Nevada City, CA: Dawn.

Prelutsky, J. (1998). *The dragons are singing tonight*. New York: Greenwillow Books.

Rau, D. M. (2005). *Fluffy, flat, and wet: A book about clouds*. New York: Nonfiction Picture Books.

Robertson, M. P. (2010). *Food chain*. London: Lincoln Children's Books.

Rocco, J. (2011). *Blackout*. New York: Disney-Hyperion.

Rosinsky, N. M. (2002). *Rocks: hard, soft, smooth, and rough*. New York: Nonfiction Picture Books.

Ross, M. E. (2007). *What's the matter in Mr. Whiskers' room?* Somerville, MA: Candlewick Press.

Rowan, P. (1998). *Big head!: A book about your brain and your head*. New York: Knopf Books for Young Readers.

Ruiz, A. L. (1997). *The life of a cell*. New York: Sterling.

Sayre, A. P. (1998). *Home at last: A song of migration*. New York: Holt.

Sayre, A. P. (2007). *Vulture view*. New York: Holt.

Seeger, L. V. (2011). *First the egg.* Shijiazhuang, China: He Bei Jiao Yu Chu Ban She/Tsai Fong Books.

Shaw, B. M. (2000). *Pass the energy, please!* Nevada City, CA: Dawn.

Sheldon, D. (2009). *Into the deep: The life of naturalist and explorer William Beebe.* Watertown, MA: Charlesbridge.

Showers, P. (2000). *Hear your heart.* New York: HarperCollins.

Shuett, S. (1997). *Somewhere in the world right now.* New York: Dragonfly Books.

Sidman, J. (2000). *Just us two: Poems about animal dads.* Minneapolis, MN: Millbrook Press.

Sidman, J. (2005). *Song of the water boatmen and other pond poems.* New York: HMH Books for Young Readers.

Sidman, J. (2006). *Butterfly eyes and other secrets of the meadow.* New York: HMH Books for Young Readers.

Simon, S. (1997). *Mountains.* New York: HarperCollins.

Simon, S. (2000a). *Bones: Our skeletal system.* New York: HarperCollins.

Simon, S. (2000b). *Muscles: Our muscular system.* New York: HarperCollins.

Simon, S. (2006a). *The brain: Our nervous system.* New York: HarperCollins.

Simon, S. (2006b). *The heart: Our circulatory system.* New York: HarperCollins.

Simon, S. (2009). *Wolves.* New York: HarperCollins.

Singer, M. (2001). *On the same day in March.* New York: Harper Festival.

Sis, P. (1993). *Komodo!* New York: Greenwillow Books.

Sis, P. (2000). *Starry messenger.* New York: Square Fish.

Sis, P. (2003). *The tree of life.* New York: Farrar, Straus & Giroux.

Skurzynski, G. (2000). *On time: From seasons to split seconds.* Washington, DC: National Geographic Children's Books.

Snedden, R. (2007). *DNA and genetic engineering.* Chicago: Heinemann.

Spickert, D. N. (2010). *Earthsteps: A rock's journey through time.* Golden, CO: Fulcrum.

Stille, D. R. (2004). *Matter: See it, touch it, taste it, smell it.* New York: National Picture Books.

Stockland, P. M. (2005). *Red eyes or blue feathers: A book about animals.* North Mankato, MN: Picture Window Books.

Swiatkowska, G. (2004). *Arrowhawk.* New York: Holt.

Swope, S. (2004). *Gotta go, gotta go.* New York: Square Fish.

Thomas, P. (2011). *For the birds: The life of Roger Tory Peterson.* Honesdale, PA: Calkins Creek.

van Frankenhuyzen, R. S. (2004). *Saving Samantha.* Chelsea, MI: Sleeping Bear Press.

Vieira, L. (1994). *The ever-living tree: The life and times of a coast redwood.* New York: Walker.

Walker, S. M. (2000). *Mary Anning: Fossil hunter.* New York: Scholastic.

Ward, J. (2005). *Forest bright.* Nevada City, CA: Dawn.

Weisner, D. (1999). *Sector 7.* New York: Clarion Books.

Weisner, J. (1995). *June 29, 1999.* New York: HMH Books for Young Readers.

Wells, R. E. (2002). *How do you know what time it is?* Morton Grove, IN: Whitman.

Wick, W. (1997). *A drop of water: A book of science and wonder.* New York: Scholastic.

Willis, J. (2008). *Daft bat.* New York: Sterling.

Willis, N. C. (2002). *Raccoon moon.* Middletown, DE: Birdsong Books.

Winter, J. (2011). *The watcher.* New York: Schwartz & Wade.

Wood, A. J., & Twist, C. (2009). *Charles Darwin and the beagle adventure*. Surrey, UK: Templar.

Yee, W. H. (2007). *Tracks in the snow*. New York: Square Fish.

Yolen, J. (2001). *Welcome to the river of grass*. New York: Putnam Juvenile.

Part Six: Paired Text in Mathematics

Aber, L. W. (2000). *Who's got spots?* New York: Kane Press.

Aber, L. W. (2001). *Carrie measures up*. New York: Kane Press.

Adler, D. A. (2000). *Shape up!* New York: Holiday House.

Adler, D. A. (2007). *You can, toucan, math*. New York: Holiday House.

Adler, D. A. (2012a). *Millions, billions, and trillions: Understanding big numbers*. New York: Holiday House.

Adler, D. A. (2012b). *Perimeter, area, and volume: A monster book of dimensions*. New York: Holiday House.

Adler, D. A. (2014). *Triangles*. New York: Holiday House.

Alda, A. (2004). *1 2 3: What do you see?* Berkeley, CA: Tricycle Press.

Allsburg, C. V. (2011). *Jumanji*. New York: HMH Books for Young Readers.

Anno, M. (1977). *Anno's counting book*. New York: Crowell.

Anno, M., & Anno, M. (1999). *Anno's mysterious multiplying jar*. New York: Philomel.

Bader, B. (2003). *Graphs*. New York: Grosset & Dunlap.

Bang, M. (2003). *Ten, nine, eight*. New York: Greenwillow Books.

Base, G. (2006). *Uno's garden*. New York: Abrams.

Berkes, M. (2006). *Over in the ocean in a coral reef*. Nevada City, CA: Dawn.

Birch, D. (1993). *The king's chessboard*. New York: Puffin.

Briggs, R. (1997). *Jim and the beanstalk*. New York: Puffin.

Bryant-Mole, K. (1995). *Fractions and decimals*. Tulsa, OK: E.D.C.

Burns, M. (2008a). *The greedy triangle*. New York: Scholastic.

Burns, M. (2008b). *Spaghetti and meatballs for all!* New York: Scholastic.

Calvert, P. (2006). *Multiplying menace: The revenge of Rumpelstiltskin*. Watertown, MA: Charlesbridge.

Calvert, P. (2011). *The multiplying menace divides*. Watertown, MA: Charlesbridge.

Campbell, S. C. (2010). *Growing numbers*. Honesdale, PA: Boyds Mills Press.

Carle, E. (1998). *1 2 3 to the zoo*. New York: Puffin.

Christaldi, K. (1996). *Even Steven and odd Todd*. New York: Cartwheel.

Cleary, B. P. (2007). *The mission of addition*. Minneapolis, MN: First Avenue Editions.

Cleary, B. P. (2008). *The action of subtraction*. Minneapolis, MN: First Avenue Editions.

Clements, A. (2006). *A million dots*. New York: Atheneum Books for Young Readers.

Cobb, A. (2000). *The long wait*. New York: Kane Press.

Cole, N. (1994). *Blast off!: A space counting book*. Watertown, MA: Charlesbridge.

Cotton, C. (2002). *At the edge of the woods*. New York: Holt.

Crew, G. (1995). *Gulliver in the south seas*. Melbourne, Australia: Lothian.

D'Agnese, J. (2010). *Blockhead: The life of Fibonacci*. New York: Holt.

Day, N. R. (2003). *Double those wheels*. New York: Dutton Children's Books.

Dee, R. (1988). *Two ways to count to ten*. New York: Holt.

Demi. (1997). *One grain of rice: A mathematical folklore*. New York: Scholastic.

Dodds, D. A. (2005). *The great divide*. Somerville, MA: Candlewick Press.

Dodds, D. A. (2009). *Full house: An invitation to fractions*. Somerville, MA: Candlewick Press.

Driscoll, L. (2003). *The blast-off kid*. New York: Kane Press.

Dussling, J. (2003). *Fair is fair*. New York: Kane Press.

Einhorn, E. (2008). *A very improbable story*. Watertown, MA: Charlesbridge.

Ekeland, I. (2006). *The cat in numberland*. Peru, IL: Cricket Books.

Ellis, J. (2004). *What's your angle, Pythagoras?* Watertown, MA: Charlesbridge.

Ellis, J. (2010). *Pythagoras and the ratios: A math adventure*. Watertown, MA: Charlesbridge.

Escher, M. C. (1992). *The pop-up book of M. C. Escher*. Petaluma, CA: Pomegranate.

Ewing, S. (2005). *Ten rowdy ravens*. Portland, OR: Alaska Northwest Books.

Falwell, C. (2003). *Feast for 10*. New York: HMH Books for Young Readers.

Felton, C., & Felton, A. (2003). *Where's Harley?* New York: Kane Press.

Fisher, D. (2007). *My even day*. Pleasant, SC: Sylvan Dell

Fox, M. (1996). *The straight line wonder*. New York: Mondo.

Franco, B. (2009). *Zero is the leaves on the tree*. Berkeley, CA: Tricycle Press.

Friedman, A. (1994a). *A cloak for the dreamer*. New York: Scholastic.

Friedman, A. (1994b). *The king's commissioners*. Chicago: Heinemann.

Friedman, M., & Weiss, E. (2001). *Kitten castle*. New York: Kane Press.

Fritz, J. (2001). *Leonardo's horse*. New York: Putnam Juvenile.

Gag, W. (2006). *Millions of cats*. New York: Puffin.

Gill, S. (2005). *Big blue*. Watertown, MA: Charlesbridge.

Glass, J. (1998). *A fly on the ceiling*. New York: Random House Books for Young Readers.

Goldstone, B. (2010). *Great estimations*. New York: Square Fish.

Goldstone, B. (2013). *That's a possibility*. New York: Holt.

Gravett, E. (2010). *The rabbit problem*. New York: Simon & Schuster Children's.

Grifalconi, A. (1986). *The village of round and square houses*. New York: Little, Brown Books for Young Readers.

Grossman, V. (1995). *Ten little rabbits*. San Francisco: Chronicle Books.

Grover, M. (1996). *Circles and squares everywhere!* New York: HMH Books for Young Readers.

Harris, T. (2008). *Splitting the herd: A corral of odds and evens*. Minneapolis, MN: Millbrook Press.

Heiligman, D. (2013). *The boy who loved math: The improbable life of Paul Erdos*. New York: Roaring Brook Press.

Herman, G. (2002). *Bad luck Brad*. New York: Kane Press.

Herman, G. (2006). *Keep your distance!* Minneapolis, MN: Lerner.

Hightower, S. (2001). *Twelve snails to one lizard*. New York: Simon & Schuster.

Holub, J. (2012). *Zero the hero*. New York: Holt.

Hong, L. T. (1993). *Two of everything*. Morton Grove, IN: Whitman.

Hosford, K. (2012). *Infinity and me*. Minneapolis, MN: Carolrhoda Books.

Hulme, J. N. (1996). *Sea sums*. New York: Disney-Hyperion.

Hulme, J. N. (1999). *Sea Squares*. New York: Hyperion.

Hulme, J. N. (2010). *Wild Fibonacci: Nature's best code revealed*. Berkeley, CA: Tricycle Press.

Hutchins, P. (1986a). *1 hunter*. New York: Greenwillow Books.

Hutchins, P. (1986b). *The doorbell rang*. New York: Scholastic.

Hutchins, P. (1987). *Changes, changes.* New York: Aladdin.

Jenkins, S. (1996). *Big and little.* New York: HMH Books for Young Readers.

Jenkins, S. (1997). *Biggest, strongest, fastest.* New York: HMH Books for Young Readers.

Johnson, D. B. (2010). *Palazzo inverso.* New York: HMH Books for Young Readers.

Johnson, S. J. (2003). *City by numbers.* New York: Puffin.

Juster, N. (2000). *The dot and the line: A romance in lower mathematics.* San Francisco: Chronicle Books.

Kassirer, S. (2005). *Math fair blues.* New York: Kane Press.

King, Z. (2004). *The story of our numbers.* New York: Rosen Classroom Books & Materials.

Kroll, V. (2005). *Equal shmequal: A math adventure.* Watertown, MA: Charlesbridge.

Leedy, L. (1996a). *2 × 2 = boo!: A set of spooky multiplication stories.* New York: Holiday House.

Leedy, L. (1996b). *Fraction action.* New York: Holiday House.

Leedy, L. (1999). *Mission: Addition.* New York: Holiday House.

Leedy, L. (2000). *Measuring penny.* New York: Square Fish.

Leedy, L. (2002). *Subtraction action.* New York: Holiday House.

Leedy, L. (2006). *The great graph contest.* New York: Holiday House.

Leedy, L. (2007). *It's probably penny.* New York: Holt.

Lewin, T. (2012). *Lost city: The discovery of Machu Picchu.* New York: Puffin.

Lewis, J. P. (2007). *Arithme-tickle: An even number of ddd riddle-rhymes.* New York: HMH Books for Young Readers.

Lionni, L. (1995). *Inch by inch.* New York: HarperCollins.

Long, E. (2014). *The Wing Wing brothers geometry palooza!* New York: Holiday House.

Long, L. (1998). *Dealing with addition.* Watertown, MA: Charlesbridge.

Loomis, C. (1994). *One cow coughs.* New York: HMH Books for Young Readers.

LoPresti, A. S. (2003). *A place for zero: A math adventure.* Watertown, MA: Charlesbridge.

Losi, C. A. (1997). *The 512 ants on Sullivan Street.* New York: Cartwheel.

Love, D. A. (2006). *Of numbers and stars: The story of Hypatia.* New York: Holiday House.

Maccarone, G. (1995). *Monster math.* New York: Scholastic.

Maccarone, G. (1998). *Three pigs, one wolf, and seven magic shapes.* New York: Cartwheel.

MacDonald, S. (1998). *Sea shapes.* New York: HMH Books for Young Readers.

Markel, M. (2009). *Tyrannosaurus math.* Berkeley, CA: Tricycle Press.

Markle, S. (2011). *Insects: Biggest! Littlest!* Honesdale, PA: Boyds Mills Press.

Matthews, L. (1990). *Bunches and bunches of bunnies.* New York: Scholastic.

Mazzola, F., Jr. (1997). *Counting is for the birds.* Watertown, MA: Charlesbridge.

McCallum, A. (2006). *Beanstalk: The measure of a giant.* Watertown, MA: Charlesbridge.

McCallum, A. (2007). *Rabbits, rabbits, everywhere.* Watertown, MA: Charlesbridge.

McElligott, M. (2007). *Bean thirteen.* New York: Putnam Juvenile.

McElligott, M. (2012). *The lion's share: A tale of halving cake and eating it, too.* New York: Walker Childrens.

McGrath, B. B. (2004). *The M&M's addition book.* Watertown, MA: Charlesbridge.

McMillan, B. (1991). *Eating fractions.* New York: Scholastic.

Merriam, E. (1996). *12 ways to get to 11.* New York: Aladdin.

Michelson, R. (2000). *Ten times better.* Singapore: Cavendish Children's Books.

Muller, R. (1991). *How big is a foot?* New York: Yearling.

Murphy, F. (2001). *Ben Franklin and the magic squares.* New York: Scholastic.

Murphy, P. J. (2003). *Counting with an abacus.* New York: Rosen.

Murphy, S. (1997). *Lemonade for sale.* New York: HarperCollins.

Murphy, S. J. (1996a). *Give me half!* New York: Great Source.

Murphy, S. J. (1996b). *Ready, set, hop!* New York: HarperCollins.

Murphy, S. J. (1996c). *Too many kangaroo things to do!* New York: HarperCollins.

Murphy, S. J. (1997a). *Betcha!* New York: HarperCollins.

Murphy, S. J. (1997b). *Divide and ride.* New York: HarperCollins.

Murphy, S. J. (1997c). *Elevator magic.* New York: HarperCollins.

Murphy, S. J. (1998). *Henry the fourth.* New York: HarperCollins.

Murphy, S. J. (2000). *Probably pistachio.* New York: HarperCollins.

Murphy, S. J. (2001a). *Captain Invincible and the space shapes.* New York: HarperCollins.

Murphy, S. J. (2001b). *Dinosaur deals.* New York: HarperCollins.

Murphy, S. J. (2001c). *Racing around.* New York: HarperCollins.

Murphy, S. J. (2002a). *Bigger, better, best.* New York: HarperCollins.

Murphy, S. J. (2002b). *The sundae scoop.* New York: HarperCollins.

Murphy, S. J. (2003). *Less than zero.* New York: HarperCollins.

Nagda, A. W. (2005). *Panda math.* New York: Holt.

Nagda, A. W. (2007). *Cheetah math: Learning about division from baby cheetahs.* New York: Holt.

Nagda, A. W., & Bickel, C. (2002). *Tiger math: Learning to graph from a baby tiger.* New York: Square Fish.

Nagda, A. W., & Bickel, C. (2007). *Polar bear math: Learning about fractions from Klondike and snow.* New York: Square Fish.

Napoli, D. J., & Tchen, R. (2008). *Corkscrew counts: A story about multiplication.* New York: Holt.

Neuschwander, C. (1997). *Sir Cumference and the first round table.* Watertown, MA: Charlesbridge.

Neuschwander, C. (1998). *Amanda bean's amazing dream.* New York: Scholastic.

Neuschwander, C. (2001). *Sir Cumference and the great knight of angleland.* Watertown, MA: Charlesbridge.

Neuschwander, C. (2003). *Sir Cumference and the sword in the cone.* Watertown, MA: Charlesbridge.

Neuschwander, C. (2006). *Sir Cumference and the isle of immeter.* Watertown, MA: Charlesbridge.

Neuschwander, C. (2007). *Patterns in Peru.* New York: Holt.

Neuschwander, C. (2009a). *Mummy math: An adventure in geometry.* New York: Square Fish.

Neuschwander, C. (2009b). *Sir Cumference and all the king's tens.* Watertown, MA: Charlesbridge.

Neuschwander, C. (2012). *Sir Cumference and the off-the-charts dessert.* Watertown, MA: Charlesbridge.

Neuschwander, C. (2012). *Sir Cumference and the Viking's map.* Watertown, MA: Charlesbridge.

Nolan, H. (2001). *How much, how many, how far, how heavy, how long, how tall is 1000?* Tonawanda, NY: Kids Can Press.

Ochiltree, D. (2000). *Bart's amazing charts.* New York: Scholastic.

Onyefulu, I. (2007). *A triangle for Adaora: An African book of shapes.* London: Lincoln Children's Books.

Otoshi, K. (2010). *Zero.* Berkeley, CA: KO Kids Books.

Packard, E. (2000). *Big numbers*. Minneapolis, MN: Millbrook Press.

Packard, E. (2001). *Little numbers*. Minneapolis, MN: Millbrook Press.

Pallotta, J. (1999). *The Hershey's milk chocolate fractions book*. New York: Cartwheel.

Pallotta, J. (2000). *Reese's Pieces count by fives*. New York: Cartwheel.

Pallotta, J. (2001a). *Hershey's Kisses addition book*. New York: Scholastic.

Pallotta, J. (2001b). *Underwater counting*. Watertown, MA: Charlesbridge.

Pallotta, J. (2002a). *The Hershey's milk chocolate multiplication book*. New York: Cartwheel.

Pallotta, J. (2002b). *Twizzlers: Shapes and patterns*. New York: Cartwheel.

Pallotta, J. (2003). *Apple fractions*. New York: Cartwheel.

Penner, L. R. (2002). *X marks the spot!* New York: Kane Press.

Pilegard, V. (2000). *The warlord's puzzle*. Gretna, LA: Pelican.

Pilegard, V. (2001). *The warlord's beads*. Gretna, LA: Pelican.

Pilegard, V. W. (2003). *The warlord's puppeteers*. Gretna, LA: Pelican.

Pinczes, E. J. (1996). *Arctic fives arrive*. New York: HMH Books for Young Readers.

Pinczes, E. J. (1999). *One hundred hungry ants*. New York: HMH Books for Young Readers.

Pinczes, E. J. (2002a). *My full moon is square*. Boston: Houghton Mifflin.

Pinczes, E. J. (2002b). *A remainder of one*. New York: HMH Books for Young Readers.

Pinczes, E. J. (2003). *Inchworm and a half*. New York: HMH Books for Young Readers.

Pollack, P., & Belviso, M. (2002). *Chickens on the move*. New York: Kane Press.

Rand, A. (2006). *Little 1*. San Francisco: Chronicle Books.

Rau, D. M. (2006). *A star in my orange: Looking for nature's shapes*. Minneapolis, MN: First Avenue Editions.

Rocklin, J. (1998). *The case of the backyard treasure*. New York: Scholastic.

Rocklin, J. (2000). *The incredibly awesome box: A story about 3-D shapes*. New York: Scholastic.

Rose, D. L. (2003). *One nighttime sea*. New York: Scholastic.

Ross, C. S. (1994). *Triangles: Shapes in math, science and nature*. Tonawanda, NY: Kids Can Press.

Sayre, A. P., & Sayre, J. (2006). *One is a snail, ten is a crab*. Somerville, MA: Candlewick Press.

Schlein, M. (1999). *Round and square*. New York: Mondo.

Schwartz, D. M. (1994). *If you made a million*. New York: HarperCollins.

Schwartz, D. M. (1999). *If you hopped like a frog*. New York: Scholastic.

Schwartz, D. M. (2001). *On beyond a million: An amazing math journey*. New York: Dragonfly Books.

Schwartz, D. M. (2004). *How much is a million?* New York: HarperCollins.

Schwartz, D. M. (2006). *Millions to measure*. New York: HarperCollins.

Schwartz, R. E. (2010). *You can count on monsters*. Natick, MA: Peters/CRC Press.

Scieszka, J. (1995). *Math curse*. New York: Viking Juvenile.

Stamper, J. B. (2003a). *Breakfast at Danny's diner: A book about multiplication*. New York: Grosset & Dunlap.

Stamper, J. B. (2003b). *Go fractions!* New York: Grosset & Dunlap.

Stills, C. (2014). *Mice mischief: Math facts in action*. New York: Holiday House.

Sundby, S. (2000). *Cut down to size at high noon*. Watertown, MA: Charlesbridge.

Sweeney, J. (2002). *Me and the measure of things*. New York: Dragonfly Books.

Tang, G. (2002). *The best of times*. New York: Scholastic.

Tang, G. (2003). *Math-terpieces: The art of problem solving.* New York: Scholastic.

Tang, G. (2004). *The grapes of math.* New York: Scholastic.

Taylor-Cox, J. (2012). *Sigmund Square finds his family.* Severna Park, MD: Taylor-Cox Instruction.

Thompson, L. (2001). *One riddle, one answer.* New York: Scholastic.

Thorne-Thomsen, K., & Rocheleau, P. (1999). *A shaker's dozen.* San Francisco: Chronicle Books.

Toft, K. M., & Sheather, A. (1998). *One less fish.* Watertown, MA: Charlesbridge.

Tompert, A. (1993). *Just a little bit.* New York: Houghton Mifflin.

Trinca, R. (1987). *One wooly wombat.* La Jolla, CA: Kane/Miller.

Turner, P. (1999). *Among the odd and evens: A tale of adventure.* New York: Farrar, Straus & Giroux.

Walsh, E. S. (1995). *Mouse count.* New York: HMH Books for Young Readers.

Walton, R. (1996). *How many, how many, how many.* Somerville, MA: Candlewick Press.

Walton, R. (2000). *One more bunny: Adding from one to ten.* New York: HarperCollins.

Wells, R. E. (1993). *Is a blue whale the biggest thing there is?* Morton Grove, IN: Whitman.

Wells, R. E. (1997). *What's faster than a speeding cheetah?* Morton Grove, IN: Whitman.

Wells, R. E. (2000). *Can you count to a googol?* Morton Grove, IN: Whitman.

Wise, W. (2004). *Ten sly piranhas.* New York: Puffin.

Wright, A. (1997). *Alice in pastaland: A math adventure.* Watertown, MA: Charlesbridge.

Index

Page numbers followed by an *f* indicate figures.